D1162752

Strategic Innovation

Strategic Innovation

Embedding Innovation as a
Core Competency in Your Organization

Nancy Tennant Snyder
Deborah L. Duarte

Foreword by Gary Hamel

JOSSEY-BASS
A Wiley Imprint
www.josseybass.com

Copyright © 2003 by John Wiley & Sons, Inc. All rights reserved.
Published by Jossey-Bass
A Wiley Imprint
989 Market Street, San Francisco, CA 94103-1741   www.josseybass.com

No part of this publication may be reproduced, stored in a retrieval system, or
transmitted in any form or by any means, electronic, mechanical, photocopy-
ing, recording, scanning, or otherwise, except as permitted under Section 107 or
108 of the 1976 United States Copyright Act, without either the prior written
permission of the Publisher, or authorization through payment of the appropriate per-copy fee to the Copyright Clearance Center, Inc., 222 Rosewood Drive,
Danvers, MA 01923, 978-750-8400, fax 978-750-4470, or on the web at
www.copyright.com. Requests to the Publisher for permission should be
addressed to the Permissions Department, John Wiley & Sons, Inc.,
111 River Street, Hoboken, NJ 07030, 201-748-6011, fax 201-748-6008,
e-mail: permcoordinator@wiley.com.

Jossey-Bass books and products are available through most bookstores. To contact Jossey-Bass directly call our Customer Care Department within the U.S. at
800-956-7739, outside the U.S. at 317-572-3986 or fax 317-572-4002.
Jossey-Bass also publishes its books in a variety of electronic formats. Some
content that appears in print may not be available in electronic books.

Library of Congress Cataloging-in-Publication Data
Snyder, Nancy Tennant, 1957
Strategic innovation : embedding innovation as a core competency in
your organization / Nancy Tennant Snyder, Deborah L. Duarte ; foreword
by Gary Hamel.
p. cm.—(The Jossey-Bass business & management series)
Includes bibliographical references and index.
ISBN 0-7879-6405-0 (alk. paper)
1. Technological innovations—United States.
2. Strategic planning—United States. 3. Organizational change—United States.
4. Organizational effectiveness—United States. 5. Industrial
management—United States. 6. Whirlpool Corporation—Case studies.
I. Duarte, Deborah L., 1956- II. Title. III. Series.
HD45.S57 2003
658.4'063—dc21
2003002024

Printed in the United States of America
FIRST EDITION
HB Printing   10 9 8 7 6 5 4 3 2 1

The Jossey-Bass
Business & Management Series

CONTENTS

EXHIBITS AND WORKSHEETS

EXHIBITS

WORKSHEETS

FOREWORD

It's hardly surprising that innovation has become the new mantra of CEOs everywhere. In our suddenly sober world, there are few alternatives to innovation. Most companies have reached the point of diminishing returns in their cost cutting: they are working harder and harder to eke out smaller and smaller efficiencies. After a decade of frantic deal making, industry consolidation has mostly run its course. In any case, investors have learned that a big acquisition is more likely to destroy shareholder value than create it. Fewer and fewer companies are generating consistent and profitable organic growth. And with customers becoming ever more powerful and value conscious, it's nearly impossible to raise prices.

So yes, innovation *is* the only alternative. Yet in most companies, innovation is more rhetoric than reality. If you doubt this, go interview a few midlevel employees in your organization and ask them to describe the "corporate innovation system." Ask them how they have been trained to be more innovative. Ask them where they go with a break-out idea. Ask them what processes and methods have been put in place to support innovation. Ask them how innovation has been baked into the company's performance evaluation system. Ask them whether they really, truly believe that top management regards every employee as an innovator, potentially capable of shaping corporate direction.

If innovation is more buzzword than core competence, it's not because top management is disingenuous. Leaders know that above-average performance demands rule-breaking innovation. The problem is that most senior executives don't have a highly developed and deeply practical understanding of what innovation looks like as a corporate-wide capability. To them, innovation is largely about new product development rather than across-the-board business innovation. Innovation is the province of R&D boffins, not the work of every employee. Innovation is a risky and only occasionally rewarding diversion from the basic job of improving operational effectiveness. One can hardly blame executives for this truncated view of innovation. Until recently, no company on the planet had succeeded, or even attempted, to make innovation an encompassing capability.

An analogy might be helpful here. Think back to the late 1960s. If you had suggested to the chairman of General Motors or Ford that there might be a payoff to improving vehicle quality, you would have received a polite nod in return. Sure, quality was important to these companies; after all, they employed a legion of inspectors. Yet no American auto industry executive could have told you about statistical process control, Pareto analysis, quality circles, or any of the other methods that would ultimately come to be known as Total Quality Management. Indeed, the notion that "ordinary" employees could and should be responsible for quality would have struck them as absurd. It took a severe drubbing from quality-obsessed Japanese car companies to open their minds to the radical idea that quality could be an intrinsic organizational capability rather than a specialized function. It then took another two decades for America's carmakers to decode and adapt the disciplines of Total Quality Management to their own organizations.

Today the bleeding edge for organizations is not quality but innovation. But like those long-departed auto executives, most managers today don't have a detailed model of how to build this new capability. Or rather, they didn't until Whirlpool committed itself to doing what no other industrial company had ever done: making innovation a corporate-wide core competence. This book is the story of Whirlpool's innovation journey. It is the story of a company intent on unleashing the imagination of every employee. It is the story of a company that refused to believe that penny-pinching efficiency and edge-of-the-envelope innovation couldn't coexist in a single organization. It is the story of a company that has demonstrated a willingness to radically reinvent its core management processes in the quest for wealth-creating innovation.

If you want to stoke the fires of innovation in your organization, you'll find this book to be an invaluable source of inspiration and practical advice. If it doesn't have all the answers, it has more than you're likely to find anywhere else.

April 2003

PROFESSOR GARY HAMEL
DIRECTOR, WOODSIDE INSTITUTE
CHAIRMAN, STRATEGOS

PREFACE

This book is a case study focused on one organization—the Whirlpool Corporation—and its journey to embed innovation as a core competency. *Embedment* is a rather new term, so it's only fitting that we define what we mean. In embedding innovation, we are referring to a wide range of actions that assimilate, incorporate, internalize, and imbue the entire fabric or lifeblood of an organization with the mind-set and skills of innovation. Think of embedment as a cross between embodiment and bedrock. We will shortly explain in much greater detail the nature and purpose of embedment and innovation.

You are probably familiar with Whirlpool and its major North American brands: Whirlpool, KitchenAid, and Roper. It also has a significant partnership with Sears as a supplier of many of the Kenmore appliances along with the Whirlpool and KitchenAid brands. In Latin America, Whirlpool operates under the Brastemp and Consul brands, both leading appliance brands in the region. In Europe, the major brands are Whirlpool and Bauknecht. In Asia, the Whirlpool brand is the major brand for the most rapidly growing appliance market in the world. In all, Whirlpool is the largest appliance company in the world.

Before the innovation initiative described in this book, Whirlpool was a traditional manufacturing company whose core competencies were manufacturing efficiencies and trade partner relationships with the retailers that sell our brands. Whirlpool began as a washing machine company in 1911, selling washers to Sears and Roebuck. Over the next seventy years, it built the leading market position in North America. During the 1990s, Whirlpool expanded its reach and became the global appliance leader, operating in every major region of the world. In North America, Whirlpool is a well-known brand name with most consumers, enjoying a reputation of quality and durability. It is also known to a large culinary segment because of the iconoclastic reputation of its KitchenAid mixer, so famous for its design that it is found in design museums around the world. The mixer is a prop in the background of nearly every cooking show and upscale kitchen set on television sit-coms.

Inside the company, Whirlpool has a solid and trustworthy reputation for fair dealing and of integrity with its employees, suppliers, and communities in which it operates. Most outsiders visiting a Whirlpool facility comment on the friendliness and unpretentiousness of the people. In short, Whirlpool is good, solid company with a significant track record and global reach.

In this book, we present Whirlpool's story of embedding innovation in our company between 1999 and 2003. Chapter by chapter, we discuss the origins of our strategy, the steps we took to implement it, what worked and what didn't, what needed to be redirected, and what we learned. On occasion, we bring in some of the literature and best practices we used to design our innovation embedment approach. For the most part, though, this book relates Whirlpool's experience in transforming itself from a cost and quality producer of appliances to a customer-focused company that is well underway in its strategic plan to embed innovation throughout the organization.

To make the book as useful as possible, worksheets at the end of each chapter will help you and your organization replicate the journey we have taken. To a large extent, these hands-on activities can serve as a programmatic guide to embedding innovation in any organization. We encourage you to use these worksheets as the foundation for your own efforts.

A LONG AND WINDING ROAD

We want to be upfront and honest in admitting that our story is not clean, neat, and pretty. As anyone who has been involved in massive change efforts knows, this is hard work. Such an effort is even more difficult in a large, global enterprise. The change process from here to there is seldom predictable. If you are looking for a precise and well-laid out picture of change, you won't find it in this book. But if you are in search of a real-life story about challenges and struggles to address change with successful results, you will find value here.

When Whirlpool was compelled by our CEO to establish and embed innovation as a core competency, we were faced with the daunting task of creating a plan and executing it at the same time, learning and adapting as we went along. We used targeted expertise in key areas but had no road map showing us the path to transformation. Other companies may have faced the same challenge, but to our knowledge, the stories of how they approached it, what they accomplished, and where they fell short have not been sufficiently told. The lack of such background is one of the primary reasons that we believed it was important to add our story to the business literature.

In the spirit of candor, we also chose not to tell our story as a nice neat, edited parable, such as those found in much of today's business literature and conference presentations. Parables crisply recited portraying initiatives that always start where they should, progress along without missteps, and end with aplomb have usually incorporated some sort of revisionist history. Instead, we decided to reveal what really happened within Whirlpool as the story unfolded. We call these boxed interruptions you will find in the body of the chapters the "Duct Tape Version." These honest and sometimes humorous anecdotes reveal a variety of missteps and midcourse corrections we made to keep on track. We are confident that you will see how the end results are, like duct tape, strong and hard to destroy, and, most important, you will see how the corrections worked for us in the long run.

Do not take away from our frankness and occasional *mea culpa* style of writing that the people who led this effort at Whirlpool bumbled through innovation embedment or mindlessly progressed forward through sheer luck and happenstance. On the contrary, these people were—and are—smart and leading-edge leaders trying to accomplish something unparalleled in any transformation effort in the world, establishing a global system that allows any one of sixty thousand people, at any level, in any job, to become an innovator.

At the time of this writing, Whirlpool has already experienced great successes in innovation, and we expect many more. This book strives to be an honest and down-to-earth account of how the leaders of Whirlpool are progressing in embedding innovation as a core competency.

WHO "WE" ARE

The account of innovation embedment at Whirlpool is extraordinary. This book seeks to share this story with as many people as possible. As Deb Duarte and I wrote, it was incredibly difficult to honor all the people who made it possible. As a result, we use the term *we* quite a bit. It is extremely important that everyone who reads this book understand that we are not implying that we, the authors, led the effort or did all the thinking and hard work that it took to embed innovation in Whirlpool. Indeed, there were, and are, many players who contributed greatly to the creation of innovation from everyone and everywhere.

Much of the hard work of innovation embedment was done at the Executive Committee level and through members of the innovation teams. Deb (through her work with me) and I were most often in the role of executors and implementers.

The term *we* therefore refers to all the people in Whirlpool who made embedment possible: the CEO and chairman of the board, Dave Whitwam; the chief operating officer, Jeff Fettig; the Executive Committee (the eight direct reports to the office of the chairman); the Chairman's Council (the twenty-five officers in the company); my staff; members of the innovation teams; the knowledge management teams; Corporate Communications; Strategos (our consulting firm); and many others. Whenever an action, thought, or idea was attributable to one person, it is spelled out for the reader.

We list all the players in Chapter One, identifying by name and title some of the many people at Whirlpool who worked hard to make innovation embedment possible. Unfortunately, we could not list them all. We also include two organizational charts to help you understand the structure that Whirlpool already had and the positions and boards we added to serve innovation.

In addition, let us tell you something about who we, the authors, are. One of us, Nancy Snyder, is the corporate vice president of strategic competencies and leadership development for Whirlpool Corporation. I was appointed in July 1999 as the global vice president of innovation to help the CEO and Whirlpool embed innovation as a core competency. I work closely with the senior Whirlpool team around the world to design and deploy innovation into every aspect of Whirlpool, from its jobs to its business processes. I led a global team of internal innovation embedment general managers to share best practices around the world and to assist the business leaders in the ramp-up of innovation to play the key role in the customer-centered business strategy that Whirlpool was and is pursuing.

The other one of us, Deb Duarte, is an external consultant with over nine years of in-depth experience with Whirlpool. My role in innovation at Whirlpool was as an adjunct professional to Nancy's staff, working on many critical projects in innovation embedment. I aimed to bring a unique perspective to this effort because I have had the fortune of being both inside and outside the transformation process. As a result, my observations are sometimes more gracious than hers and at times more critical. My role in creating the content for this book was to ensure that the story was told in an even and balanced manner, honoring and sharing what really worked, including areas that we may have taken for granted but that readers will find useful.

Finally, Deb and I would like to acknowledge that this book is written from our point of view and perspective. There are many other points of view from within Whirlpool that are important and valid. This is ours. We recognize that we might have biases toward how events unfolded and played out. Any mistakes or errors in reporting belong solely to us. We have tried to be objective and true to the spirit of innovation at Whirlpool.

WHO SHOULD READ THIS BOOK

We wrote this book for a multifaceted audience. It is for business leaders whose business model of success depends on innovative solutions for their customers. It is for strategic organizational development practitioners who help organizations with large, complex change relating to the strategic mandate of innovation. It is for academics and business students who want to learn from Whirlpool Corporation as a case study in changing a large enterprise to become innovative. And it is for the business press to learn how innovation will soon change the face of many global industries.

April 2003

NANCY TENNANT SNYDER
Benton Harbor, Michigan

DEBORAH L. DUARTE
Incline Village, Nevada

To all the people of Whirlpool Corporation:
The greatest ideas are nothing without the commitment
and energy to make them reality.

ACKNOWLEDGMENTS

Innovation and writing a book share some common characteristics: you never know where either will take you when you start, they take enormous passion and personal commitment, and they require many dedicated people to produce the finished result.

We have been unusually lucky to have worked with so many wonderful people on this book. The following is really a short list of all who have made this story possible.

We start with a special acknowledgment to David R. Whitwam, chairman and CEO of Whirlpool. He was, and continues to be, an impressive and inspirational leader, an unparalleled visionary. He trusted us to write a book that would ring true to the people of Whirlpool while at the same time using a candid and open writing style to depict Whirlpool's spirited journey. In writing this book, we could reflect on what a unique CEO Dave is for setting this path and then sticking to it with all the passion and commitment that defines his leadership of Whirlpool.

Other important Whirlpool players in the formation of the book were Jeff Fettig, our chief operational officer. Jeff has been key in making sure that innovation was always top of mind from an operational perspective and didn't become set apart from our "real business." We are also beholden to the members of Whirlpool's Executive Committee, whose members had the passion, commitment, and perseverance to lead the innovation effort, run the business, and stay the course.

We express our gratitude to the regional innovation leaders, especially Andrew Batson, Ricardo Acosta, and Phil Pejovich and their teams, and for the people on the knowledge management teams for giving us the "real deal": working hard to make sure that innovation became a reality for everyone, everywhere. Nancy's staff in the Leadership and Core Competencies group—Giuseppe Geneletti, Tammy Patrick, Joe Frodsham, and Makini Nyanteh—were critical to providing the infrastructure that we used for many embedment activities. We owe a very special recognition to Nancy's executive assistant, Blythe Handy, for her patience with us and follow-through on all our special requests. We also thank our long-time colleague, Monica Brunkel. Just knowing she is there is a comfort!

We are also blessed to have such a long and rich relationship with our publisher, Jossey-Bass. Special thanks to Susan R. Williams for her trust in us and in seeing the potential in our story and to Byron Schneider and Rob Brandt for their support and good counsel.

We wanted to do the writing ourselves and shunned any notion of ghost-writers. We also wanted a personal and candid writing style and an editor who shared that vision. To pull this off, we knew we needed a strong and skillful editor. We were very fortunate to be introduced by Byron at Jossey-Bass to Rick Benzel, our developmental editor. Rick worked with us at each turn making excellent suggestions and supporting our decisions along the way. His deft professionalism and editorial prowess helped the book enormously.

We also were privileged to work with the Strategos team and continue to have a rich relationship with them. Thanks to Gary Hamel for writing the thought-provoking seminal articles that started this revolution in the business world and for agreeing to write the Foreword for this book. Also special thanks to David Crosswhite for input to the book and for his ongoing support for innovation at Whirlpool.

Special appreciation goes to Heidi Thibodeau for helping us with the research. She came through in the eleventh hour and was a pleasure to work with. We also thank Tom Wright for the graphics work on the embedment wheel.

We have great and loving families who keep us tuned to the world outside our insular corporate focus. They also are loads of fun and only *slightly* dysfunctional. Nancy thanks her sisters and their husbands—Janet and Larry, Linda and Fred, Diane and Bill—and especially her nieces and nephews—Natalie, Michael, Tyler, and Danielle. Thanks to Mike and Steve, Deb's brothers; their wives, Audrey and Sally; her mother, Jackie; and Brett, Abby, Meagan, and Allison for putting up with the writing and distraction during family events.

Deb thanks her husband, Clay, for not only living through but encouraging another book. Nancy thanks her husband, Robert, for all his help and support, especially in the last frantic hours of producing and mailing the final manuscript. Also thanks for taking such great care of Minnie (Me), Max, and the cat.

N.T.S.
D.L.D.

THE AUTHORS

Nancy Tennant Snyder is currently the corporate vice president of core competencies and leadership development for Whirlpool Corporation. In this capacity she is responsible for creating and implementing global strategies that facilitate innovation, customer centered operational excellence, and customer loyalty as core competencies and leadership development as an enterprise capability. She has consulted at many companies on a wide range of business topics. She holds a doctorate in organizational behavior from George Washington University. She is the author of numerous articles on globalization, virtual teams, and organizational capability and is the coauthor of the best-selling book *Mastering Virtual Teams.*

Deborah L. Duarte works with a wide range of clients from Fortune 500 companies that span a number of industries, including telecommunications, durable goods, pharmaceuticals, and industrial products, and from leading government and not-for-profit agencies, such as the National Aeronautics and Space Administration, the Federal Aviation Administration, and the United Nations. Her work integrates approaches from a broad range of disciplines, including organizational behavior, social psychology, computer-supported collaborative work, and anthropology. Duarte holds a doctorate in organizational behavior from George Washington University. She is the coauthor of the best-selling book *Mastering Virtual Teams.* She lives with her husband, Clay Durr, in Incline Village, Nevada, and in Herndon, Virginia.

CHAPTER ONE

Introduction

Innovation as a Core Competency

If you grew up in the United States between 1950 and 1999, hearing the name *Whirlpool* probably makes you think of gleaming white washing machines and dishwashers. In your mind, you may picture an old-line manufacturing company with lines of factory workers assembling parts and shooting screws, along with shipping docks laden with heavy brown boxes filled with appliances for the kitchen and laundry room. Actually, your vision would be somewhat accurate for that period of time.

With that picture in mind, the Whirlpool of today would surprise you. We are sixty thousand employees around the world in 170 countries, with efficiency and productivity unparalleled in any industry. We have thirteen high-tech manufacturing facilities and eighteen world-class technology centers with engineers designing in virtual teams from around the world. We produce numerous product lines, including washers, refrigerators, microwaves, and high-end KitchenAid small appliances like mixers, coffee makers, and toasters, and dozens of other new products are on the drawing board. Hundreds of innovators from all levels and types of jobs, sometimes from where you might least expect them, are working to invent on behalf of the customer, enjoying and maximizing their contribution to the company. You would see innovations across all touch points with the customer: purchase experience, service, communication, relationship building, and product.

To highlight the degree of innovation Whirlpool has achieved, consider this short list of newly launched and drawing board innovations:

1

- Gladiator GarageWorks, a line of modular garage accessories and appliances targeted at male consumers who thinks of the garage as more than a place to store the car
- Polara, a range with refrigeration capabilities, representing a new-to-the-world technological innovation
- Duet, a high-tech, energy-efficient, front-loading washer and dryer system marketed in every premium market in the world
- Gator Pak, customizable units for tailgate parties that feature such options as grills, cooling and warming drawers, beverage taps, microwave ovens, and sound systems, created by enthusiastic and dedicated innovators from a manufacturing plant
- Personal Valet, a closet-like appliance that removes wrinkles and odors from clothes
- Briva, a double-tub sink that features a small, high-speed dishwasher on one side
- Pla (pronounced "play"), a line of orange-and-silver personal appliances for the age eighteen- to thirty-four-year-old crowd, created by a global team of innovators
- Cielo, a line of the company's first whirlpool baths
- Shredpactor, a paper shredder that also compacts
- Coolbox, a small bedside cooling unit for storing medication, baby bottles, and other items requiring refrigeration
- Kitchen utensils bearing the KitchenAid brand
- Water purification system for the Latin American and European markets with new economic engines like leasing
- A voltage regulator accessory for India consumers
- A basic Indian refrigerator for rural areas selling for under seventy-five dollars

Why did Whirlpool make this transition? More important, how did it do this? The answers are diverse and wide ranging, but they essentially come down to the simple truth that Whirlpool needed to break out of its commodity-based industry by changing its strategy in order to become innovative. As with many other large multinationals from America in the 1990s, our corporate strategy of globalization established a solid footprint in our corporate evolution. However, our global leadership position was not creating sufficient value for our shareholders. The next stage in Whirlpool's evolution was to create growth through unmatched levels of customer loyalty driven by innovation.

THE END OF AN ERA

By the end of the twentieth century, Whirlpool was not very different from many other industries that faced new levels of expectations to create shareholder value. Companies of all kinds grappled to find strategies that would yield the most growth opportunities.

Some companies adopted strategies to increase shareholder value by relying heavily on improvements in cost, quality, and productivity. Big savings were sought, largely through cost-cutting measures. Other companies in the manufacturing, service, and retail sectors put their emphasis on internal efficiencies. Some took cost and quality to a new level using techniques such as Motorola's Six Sigma program, in which Six Sigma experts commonly called "black belts" were trained in a set of techniques that focused on cutting cycle time, cost, and waste in repetitive activities.

INNOVATION TO THE RESCUE

In the late 1990s, it became apparent to Whirlpool's CEO and Executive Committee (the top nine leaders in Whirlpool) that one of the best ways to create growth was through a long-term strategy focused on customer loyalty, whereby customers would demand and pay a premium for Whirlpool brands. (For the purpose of this book, we use the term *customer* to mean the end user.) In order to sustain this type of loyalty relationship, Whirlpool first had to satisfy customers' expressed needs on the basics. But we had to create more than just the basics. We determined that we had go beyond satisfaction to providing unique solutions for new and unarticulated needs.

Think about how you experience relationships with your favorite brands. Merely satisfying your basic needs does not create passionate loyalty on your part as a customer. It may develop a transaction but not a relationship. It does not differentiate the brand, except on a cost and quality axis. Distinction is based on price. This sets up a cost and quality business model for a company and the resident processes and skill sets that drive it like operational excellence, quality disciplines, Total Cost Productivity, and sales, general, and administration reduction.

Many companies choose this path to create value. In fact, Whirlpool too had used this business model to great success in the past. But at this point in our evolution, we realized that for true long-term sustainable growth, cost and quality alone would not produce the results we desired.

Real customer loyalty required our taking a different path. It required a new mind-set and performance level from Whirlpool, a transformation in the way relationships with our customers were formed. Loyalty had to be based on deeper customer insights and a relationship of trust that would last a lifetime.

The major question on our minds was this: Did Whirlpool customers want a lifelong relationship with the company that makes their washer?

Whirlpool's strategy predicted that many customers would answer yes to this question, but only if they were presented with the right offerings and solutions to meet their needs. How big a change would it be for Whirlpool to create this type of loyalty? First, Whirlpool had some barriers to address:

Barrier 1: In the appliance industry, product life cycles are some of the longest in the consumer industry. There is a saying in this industry: "Old refrigerators never die; they just move to the garage." With that dynamic in the customers' mind, along with the world-class quality standards we had put into place in our products, a customer may be in the market for a new refrigerator only once every fifteen years.

Barrier 2: Add to that a relationship of very little direct contact between Whirlpool and the customer. Customers purchase products through retail stores like Sears, Lowes, Ikea, or Carrefour, or they move into a house where the builder has already made the choice for them. In addition, the retail experience of buying an appliance may not always be the most pleasant one. One woman we talked to facetiously compared buying a washer in the retail environment today to the "joy of buying tires . . . only worse."

Barrier 3: Many customers think about appliances as lackluster: all products seem to look and act the same. They do not think of appliances as experiences that can inspire in them deep loyalty to the brand. Customers just want their products to work, to be safe, and to have little hassle if they need service. As one customer put it, "Hey, I don't want to hug my washer."

REMOVING THE BARRIERS WITH INNOVATION

After much research and strategy development, Whirlpool's leadership made some bold decisions and realizations. They determined that all three barriers could be overcome through innovation. Changing purchasing cycle times could be done by bringing to market new and exciting innovations that customers would come to demand. These innovations did not have to be just around the *product* itself; they could also be in how the product was *purchased,* how the customer was *communicated* to, and the nature of a long-term *relationship* that could be developed through *services* such as repair and customer assistance. We refer to these five elements (including products) as customer touch points.

Second, we realized that Whirlpool could have more contact with the customer than we originally thought. Although parts of Whirlpool had always focused on the customer, the overall mind-set of the enterprise in the past was not truly focused on understanding our customers' needs through rich insights. Because our previous strategy focused on manufacturing cost, quality, and globalization, Whirlpool was not organized in a way, and did not have the internal processes in place, to maximize contact with customers across the entire enterprise. This could change through our efforts at innovation that would bring us much closer to our customer. In addition, by using retail stores as partners, we could add innovations to the purchase experience so that not only the customer benefited, but so would Whirlpool and its retail store partners. Customers would demand the Whirlpool brand in the retail store and with builders if they were provided unique products and services that met their needs.

Finally, the lackluster image with customers could be changed using innovation to create unique ideas and solutions. Innovation across products and services could change the way customers thought of our brand, while also changing the way they preserved and cooked their food, cared for their fabrics, and met the needs of their families.

DEFINING INNOVATION

Whirlpool thus determined that innovation was needed to create unique solutions for our customers. But what exactly does innovation mean? What does it entail in terms of transforming an organization? We need to pause in our story for a moment to provide some important background about innovation and embedment.

Not surprisingly, the literature on innovation contains a wide array of definitions. One useful distinction comes from Kim Cameron and Dave Whetten (1998), who draw a line between continuous improvement and innovation. In their view, continuous improvement refers to incremental steps, while innovation involves discontinuous changes and breakthroughs. According to Peter Drucker (1985), innovation is the set of tools to create a new business. These tools can be learned and practiced. Gary Hamel (1998) redefines innovation as strategic innovation—the capacity to reconceive the existing business model in ways that create new value for customers and stakeholders and advantage over the competition.

Meanwhile, a small population of innovative companies each seem to have their own definition of innovation. At Harley-Davidson, innovation is ensuring that its products are newer and more leading edge than those of competitors. At IBM, the number of new patents defines innovation. Volkswagen defines innovation as a way of fulfillment and connection with customers by creating something novel that also pays off. The payoff may be in a new product or something as intangible as a new way to do things.

In the light of this diversity of definitions, Whirlpool looked to define innovation for ourselves in order to meet our own unique strategic needs. We now define *innovation* as any product or service that creates unique and compelling solutions valued by our customers, real and sustainable competitive advantages, and extraordinary value for our shareholders. In addition, innovation should create a clear linkage to our customer loyalty mission, drive breakthrough levels of thinking, and include a wide scope of work from core products to new-to-the-world offerings—from high-end products to innovation for the masses and across all customer touch points. It must also drive a reallocation of our resources to be more focused on our strategic objectives.

ORGANIZATIONAL CORE COMPETENCIES

Once our strategic decision was made, the next question was how to transform Whirlpool into a brand-focused innovative company. To do this, innovation had to reside in more than just the engineers or the leadership team. It had to be developed as an organization-wide capability, or what has come to be called a core competency.

The notion that organizations have core competencies has gained extensive credibility in recent years. In particular, the research and writing of C. K. Prahalad and Gary Hamel (1990) has been instrumental in reconceptualizing how competitive advantage can no longer be sustained solely from price and performance attributes such as features, cost, and quality. Instead, sustainable competitive advantage must now be attained by defining, building, and leveraging unique organizational knowledge, skills, and experience in ways that competitors cannot imitate. Their view of strategy and strategic advantage involves orchestrating all the resources of an organization toward creating future opportunities and markets in areas where they hold the advantage.

Many organizations confuse core competencies with employee or functional knowledge and skills. Indeed, functional-level knowledge and skills are important, but these are ubiquitous skills employed in every company regardless of the strategy. For example, any company in the private sector requires a common set of functional skills to conduct business, from finance to manufacturing, or process skills like product development that cut across many disciplines.

In contrast, core competencies are derived from the organization's strategic mandate. They can be resident or aspirational in nature. Core competencies need to exist at the organizational level and be embodied in the very lifeblood of the organization. As strategic mandates, they must be embedded across a wide range of employees, thereby becoming an enterprise-wide competency.

A competency must meet three tests to be considered core. First, the competency must exist in more than one or two businesses, markets, or product lines. For example, if marketing is to be a core competency, it must permeate all products and businesses, not just one or two. Second, a core competency must make significant contributions to perceived customer benefits. If your customers do not perceive value from your core competency, it cannot be considered core. Finally, a core competency should be very difficult for competitors to copy or acquire.

Firms can embody several competencies or capabilities and in many different ways, ranging from logistics, to distribution, to trade partner relationships, to branding. However, given that resources in organizations are usually limited, most organizations have at the most five to six core competencies related to attaining and sustaining their competitive advantage. Whatever they are, a set of core competencies needs to create a uniquely bundled system that integrates and aligns diverse products, customers, projects, technologies, and other experiences into the organization's competitive advantage.

For example, consider a consumer products company that has identified "being first to market" as its core competency, compared to another that has identified "fast follower" as its core competency. You can imagine the completely different skill sets required across the entire enterprise.

Wal-Mart's success is often cited as a perfect case study in leveraging multiple core competencies—including customer focus, logistics, transportation, and informal cooperation among store managers—into sustainable competitive advantage. These competence areas create a set of capabilities that its competitors have been slow or unable to imitate or recreate.

THE STRUGGLE TO EMBED CORE COMPETENCIES

Many organizations try to become innovative, but few have succeeded in embedding innovation as a core competency. Prahalad and Hamel and others who write about core competency creation especially stress that sustaining core competencies for the long run is critical to creating value. Prahalad and Hamel (1990) outline five key leadership tasks that are essential to embedding a core competency:

1. Leaders must identify core competencies as specific, deep, shared understandings around the critical few core advantages of the organization. They must assess if each competency meets the core

competence test of running across market and product lines, customer benefits, and difficulty of imitation.

2. Leaders must establish a core competence acquisition agenda or mapping of how current or new core competencies can strengthen positions in existing or new markets. This should include determining areas that leverage existing competencies, areas that might be obsolete, and areas that require building new competencies.

3. Leaders need to recognize that building core competencies requires sustained effort over a long time period, roughly five to ten years.

4. Leaders need to deploy core competencies across multiple business units and divisions in a manner that is aligned but flexible.

5. Leaders need to protect and defend core competencies over time. Core competencies may be lost in many ways, including lack of funding, loss of interest, fragmentation, or divestiture. Maintenance of core competencies is a critical aspect of strategy that can be easily overlooked.

The last three actions listed constitute the real process of embedment. They focus on sustaining the organization's core competencies and are clearly the most overlooked in organizations. Although the methods for identifying core competencies and mapping them are fairly well developed, there is not a common approach or a set of agreed-on methodologies regarding how to build, deploy, and protect core competencies.

Embedment has to do with making an enterprise-wide competency, like innovation, a permanent change in the organization. Although there are many models of organizational change and transformation, there is no blueprint or set of recipes that even begins to describe exactly what actions to take to embed core competencies. Business leaders focused on the strategic core competencies required to give their businesses and companies an advantage over their competitors are often frustrated with how to embed these competencies across a large group of people, an existing culture, and a set of processes and systems in a way that ensures they are long lasting.

The mistake many companies make is to move directly to skill training in innovation techniques or to small process modifications when they are trying to make this type of strategic change. This approach may work as a short-term solution, but it is usually ineffective at dispersing skills over wide groups of people. In contrast, while the process of embedment may require skills training, the emphasis is much more focused on creating systemic change in the infrastructure in order to reinforce the new skills and on leadership development to guide the embedment process and the skill acquisition itself. Embedment is thus a broad and inclusive approach, whereas training is a narrower, more targeted approach generally reserved for a defined set of people in the organization. To put it another way, training is analogous to changing the outer skin of the organism, whereas embedment changes its DNA.

Some organizations have managed to build, deploy, and protect their core competencies in certain common business areas such as marketing, customer service technology, and distribution. However, embedding innovation as a core competence seems to be among the most slippery and difficult to master. An Arthur D. Little survey (1992) found that less than 25 percent of executives from over 650 global companies believed that their performance in innovation was where it needed to be. Even organizations known for one or two big innovations have not been able to replicate their behavior at a high level reliably over time. Indeed, making innovation a core competence seems to be a serious challenge—even with all the literature on innovation.

THE BEGINNING OF INNOVATION AT WHIRLPOOL

Given this conceptual background, we're now ready to come back to our story concerning the events that occurred at Whirlpool that have taken us on the path to innovation embedment.

The idea to embed innovation as a core competence at Whirlpool began in September 1999 and came from our CEO, David Whitwam. At that point, Whitwam had been at Whirlpool for thirty-one years and had led the company for twelve years as the chairman and CEO. Most people assumed that we were in for more of the same when Whitwam was announced as the new CEO because he came from inside. But we soon learned that he thought like an outsider.

Whitwam started his tenure as CEO in 1986 by simultaneously creating a new vision and set of strategies to globalize the company, reorganize its divisions by brands, and change our long-held loyalty compensation system to a performance-based approach. From day one, it was clear that he was a CEO who was both comfortable with change and impatient with the status quo. The vision he embarked on took Whirlpool from a domestic U.S.-based company to the largest global appliance player in the 1990s. Once he had put our global footprint in place, he began leading the company to a brand-focused strategy, building our brands in the marketplace through customer loyalty.

But that was not the end of his vision for change. In September 1999, Whitwam issued his provocative new vision: "Innovation from Everyone and Everywhere." He was referring not just to innovation in the sense of more creativity in our jobs, but to innovation across the board, including our products, customer touch points, business methods with suppliers and vendors, and our entire strategic focus.

His statement was infused with values of inclusion and human potential. Using just those five words, he stirred an amazing reaction throughout the organization: curiosity. In an old-line manufacturing company, the idea that innovation could come from anyone was a stunning concept. Because it was out of the ordinary, it instantly provoked curiosity in people who heard it for the first time.

SEEKING MODELS AND PARTNERS

As a first step to embedment planning, we scanned the literature to see what other companies were doing to transform themselves into innovative organizations. We found very few examples that fit with our innovation vision, especially our approach to involve everyone and everywhere. With no models among other organizations, we sought a consultant to work with as a partner in the creation of our embedment plan. We also wanted to learn specific innovation tools that would be needed to fuel the endeavor.

We began by contacting a field of large, well-known consulting firms. We invited them to come in to pitch their ideas and approaches. We intended to evaluate their approaches according to five primary tenets:

1. Innovation must be possible from anyone.
2. Innovation was not just product focused.
3. Innovation must permeate to the fabric of our culture and business.
4. Innovation must create new business opportunities: it was not focused on individual- or functional-level creativity.
5. Innovation must be sustainable.

This process was both surreal and eye-opening. We watched in great amazement as a variety of consulting firms paraded in with their perspective of how to do this. It was reminiscent of a casting call where young stars come in and read their favorite scene, but not the one the movie or play needs. In the field of embedding innovation, much less in embedding any core competency, we found few consultants who had an interest or experience in this domain. Most simply wanted to come in and run a limited-time project on innovation, or conduct a detailed analysis of our culture, or show us how to turn our ideas into products.

We soon understood the deep value of the CEO's innovation vision as we went through this process. It forced us to realize that the ideal partner needed to share our enthusiasm for wide involvement and for sustaining innovation over a long period. The consultant needed to teach us how to become self-sufficient in the tools and embedment methodology that would drive the systemic change required.

DUCT TAPE VERSION
A Farsighted Confession

If we were writing for a management journal, we would say that our CEO, top leaders, and embedment practitioners were so farsighted that we already knew the detailed steps to embed innovation from the start and had them neatly laid out. But in the "duct tape version," we need to admit that no one really had an idea of what had been unleashed with the words spoken by the CEO: *Innovation from Everyone and Everywhere*. From the moment he said it, though, it clearly raised people's awareness about innovation as a new initiative, and it created enormous curiosity. People became highly motivated by the idea. A few wondered why it took leadership so long to focus on innovation for the customer. All of these reactions gave us more food for thought in creating a wide-ranging approach to innovation embedment.

What was interesting was that only one consultant focused on, or provided a foundation for, embedment of a core competence in innovation. The rest provided us with a wide range of what we considered off-the-mark concepts, which we categorized as follows.

Great Man Theory

Several consultants told our CEO, "Don't bother with innovation from everyone. It can't be done. New businesses or major game-changing customer solutions come from maybe five or six people in a firm." In their view, the strategy should focus on a few geniuses at the top of Whirlpool, and, paired with their own consulting genius, this would generate innovation.

We called this approach the "Great Man Theory." It is clearly popular. Just look at magazines and journals such as *Fast Company* that highlight the top fifty innovative individuals on a regular basis. This approach, however, violated tenet #1: innovation from everyone.

Skunkworks

Some firms suggested that we adopt a dated but repackaged idea called skunkworks. In a sense, skunkworks is simply an extension of the Great Man Theory, only with more people. The logic of skunkworks is based on the precept that great minds are not able to work well when bogged down with everyday details, associations with common folk, bureaucracy, and limited resources. Such great minds need to be isolated from others into skunkworks, segregated units of brilliant minds. Skunkworks can be effective because of the caliber of the people selected, the almost unlimited resources provided, and the impact of removing the people from the office environment into a sheltered setting devoid of any barriers associated with the formal hierarchy. Many examples of great skunkworks were cited, but in each case, the settings were usually one of a kind, and the prototypes developed were not focused on large-scale production of products or services.

We appreciated the strong legacy of skunkworks, but we decided that this approach could not create innovation from everyone, and it did not create an organization-wide climate or culture that fostered innovation.

Creativity and Games

Some consultants we talked with viewed innovation as an offshoot of individual creativity and focused on games such as sorting cards or wearing colored hats. We heard about creativity simulations, seminars, motivational speakers, and bus trips to innovation "museums" where we would be "inspired" by the ideas of great innovative people of the past. And, of course, we heard a lot about benchmarking visits to innovative places and companies.

Certainly, creativity is important, and culture and climate do have an impact on people's abilities to be creative, but we did not see this approach as robust enough to embed innovation into our culture.

Technology

Some of the consulting groups saw innovation as a technology utilization process and wanted to train our engineers on ways to innovate products using more technology. Although we believed technology was part of the answer, we were trying to steer clear of focusing our total attention on a one-dimensional answer.

Strategy (re)Formulation

A few consulting firms offered the perspective that innovation must take the form of strategy formulation in which they (naturally) would lead the work. One was positive that we had an inadequate strategy and needed to go back to the drawing board and do more strategy formulation.

But although strategy is critical to us and it was crucial in our decision to adopt innovation as a core competence, it was clear that we needed to move on to execution. This approach did not fulfill even one of our primary objectives.

Product Bells and Whistles

In the past, innovation at Whirlpool was often thought of strictly in terms of product innovation. Indeed there was a rich and worthwhile set of literature and practices around product development innovation that ranged from ideation to ensuring that the best ideas get through the product development pipeline and to market in a timely manner. Product innovation falls into two main categories: products that are new to the world such as the Palm Pilot and products that have new bells and whistles, such as extensions or expansions. Companies such as Johnson & Johnson and 3M are known for both their new products and product line extensions. For example, you can buy Tylenol in a dizzying range of options—capsules, caplets, PM, and Extra Strength to name just a few.

Although product innovation was certainly an important part of our objective, we did not want to focus exclusively on it. We were after a much broader range of innovation, including all our customer touch points.

Training and More Training

The last category of consultants was one group that wanted to train us in innovation. They offered a lovely curriculum and a host of expert instructors. Their remedy was to take everyone in Whirlpool through a three-day boot camp. It was akin to a Six Sigma approach to innovation.

But although we knew that skill and knowledge about innovation were critical to our success, this approach did not fulfill our primary objective of innovation as a cultural and permanent change in the way we do business. Training alone was not the answer.

DETERMINING TO TAKE OUR OWN JOURNEY WITH A LONE GUIDE

We eventually realized that all these approaches were ignoring a major tenet of our vision: the need to create and maintain a core competence in innovation. At this point, we understood that no one consultant group had all the answers to the process of embedment. Surprisingly, although much of the business literature also supported the need for innovation from everyone—as opposed to a product-only focus, simple culture change, or better leadership and business strategy—there was not one strong, well-conceived program that embodied what we were looking for. We concluded that we had to make this journey mostly on our own.

However, we found one company to serve as our guide, the consulting firm Strategos, located in Chicago, which shared our passion for innovation from everyone. Strategos did several things that the other consultants did not. First, these consultants shared our passion for creating innovation across a broad group of people. They did not see innovation as an elitist set of skills. Second, they possessed a set of tools that were easy to teach, easy to learn, and were proved to generate innovation. Next, they had many ideas about embedment and wanted to co-create with us a process that would be comprehensive and fit our needs.

What also intrigued us about Strategos was that the consultants did not want a long-term relationship with us and would not create consultant dependency. They admitted that they did not have all the answers and wanted to work with us to discover new ways to embed innovation. Their refreshing approach put the emphasis on learning for ourselves and, in the process, creating a systemic approach to embedment that would become self-sustaining.

We agreed that Strategos would transfer what they knew to about seventy-five of us over a twelve-month period. The plan called for teaching us a well-thought-out methodology for innovation that included a set of tools and processes that represented the required knowledge and techniques we believed we needed. Strategos had experience teaching the techniques and processes of breaking out of orthodoxies, idea generation and development, idea migration into full-blown opportunities, business opportunity analysis, and other tools and techniques.

HARNESSING THE RESOURCES AND LEADERSHIP

Once we had the vision and an external guide to provide the upfront tools, systems, and approaches, our leadership began to think about and acquire the resources and additional leadership needed for the long-term embedment effort. To start, we needed to focus on obtaining sufficient resources and enrolling our top leaders.

People Resources

We determined that we first needed to create "embedment practitioners" or general managers. Actually, we did not use those terms at that time, but it is a good description of the role those people needed to serve, and so we will use the term throughout this book. These general managers would be people who were accountable to create a plan to embed innovation working with Strategos and the CEO and other key leaders.

The first role to be filled was a Global vice president of innovation (the role that one of us, Nancy, took on). This role was to be the lead internal embedment practitioner. The position reported to the CEO and was located in corporate headquarters. The reporting relationship gave the role a status that was critical to future success.

The CEO chartered this role to help himself and our Executive Committee select the outside consultant and to get the leadership of Whirlpool ready for the innovation initiative. The ongoing accountability for this role was to be the global leader for embedment. Initially, this meant coordinating with the consultants, selecting the first seventy-five people to learn the innovation methodology, ensuring consistency across the globe, and leveraging best practices. But in the long run, the position would become much more complicated, given that creating the infrastructure and culture to embed innovation as a core competency was an unrivaled challenge.

In addition to this lead person, we needed embedment general managers at the local level. Whirlpool is like many other companies in that programs that come out of corporate headquarters are always suspect. We needed a strong regional business focus to ensure the success of innovation embedment. The CEO knew that for this to work, it could not be seen as a corporate-only initiative. Whirlpool is a global company with regional strategic business units in North America, Latin America, Europe, and Asia. (See Exhibit 1.1 at the end of the chapter for the organization chart.) Each region had to be accountable for innovation to succeed. But ultimately, the CEO insisted that we start simultaneously in the three biggest regions, excluding Asia for reasons related to size and scope. In a large global complex enterprise, this was still a tall order.

We therefore selected three regional innovation embedment general managers to work for the head of each region, in senior and visible positions. We called people in these roles vice presidents or general managers of regional innovation.

We also added a knowledge management (KM) resource in each region. Although we did not yet have a KM system, we felt that knowledge management would be an important component of innovation embedment. When we thought about embedding innovation into everyone and everywhere, we knew that we needed a knowledge distribution and collection system that would democratize knowledge and information. Our KM efforts are described in Chapter Seven, and as you will see, they played an important role in the effort.

The next steps in filling positions to support innovation embedment represented a significant organizational commitment. At the advice of the Strategos and the behest of the CEO, we selected twenty-five people from each of the three starting regions (seventy-five in total) to become the core group of people whose full-time job would be to learn the innovation methods, skills, and processes from the consultants. In each region, the twenty-five Innovation team members, or I-Team, were to become the first individuals who would learn the innovation tools that would eventually be embedded into the entire Whirlpool culture and business strategy. Their goal was to learn how to use the process to generate business ideas and move them toward reality in the marketplace with customers. In essence, they were the first genetic carriers of innovation.

The long-range plan was to have these I-Team members work at acquiring the skills for nine months. Then about one-third would return to their previous jobs and spread the innovation "virus," another third would be assigned to the new innovations that were created, and the final third would move into a teaching capacity as full-time Innovation Consultants, or I-Consultants, within

Whirlpool. Their role would be to teach the skills and replace the role that Strategos had played at the beginning.

Although these people had to separate from their normal work, they were not intended to be a skunkworks. The proof of this was evidenced in the words of our CEO, who told them, "I don't really care if innovations come out of the first seventy-five as long as they learn the skills of innovation." He expected this group to learn the tools and teach others and then, and only then, to create innovations that could be tested and scaled up in the marketplace. The emphasis for this group was clearly on knowledge and skill transfer. This is the distinction between embedment and a skunkworks: the former is to teach and learn, and the latter is to innovate and produce bottom-line results.

The selection of these first seventy-five individuals was significant. They included some of the top talent in the organization, pulled from their operational roles at a time when the business really needed them. They were intentionally selected to be seventy-five of the most diverse people ever assembled at Whirlpool. Members ranged from vice presidents to shop floor operators and included people from every functional group. They were diverse in terms of nationality, culture, and demographics. We chose the members based on the following characteristics:

- New voices as well as experienced voices
- Whirlpool-only experience as well as those who had worked outside Whirlpool
- Many organizational levels, ranging from entry level to top leadership
- A variety of functions, from operationally focused to customer focused
- Male and female
- Diverse backgrounds based on how diversity was defined in their region
- Regional and nonregional experience
- Divergent and convergent thinkers
- Courageous and willing to be a "heretic to convention"
- Ability to work well in a team learning environment
- Candidate for developmental experience
- Assessed as promotable in our talent pool system

As a result of these characteristics for the team, the I-Teams were the most diverse teams or groups of people within Whirlpool.

The I-Team members were asked to join the innovation effort in an ultimate leap of faith. One day, they received calls from their bosses to join the new I-Teams as full-time members. However, their bosses knew little about what the people were being called on to do, and the first team members were not even informed of much on that day. They were not given clear job descriptions, the description of new career paths, or the certainty of returning to their old jobs. They came from many different locations, so many of them had to move or commute from homes, countries, or regions far away.

Many I-Team members recall the first day of work in their new group. There were no fancy offices, sized and accessorized according to their rank as most of them had been used to. Instead, there was a bull pen with telephones, computers, and pads of sticky notes. Like the first unsettling day of high school, each group met, got settled, and waited to find out if they had made the right choice. They were pioneers in an uncharted endeavor, first to arms in innovation embedment.

Leadership Enrollment

The Executive Committee is the first level of leadership at Whirlpool (see Exhibit 1.1). These individuals all agreed that innovation was a primary way to maximize customer loyalty, which would lead to shareholder value. What was now needed to begin the effort in earnest was to engage the next level of leadership: the senior officers who ran the business units. These twenty-five top leaders (called the Chairman's Council) ultimately would be in charge of embedment; their time and attention were scarce due to the everyday demands of the business. But they also deeply understood the magnitude of the change that would be required.

We made a first effort to engage this level of leadership in January 2000 at a senior leadership conference, which we made into an innovation workshop, the joint idea of Strategos and the CEO. The idea was to hold an event as soon as possible that gained the understanding and commitment to innovation from the senior leadership team. The goal was to confirm with this level of leadership two things: that innovation was vital to the success of the business and that it was an undeniable core competence that Whirlpool needed to embed into the DNA of our business.

Most leaders were interested as they realized the business requirements and were excited about the approach. We knew that getting the leadership behind the embedding innovation was critical to success. At the time of this meeting, we knew few details about what these leaders would be required to do to embed innovation, but we knew their commitment was essential. The leaders left the meeting excited and ready for next steps. At this point, that was all we could ask for. We will describe in later chapters the ongoing process of engagement and leadership from people at this level as well as the entire workforce.

Creating I-Boards

The final resource structures that were established early on were Innovation Boards, or I-Boards. This group, comprising senior leaders at the regional business level, was charged with overseeing the entire innovation competence creation and embedment effort. Three I-Boards were set up, representing the three major business regions of Whirlpool: one in North America, one in Latin America, and one in Europe. The I-Boards would meet on a regular basis, set financial and embedment goals, allocate resources, and review processes and new innovation ideas for further funding.

The I-Boards turned out to be one of the most important and vital resources for the effort, but perhaps also one of the major sources of frustration. They became a place for leaders to get out of their day-to-day activities to think more about innovation and embedment. The I-Boards slowly began to change the Whirlpool mind-set about experimentation and risk taking. This change centered on moving from focusing on only big "bet-the-farm" risks to recognizing the value of smaller successive risks through experimentation. The I-Board also became a model for what was now expected of our leaders: thoughtful deliberations about innovation, interaction with innovators in a co-creation role, and overall management and oversight of individual innovation projects as well as the portfolio of innovations. For the most part, I-Boards proved to be a successful mechanism for leadership involvement and guiding the innovation embedment efforts. In Chapter Four, we will share what happened in these I-Boards and what our leaders learned. Exhibit 1.1 contains an example of a regional I-Board.

THE WHIRLPOOL ORGANIZATIONAL STRUCTURE FOR INNOVATION

Exhibit 1.1 sets out Whirlpool's main organizational structure, shows how we fit in the new structures established for innovation embedment, and lists the key players who worked in innovation.

WHAT WE LEARNED

- Innovation is difficult to embed as a core competence for many organizations.

- Although there is a significant amount of literature on innovation, there is no road map or set of rules for embedding innovation as a core competence. The road map for building the competence in any given organization most likely has to be custom-built. The specifics of each situation dictate the specific design of the road map for building the competence.

- No one consulting firm will likely offer all the answers. The effort may need to be your work—and your work alone.

(continued on page 22)

Exhibit 1.1. Whirlpool's Organization and Players

Executive Committee, Chairman's Council, and Innovation Boards

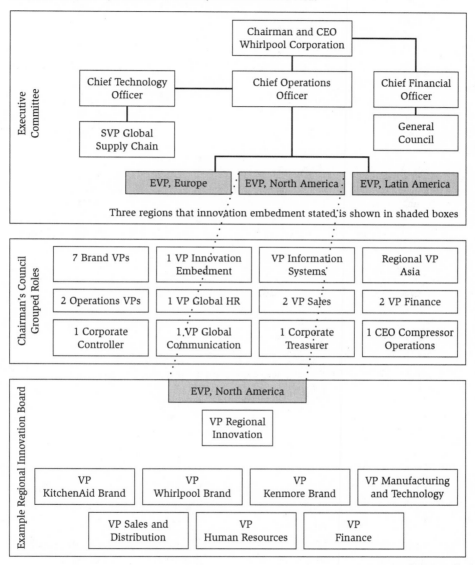

(continued)

Exhibit 1.1. Whirlpool's Organization and Players *(continued)*

Organization Chart for Innovation-Related Roles

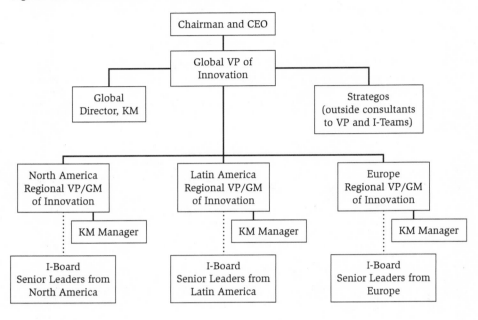

I-Teams

75 I-Team members—25 from each region above.
After training, one-third return to their work,
one-third become I Consultants,
and one-third are assigned to new innovations.

The Players

- Chairman of the board and CEO: David R. Whitwam. In addition to serving as CEO, he is the visionary and the chief architect of innovation embedment at Whirlpool.

- Chief operations officer: Jeff Fettig. In addition to serving as COO, he is a primary architect of innovation embedment at Whirlpool.

- The Executive Committee: Nine individuals: the CEO, the COO, and the seven direct reports to the Office of the Chairman. These senior officers also head the major regions, technology, or corporate center functions like finance and legal. They are also referred to as EVPs (executive vice presidents) or SBU (strategic business unit) heads. Key to the embedment process were:

Paulo Periquito, EVP of Latin American and key architect of Whirlpool's change management process discussed in Chapter Eight

Mike Thieneman, EVP for North America at the start of embedment and now the chief technology officer and key architect of Whirlpool's change management process that we discuss in Chapter Eight

Jeff Fettig, who ran Europe when we started embedment and is now the COO

Mike Todman, who was the North American EVP for a period during embedment and is now the EVP of Europe

David Swift, EVP for North America

Mark Brown, who was the CFO for a period and is now senior vice president of global strategic sourcing

Dan Hopp, senior vice president of corporate affairs and general counsel

Steve Barrett, CFO and the newest member of the Executive Committee

- The Chairman's Council: The twenty-five senior officers of the company. These include Garrick D'Silva, senior vice president for Asia; Dave Binkley, corporate vice president of global human resources; and Barry Holt, corporate vice president of global communications. The rest of these members are functional, brand, or strategic business unit heads who played key roles in innovation embedment as I-Board members or as leaders in their business group or function.

- Senior leaders: The senior 110 leaders of Whirlpool. These are key senior leadership positions within the company.

- Global vice president of innovation: The CEO created this role at the start of innovation embedment. Nancy Snyder, the coauthor, held this title.

- Regional vice president or general manager of innovation: Regional leadership roles established as the head of innovation. They reported to the EVP of the region and were facilitators of the Innovation Board for the regions. All I-Consultants within the region report to this role, which has a dotted line relationship with the global vice president of innovation. Key regional innovation vice presidents or general managers include or included:

Ricardo Acosta, Latin America

Guiseppe Geneletti, previously general manager of innovation for Europe and now global director of innovation

Andrew Batson, previous North American vice president of innovation

Phil Pejovich, vice president of innovation for North America

Kathy Nelson, current vice president of innovation for North America

P. O. Nyman, current head of innovation for Europe

Innovation consultants: Full-time highly skilled innovation positions within a region who report to the vice president or general manager of innovation and may also report to a business head. They included James Summers, the head architect and I-Consultant for Innovation Days, which we write about in the book.

(continued)

Exhibit 1.1. Whirlpool's Organization and Players *(continued)*

- Innovation mentor: Part-time role within a function or business
- Innovation Team: Original group of seventy-five (twenty-five in each of the three regions) full-time people who learned innovation skills from Strategos so that we could begin to embed innovation.
- Knowledge manager leads: Regional or global knowledge managers—full-time professionals who are accountable to ensure that knowledge management for innovation is current, user friendly, and interactive. They include:

  Tammy Patrick, global director of knowledge management who oversaw the innovation audit head of the knowledge management professions
  Roberta Vanetti, who played a key role in getting knowledge management up and running.

- Innovation Board: SBU or EVP senior staff who meet monthly to oversee innovation and innovation embedment
- Strategos: The consultant group that we partnered with in the first year. Gary Hamel is the principal of Strategos. David Crosswhite from the Chicago office was our lead consultant.

- A specific, understandable, and simple vision for innovation, originating at the top of the organization, is essential for guiding initial efforts.
- A good vision and a custom-built road map to get there may not be enough. You need a significant set of resources set aside for beginning the effort: money for consultants, a leader for the effort, senior leadership's time and attention, and, most important, the commitment of top people throughout the organization.
- You must craft your journey as you make it and be willing to adapt it as you go along.
- You have to prepare the workforce for the long term, and this means having staying power. Embedment requires a long-term perspective and the ability to view the changes required in a comprehensive manner and to understand the levers that drive embedment.

SELF-ASSESSMENTS: GETTING STARTED IN INNOVATION

At the end of the following chapters, we provide you with worksheets to help you bring innovation into your organization.

CHAPTER TWO

Reinventing the Wheel

Embedding a core competency is a long-term value proposition. It requires putting in place accountabilities, systems, structures, policies, procedures, and measures that will support and enable the competency long after the leaders who initiated the effort are gone. Real embedment includes ensuring that there is capability for innovation to occur and conditions for it to thrive on an ongoing basis. Many organizations can force the creation of capability or competency on a temporary basis, relying on the will of individual leaders to push their initiative or process onto a small group of people who possess the requisite skill sets.

But real and long-term capability is reached only when the core competency becomes a part of the DNA of the organization. It exists when the competency is embedded in the skills of all people, in the core of all systems, in the customer's perspective of the organization, and in the heart of the organization's identity. We knew it would exist for us when it became part of Whirlpool's very essence.

This chapter sets the stage for the remainder of the book by outlining the process that Whirlpool used for innovation embedment. It discusses the way we arrived at our embedment strategy and the categories of action we used in the embedment process.

FROM LEADERS' REACTIONS TO THE EMBEDMENT WHEEL

When we began thinking through the concept of embedment as a long-term strategy, we were uncertain how best to communicate it to everyone. We needed a way to ensure that this new way of thinking, new skill sets, and measures and business strategies would become part of our culture in a way that could not be easily dismantled. But we did not know what to call it or how to explain it. To make matters worse, when we tried to discuss embedment, many of Whirlpool's leaders looked at us as if we were from another planet. We were just not getting our point across—and it showed on their faces and in their reactions.

After weeks of discussions, we could see that we needed a different strategy to define and communicate the concept of embedment. As anyone who works in organizations and with teams knows, sometimes it is best to take a concept off-line, do some concrete work on it, and then bring it back for discussion. The time had come for us to do just that. A conceptual debate about embedment was getting us nowhere. We were getting the "dreaded agreement nod" that means, *I have no idea what you are talking about, but keep going because I have another meeting to go to.* It was clear that we needed a different starting place to be able to explain ourselves in more concrete terms.

Taking the discussion off-line proved useful. It allowed us to begin to differentiate between change management and embedment, a critical step for us in defining embedment. Most models of change management follow some form of Kurt Lewin's "unfreeze, change, refreeze" model (1999). John Kotter's model of change (1995), one of best we have found for leading change, ends with a

DUCT TAPE VERSION
When It Gets Murky

Over many meetings with leaders, we struggled, and the leaders suffered through a painful trial-and-error process of testing and refining ideas about how to define, create, and disseminate the concept of innovation embedment. We grappled with many salient questions, such as why it was not enough to focus on the results of innovation rather than on this extra step of embedment. If we could innovate and be successful in the marketplace, was it not reasonable to assume that people's skills as well as the back-end systems and processes would change to support and reinforce that success? We faced other questions too: Whose job was it to embed innovation? What role did leaders play in that process? Couldn't we have consultants do it for us? Was it a corporate function? And finally, Why was this any different than change management?

We felt that if innovation embedment were to be successful, we needed to start with a shared mental model of embedment. We also felt this was best accomplished by creating a simple model that had face validity with our leaders.

step that he calls "institutionalize new approaches." In essence, embedment is the "refreeze" or "institutionalize" part of these change models.

Armed with this realization, we began to define what elements any organization would need to permanently transform or modify to ensure that change became frozen or institutionalized. We could have used one of the traditional management paradigms or frameworks to describe the innovation embedment process such as McKinsey's seminal Seven Ss or the process described in "Organizing Levers for Capability Building." Our goal, however, was to find a fresh framework that would describe the stages, levels, and processes that needed to happen to embed innovation deeply into the Whirlpool bloodline. We could not just lift a framework from somewhere else.

We created a simple list of embedment actions using concepts, ideas, and tools from many different areas, including the literature referred to in Chapter One on strategy, organizational change, structuration, organizational learning, culture change, and knowledge management—to name a few. The list included items such as vision, measures, resources, tools, and other elements that we had identified through our conversations with leaders, the literature, and best practices.

Slowly, our new approach and the list of embedment actions did the trick. People began to nod their head affirmatively. However, we wanted more than just agreement. We were after passion and commitment, yet the list still did not awaken the zeal for innovation embedment that we had hoped for and needed to accomplish our goal at the deepest level within Whirlpool.

We debated whether the lack of passion was due to the list itself, or to the concept of embedment being inherently boring, or perhaps to our own presentation of it. But we were sure that the elements in the list were correct, and we chose to ignore the possibility that embedment was boring to those around us. That left just one culprit: our presentation. We retackled this, organizing the same categories of the embedment process into a visual device. Sure enough, this did the trick! We created a circle, which we named the embedment wheel (see Exhibit 2.1).

Our visual device became a hit. It immediately made far more sense to Whirlpool's leaders, and they became more energized about embedment. The wheel allowed everyone to see the elements of embedment in a far more interesting and integrated way. This simple change worked remarkably well. In fact, the joke became that through describing innovation embedment, we had reinvented the wheel.

The embedment wheel became a valuable framework that resonated with senior leadership. The lesson here was that clear language and a visual framework can make a great deal of difference in getting agreement among people about how to move forward and in building the energy and commitment needed to achieve results.

Exhibit 2.1. The Embedment Wheel

Source: © 2002 Whirlpool Corporation. All rights reserved.

ELEMENTS OF THE EMBEDMENT WHEEL

Our embedment wheel consists of three layers. The outer layer contains the vision and goals, representing the desired and hoped-for outcomes of the embedment effort. The vision and goals embody the hopes, dreams, and desires of the process. The next layer contains the infrastructure that supports innovation embedment at every level of the organization. The infrastructure includes many elements, such as leadership, culture and values, resources, knowledge management and learning systems, change management and strategic communications, rewards and recognition, systems alignment, and measurement and reporting systems. The third layer of the wheel on the inside focuses on capability development, which includes the actual processes and tools that are required to innovate.

Following is an overview of these layers. The remaining chapters in the book provide far more detail about the embedment wheel and how we crafted the approaches for the outer and inner layers.

THE OUTER LAYER: A GREAT VISION

Unquestionably, embedment must begin with a clear, compelling vision for innovation. This provides the keystone, or "North Star," that guides the journey. We strongly believed that the vision must describe the desired future state for innovation. It had to be compelling enough to motivate and guide the actions of people at all levels of the organization—from leaders to middle managers to the people on the shop floors in manufacturing. To achieve the goal of embedment of innovation from everyone and everywhere, our vision needed to be unique in order to capture the imagination and desires of sixty thousand people. It also needed to be specific enough to guide our actions and inform our decision making. We wanted our vision to be short and memorable and to speak with passion and excitement. For each person in the enterprise, it needed to answer two questions: *Why should I want to get involved?* and *How will my life change because of it?*

The Vision

Our vision, "Innovation from Everyone and Everywhere," started from the belief of our CEO, David Whitwam, that anyone in the company could innovate. The first part of the vision became even more important over time. *Everyone* spoke to the wide range of diversity we had at Whirlpool. It included all levels, functions, and jobs. *Everyone* strongly implied that innovation would come not just from people at the top or in certain functions. It endorsed the belief that anyone, given the right tools and support, could develop a business concept into a customer solution.

The second part of this vision, *everywhere,* denoted geography, relationship, and lack of proximity. It did not limit innovation to Whirlpool people, because *everywhere* is boundaryless. It acknowledged that innovation could come from both inside and outside the company, meaning that everyone in the company could listen to customers and suppliers for innovation. This broad vision about everywhere also counteracted the tendency of most large multinational organizations to engage in headquarter ethnocentrism. Everywhere meant *anywhere* in the company.

We were fortunate in many ways, in that we had what immediately seemed a great vision for embedment. This vision proved to be invaluable. For us, our vision was both poetic and literal at the same time, reaching out to both sides of the brain. It appealed to passionate people everywhere in the company who felt that they could make a difference in our business and for our customers.

The Goals Behind the Vision

With this great vision, we also needed goals to make the vision real. Goals are the ways that the innovation vision is actualized through focus and action. We created embedment goals that were "big, hairy and audacious," or BHAGs, as they have been dubbed by James Collins and Jerry Porris (1996). We believed that embedment goals in innovation must be by nature big, bold, and discontinuous from the present. We needed them to spur us toward a drastic departure from our current state. We could not live with goals that were incremental in nature. We wanted to make a strong, inspiring statement about what Whirlpool could be.

We had many important discussions about embedment goals, which allowed us to explore what embedment really meant to us. However, we often got stuck in understanding the difference between the goals of innovation effort itself and the goals of embedment. We soon realized that there were really two sets of goals: results goals (our final destination) and embedment goals (the journey we were taking). (You will also read in Chapter Three that two years into the embedment, we uncovered a third type of goal: individual goals.)

Results goals are analogous to business outcomes. They represent the ultimate outcome or business result from innovation efforts. They let you know that you have arrived at your destination. Examples of results goals include the amount of new revenue generated from innovation, the number of new products or services, the number of new-to-the-world products or services, or changes in customer loyalty measures. These goals are critical to ensuring that innovation obtains true business results.

In contrast, embedment goals are learning goals, or as the popular literature calls them, process goals. Embedment goals let you know if you are on track getting where you want to be. They are necessary to know that you are moving forward. Their curse is that even with the best definitions, they can come across as "touchy-feely" and soft. They are often by nature less tangible than destination goals, partly because they do not fall directly to the bottom line. Among the embedment goals that Whirlpool began using are these:

- Exposing everyone to innovation through reading, joining an innovation project, or some other means of engagement
- Establishing new career paths in innovation
- Including diverse people on innovation teams
- Measuring the number of people involved in innovation projects

- Counting the number of innovation mentors (I-Mentors, part-time innovation consultants) available to help on innovation projects

As you will see from time to time in our story, the distinction between results and embedment goals was both useful and confusing. But in the end, the goals clarified our thinking about how to approach innovation embedment and provided a useful framework that helped us to avoid confusing embedment measures with business results. Along the way, however, they fostered frustration and added a level of complexity that we often felt we could have lived without.

THE INFRASTRUCTURE ELEMENTS OF THE WHEEL

Vision and goals set the context for embedding innovation. The real work of embedment, however, comes from those elements that reflect the tangible and structural foundations that make innovation as a core competence not only come alive but be long lasting.

For our infrastructure, we selected elements that represented five main areas: resources, leaders, culture, systems, and processes. These elements circumscribed the many changes that Whirlpool would need to make in its infrastructures. Here is a brief review of each infrastructure element of the wheel in the sequence shown in Exhibit 2.1.

Leader Accountability and Development

It is an absolute truth about strategic change initiatives that they are impossible to accomplish purely as grassroots movements. At the front end, embedment must be the domain of leaders who, by definition, have access to resources and can implement the massive changes required to push innovation across a broad group of people. We discovered this when noting that although all senior leaders might passionately share the vision for innovation and embedment, we still needed action from them to make embedment successful. There was no doubt that leadership had to be the engine that drove embedment.

Leader focus required a dual set of responsibilities: accountability for embedment of innovation in their own way of thinking and acting and accountability for the creation of an environment and systems that made everyone else capable of leading or engaging in innovation. We found that defining these accountabilities was actually more complex than we thought at first but that we needed to define exactly what leaders would be responsible for.

We thus created a set of primary areas of accountability for leaders with regard to innovation embedment:

- Co-creation of the innovation process itself with a focus on leader involvement in not only reviewing new products or services but accountability for, and creation of, processes and systems that facilitated innovation embedment.
- Creation of time and space for learning about innovation, both for themselves and the people in their work units. All leaders were asked to set aside time for themselves and their work units to engage in innovation learning and projects. This was not a forced function and could vary based on the work unit demands, but it sent a strong signal that leaders needed to set the stage for everyone to have an opportunity to be involved.
- Engaging in and stimulating out-of-the-box thinking. Whirlpool culture had been a strong process-oriented culture for many years. As a result, novel and different ways of thinking were often discouraged in order to foster reliability and predictability. Leaders would therefore need to model new ways of thinking and pay strict attention to ensuring that they were not unintentionally squashing nontraditional or innovative, creative ideas.
- Creating an innovation-rich environment with opportunities for development. Leaders were accountable for creating the right type of environment for innovation to foster. One of the tenets of our innovation effort was that it not become bureaucratic or hierarchical. Leaders were accountable for setting the climate of the organization so that standards, expectations, rewards, recognition, relationships and results all focused on innovation.
- Balancing the day-to-day business pressures with innovation embedment. Even in the economic environment of the times, which might best be described as difficult, we gave leaders the accountability to balance the short-term and long-term demands of their business. The paradoxes of managing short- and long-term results were expected to be balanced in an intentional manner, no matter what the level in the organization.

Culture and Values

The second element of infrastructure we focused on was organizational culture. As we know, culture plays an important role in any change effort, and it functions as a particularly significant role in embedment. Culture consists of the implicit and often unstated organizational values, norms, and ways of doing business that subtly reinforce and guide many behaviors and decisions. Culture and values are a central part of a company's DNA and so affect all elements of the embedment process.

If the culture and values of the organization are at odds with the embedment effort, chances are that the embedment effort will be more difficult, perhaps even fail. For example, it is well known that encouraging ideas from everyone in a culture where risk taking is valued will be easier than in a culture where risk taking is punished. Similarly, a culture that has a strong process orientation makes thinking differently more difficult because of people's discomfort with changing their existing methods of operation. A culture that is open to change often finds innovation easier.

We found that Whirlpool possessed certain cultural characteristics that would clearly have an impact on our innovation embedment. We knew from previous efforts that we had a culture that tended to be risk averse and process oriented. But we also knew that this culture could effectively manage change.

Our surprise was that our embedment endeavors actually changed our culture. For example, through modeling new behaviors, our leaders set the stage for new cultural assumptions such as risk taking or making innovation a priority. If we had waited to change our culture so that it was ripe for innovation, we might have waited forever. The lesson we learned was that embedment efforts should not be slowed because the culture is not perfectly suited for innovation. Changing the culture happened for us through action.

The bottom line is that culture and values to support embedment are critical to success, whether they exist before the effort begins or are developed as a result of embedment. If the embedment effort is contradictory with existing culture, it can become a problem for leaders because innovation is by its character disruptive and chaotic. In Chapter Five on culture and values, we will more fully discuss how culture influenced innovation at Whirlpool and outline what we did to ensure that our culture was supporting innovation embedment.

Resources: Funds and People

Resource creation and allocation is the backbone for the embedment of all competencies. We all know that underfunded efforts not only have less chance of succeeding but often make the people involved in them look incompetent in the process. Having the appropriate resources is the ante to get in the game of innovation from everyone and everywhere, but it does not ensure embedment. Resources are required as a start-up proposition and then as ongoing support.

We divided resources into two major categories: funds for innovation and embedment activities and people or talent for those same activities.

Funds. Getting the funds and capital right for embedment is critical to the long-term success. In a start-up mode, we decided that funding the initiative from headquarters out of a corporate pool of money would initiate and sustain embedment best. A corporate fund reduced the temptation for business units facing day-to-day pressures to cut embedment start-up expenses if they were under their own control. Onset funding for innovation balances corporate or central nurturing and distributed ownership of all embedment resources. Innovation embedment has to survive its own childhood and not be distracted by other priorities. Start-up funds from corporate center were the way we did this.

One of the most important devices we found to embed innovation was to move the funds close to the ideas. A popular axiom in the venture capital world is: "Keep shopping your idea through the no's until you hear one yes." This was the attitude that we wanted our innovators to have. We wanted people to understand that if they were passionate and had a good idea, there were people close to them with money. They would not have to go through twelve layers of hierarchy to get their ideas heard and funded.

This attitude is contrary to the traditional, old-economy company axiom where it takes only a single no to kill an idea and where everyone can usually say no. We believed that if innovators had to climb through multiple levels of people who can say no to get funding, ideas from everyone would not bubble up or they would be quickly silenced. Setting up innovation seed funds close to the ideas, with open access to anyone with a good idea, was in our view a requirement for innovation embedment to succeed.

The other important nuance of this device was to make the funding idea driven rather than calendar driven. Most corporate budgeting systems hand out all their money at the beginning of each fiscal year. Departments and people line up at the trough to get their fair share, and if you miss out, too bad. In contrast, in an idea-driven model, funds are available whenever good ideas surface, no matter if that happens at the beginning, middle, or end of the fiscal year. Without funds, the system will slow or stall innovation rather than enable it.

People. Embedment of innovation from everyone requires a drastic rethinking of how people move about—or are moved—in an organization. Traditionally, supervisors or human resources move people around jobs. But innovation from everyone requires fluidity of human capital. People need to move to where the ideas are, especially if they have the passion to work on them and the skills needed. The assignment of jobs in innovation has to be based on a system that recognizes free will. Of all of the embedment components, this might have been one of the hardest for us to implement. It involved removing barriers to free movement and taking the control of job mobility out of the hands of supervisors who were usually reluctant to lose their best talent. But we learned a more important lesson about people and embedment: if embedment is successful, not only do people move to ideas but innovation comes to them in their daily jobs. In Chapter Six, we discuss these learnings in detail. At the end of the day, as hard as funds and capital are to come by, your most precious resources always turn out to be people's time and talent.

Knowledge Management and Learning Systems

We found that innovation from everyone required at least two parallel learning channels. We've discussed one: leaders who could teach others. The other was a knowledge management system that let people teach themselves about innovation.

Knowledge management and learning systems have a practical application when you want innovation from everyone and everywhere, especially where "everywhere" is spread over five continents and tens of thousands of people. Knowledge management involves how a firm creates, collects, stores, and shares knowledge. An effective knowledge management system can provide most people in an organization with access to knowledge and information about innovation as well as related topics.

We found that knowledge management and learning systems became most interesting when they circumvented hierarchy and allowed people with passion to learn about working on innovative ideas and projects. We wanted no permissions or letters of introduction required in the knowledge-based organization we were trying to create. Instead, we opted for informal networking, not organizational charts, to become the currency of information sharing and meeting others. Our knowledge management systems (we had both electronic-based and nonelectronic-based systems) encouraged people to explore and learn about the customer, new ideas, the innovation process itself, and others who wanted to work with them on projects.

Change Management and Strategic Communications

Change management and strategic communications also support the infrastructure in the embedment wheel. Change management is intimately related to core competency embedment. Effective embedment requires an active change management process that can have an impact on the redesign of systems and processes that support embedment. In a way, we found that change management started the embedment of innovation as a core competency at the enterprise level and was again required, perhaps in a scaled-down version, at all stages of the embedment process.

Fortunately, Whirlpool had a very well-developed and well-understood change management process. The robust nature of this process was a real strategic advantage in embedment.

Similarly, we found strategic communications to be one of the most paradoxical elements of the embedment infrastructure. Effective communication can help everyone know about innovation, yet too much communication too fast can set up expectations that the organization cannot meet. We discovered, for instance, that the timing of messages to everyone was critical. If they came too soon, expectations would be too high. If they came too late, the communication was not effective in leveraging the desired behavior. In addition, we discovered that the person communicating a message is as important as the message communicated. In some organizations, it is the accountability of the headquarters for enterprise-wide communication, but at Whirlpool, for our innovation activities, we saw that the communicators must be closer to the ideas.

Finally, we noted that it is also important that there be a consistency of language and approach to communications, which might best be handled by a central group. Designing and implementing a strong strategic communications strategy that balances the tensions of central and coordinated communication with those close to ideas is critical.

Rewards and Recognition

Rewards and recognition are a requirement to ensure that activity around innovation embedment is reinforced by formal organizational systems such as career development, compensation, and informal recognition practices. This element answers the question, "What's in it for me?" Rewards and recognition should reinforce the attainment of the new innovation skill sets, as well as recognize leaders and others who apply those skills toward the goals of the organization.

We used rewards, monetary and nonmonetary, as rewards and recognition practices in a number of different ways. One goal was to provide incentives to people to try new career paths or acquire new skill sets without changing jobs. We also included incentives that would encourage managers to alter their existing roles and job descriptions. Instead of focusing only on doing more of the same but constantly better, faster, and cheaper, we wanted to drive a portion of their focus in the direction of new and different—that is, innovation in their core business.

One school of thought around innovation compensation involves bringing Silicon Valley approaches to the organization, more or less structuring compensation around a venture capital approach where people are rewarded based on the revenue their ideas brings. However, the amount of angst that this approach created for us when we discussed it was astounding. The anxiety started and ended with the following premise: if an innovator or a team of innovators created a customer solution worth millions to the firm, should they not share in the gains or, as some say, become millionaires? A second, juxtaposing premise went: if people in organizations wanted to be millionaires and live the life of a garage entrepreneur, they would have chosen a life that does not start and end with an employee number.

Many of us who join companies do not expect to become millionaires from an idea, but we do expect to be rewarded. We are still wrestling with this question, and our approach is still evolving. In Chapter Nine, we discuss where we are currently in this debate. We also share our learnings about rewards and recognition as well as the system that is beginning to work for us.

Systems Alignment

Another infrastructure element in the embedment of innovation is the combination of strategic, operations, and management systems that drive organizationwide behavior. These purposeful systems need to be aligned to support innovation. By nature, this forces questions of fit, alignment, and coexistence.

If innovation embedment does not fit or align with current financial, human resource, or other administrative systems, leaders need to redesign them over time as the embedment unfolds or as problems and opportunities arise.

For us, this was a long-term proposition that we planned and executed over a number of years. We began by conducting an audit of the systems that were critical for fit and discovered that these included all the major systems in our organization: profit planning, strategic planning, performance management, pay incentive systems, rewards and recognition, product development, operational excellence, operations reviews, staff meetings, balanced scorecard or organization goal-setting processes, employee or human resource systems such as talent pool, employee satisfaction, and still others. We soon realized that most of our systems and processes would need at least some adaptation to support innovation. We also knew that any new systems, practices, and policies would need to be designed to support innovation.

We were aware, however, that many change efforts or capacity development systems fail because they do not address these titanic performance-driving systems and mechanisms. We clearly faced a daunting task; many of these processes or systems were incredibly complex and embedded in their own way in the business. Yet introducing innovation into the organization created the opportunity to refresh all strategic, operations, and management systems that run the business.

Measurement and Reporting Systems

Measurement and reporting systems are critical to understanding and tracking new behavior and change. If measures and reporting are lacking, we can expect at the very least to fail in understanding our progress toward embedment, let alone be able to make any necessary midcourse corrections. Furthermore, since embedment does not occur overnight or in the first year, innovation results, by their nature, are impossible to post to the bottom line in the twelve-month period following the innovation launch. Just as with measuring progress toward vision and goals, measurements in the first years of embedment needed to include both measures as well as embedment measures.

Results Measures. Even before there were any business results, it was important to establish the footprint for measuring them. Our initial cut at results measures focused on new revenue generated as a result of innovation, number of products or services created from innovation, and customer measures that indicated the impact of innovation on customer loyalty. We found that these measures changed over time to reflect changes in our goals and the realities of the business. One of our learnings was that we needed to remain agile and revisit measures often to ensure that they matched our strategy. We will revisit our current state of results measures in Chapter Ten.

Embedment Measures. Embedment measures also need to assess the capability-building or learning accomplishments. These measures need to acknowledge the fact that when a core competency is new, people in the organization have a learning curve to go through before the competency is embedded. At some point, we assumed, the embedment measures will drop away entirely because the organization will have passed through the learning curve and we would be left with results measures. However, there were embedment milestones that existed along the path, and these could be measured.

We focused on a broad array of embedment measures, such as how many people were using the tools and innovation process, how many experts we had in innovation (I-Consultants or I-Mentors), the number of people volunteering for innovation projects, and people's awareness of innovation as a goal, to name a few.

It is noteworthy that many embedment measures focused on the individual. We realized at a certain point that the true test of embedment lay at the individual level. Did people's job change as a result of embedment? Were they approaching their work differently? Did they understand how to use the tools? These areas of measurement became the most meaningful measures for action planning because they told us how far we had come and how far we needed to go to embed innovation at the real point of action: people's everyday lives on the job. We therefore put into place a robust process to measure embedment at the individual level, including electronic surveys, focus groups, and work unit audits of people's job activities.

A Tension Between Goals. One important point to note is that results measures tend to be seductive to business leaders. They are the real deal, the way leaders are accustomed to thinking about business. The early tension between embedment goals and results will be acute if the organization does not have a culture that supports learning and knowledge creation. This type of culture creates the opportunity for people to understand and relate to embedment as a concept. The bottom line is that two types of measures are required to track and report progress accurately: embedment and results.

CAPABILITY DEVELOPMENT: INNOVATION PROCESSES AND TOOLS

Processes and tools are found in the very inner layer of the embedment wheel. This element has to do with the selection of tools, processes, and techniques that create innovation. There are a number of very valid and useful tool sets and processes that can be used here. It is not our intention to have this book be a treatise on the many different types of innovation tools, techniques, and processes, but a short overview here might be useful in helping you understand how we selected the tool set that we did, largely using Strategos as our guide.

First, we were adamant that the selection of the tools and process match our strategic objective: innovation from everyone and everywhere, with a strong link to transforming our business. To get started, we sorted innovation tools and process into three major categories: those that focused on creativity, those that focused on modified version of skunkworks, and those that focused on an entrepreneurial approach to innovation. Some consultants might argue for a different type of categorization, but this one worked for us.

Creativity Techniques

The tools and techniques in the creativity category tend to focus on teaching skills and techniques aimed at individuals or teams charged with product development or service ideas. Often they use the set of approaches that are well known to create innovative ideas, such as lateral thinking (a phrase and set of techniques coined by DeBono, 1992), where individuals put together unrelated concepts to arrive at new and creative ideas. These creativity sessions are usually performed in teams or groups within a strict set of norms around acceptance of all new ideas as possibilities without making any prejudgments. The goal of lateral thinking is to generate as many new and creative ideas as possible.

During these sessions, ideas are usually generated by starting with a customer problem or competitive issue in mind. Ideas are then evaluated against a set of business requirements to see if they are worthy of further development or should be shelved for later use. Ideas that are selected for further development get placed into a product development process.

This approach to creativity has been adopted by some consulting firms that have created idea labs where teams can go to examine customer needs and wants and use creativity techniques that will help them obtain new ideas about how to approach this market. This approach has also been used at the front end of many product development processes to feed the ideation part of the process or as part of a pipeline where new ideas are formed and tested for their initial feasibility.

Skunkworks

A second category those that can be described as a modified version of skunkworks. As we noted in Chapter One, a skunkworks is a group of people who work on a project in a way that is outside the normal way of doing business. A skunkworks is often a small team that assumes or is given responsibility for developing something in a short time with few management constraints. It is sometimes used to spearhead a product design that later might be developed according to the usual procedures. A skunkworks project may be secret.

Skunkworks usually involves separating a team of people from the formal bureaucracy, systems, and structure of the organization to allow them time and space for innovation. They are usually provided with all the resources they need and are separated from their everyday responsibilities. Often the people in a skunkworks are selected for their intellect and talent. Lockheed Martin (formally Lockheed Corporation) has used this approach on a number of defense-related projects for over forty years. One famous example is the situation described in Tracy Kidder's Pulitzer Prize–winning book, *The Soul of a New Machine* (1982), where two technical teams were tasked with developing a new computer and were pitted against each another to see who would come out with the best design first.

Entrepreneurial Tools

The last group of innovation capability approaches are those that focus on tool sets that create or mimic what happens in an entrepreneurial setting. Much of what we did with Strategos fell into this category. These tools contain elements of creativity, product development processes, and skunkworks, in that they rely on getting people to generate new ideas. However, this approach and tool set has a different focus on how to use customer insights and trends to create business opportunities with potential. It goes beyond creativity techniques, product development processes, and skunkworks to teach a set of tools that people in the venture capital world use to evaluate new ideas, fund their development, and bring them into the market (or kill them if they do not work).

This set of tools targets creating a skill set around how to think, act, and evaluate ideas from a venture capitalist perspective. These tools also offer methods to scale up ideas into full-blown businesses. They provide methods to translate ideas into quick experiments in the market, procure resources to move ideas to the next level, and use financial and market research tools to determine whether an idea has long-term business potential. Many of the people involved in our innovation process commented that they had a better education in business using this tool set than they did in their M.B.A. program. Most important, they were targeted to everyone with a good idea. Just as level or occupation doesn't bind entrepreneurship, these tools were open for use for anyone with a good idea.

Selecting which tool set that was right for us was highly influenced by our vision for innovation from everyone and everywhere. We did not feel that a creativity approach alone would provide the business depth we needed or that a skunkworks approach allowed for innovation from everyone and everywhere. The third approach and tool set seemed to fit our strategy and objectives best while at the same time containing some of the elements of the first two approaches.

WHAT WE LEARNED

- The concept of embedment is analogous to the institutionalization of a core competency.

- A strong visual picture (in our case, the embedment wheel) is a good organizing framework to explain innovation embedment and motivate others to join.

- Creating categories of embedment must build on change management, but it must be strongly differentiated in people's minds and in practice that embedment needs change management practices.

- Leaders need both to understand embedment and be excited by it. Embedment will not work without leadership passion, commitment, and accountability to stay the course.

- Dialogue and debate about the worthiness of embedment is an essential process to define what embedment means. This might take time but is a vital part of the process. Dialogue and debate are moved forward by having formal forums, such as the I-Boards, where this type of discussion can take place.

- Goals, measures, systems, processes, rewards, recognition, communication, knowledge management, and other infrastructure areas always need to align to the vision and goals of embedment. This is not a one-time check but an ongoing process to ensure that alignment meets the demands of current reality and changing business requirements.

SELF-ASSESSMENT: DETERMINING YOUR EMBEDMENT READINESS QUOTIENT

The Innovation Embedment Baseline Readiness Assessment (Worksheet 2.1) will help you gauge the readiness of your organization to embark on embedding innovation. The worksheet is not scored, but the analysis that follows can be used to point you to those categories of the embedment wheel on which your organization might need further preparation or focus.

Worksheet 2.1. Innovation Embedment Baseline Readiness Assessment

Instructions: Using the questionnaire, assess your company's readiness for innovation embedment. *Innovation* is defined as creating nontechnical unique customer solutions. This includes products and services.

1. Our performance systems (for example, appraisals, promotions, assessment) reinforce innovation.

1	2	3	4	5
Not at All		To Some Extent		To a Great Extent

2. We have tools and processes in place to help all people learn innovation to create customer solutions.

1	2	3	4	5
Not at All		To Some Extent		To a Great Extent

3. We have a simple system (electronic or nonelectronic) in place that captures and shares innovation ideas.

1	2	3	4	5
Not at All		To Some Extent		To a Great Extent

4. Our firm has a process for innovators to get funding, time and space, and other types of support to work on their innovation ideas.

1	2	3	4	5
Not at All		To Some Extent		To a Great Extent

5. Our leaders are out-of-the-box thinkers who encourage innovation and support different ideas and nontraditional ways of thinking.

1	2	3	4	5
Not at All		To Some Extent		To a Great Extent

6. We have transparent and simple measures to show how our firm is progressing on innovation embedment.

1	2	3	4	5
Not at All		To Some Extent		To a Great Extent

7. People who innovate are appropriately compensated for their ideas.

1	2	3	4	5
Not at All		To Some Extent		To a Great Extent

8. Innovation is critical to our company's success.

1	2	3	4	5
Not at All		To Some Extent		To a Great Extent

9. Our organization believes that innovation can come from anyone at any time in any role.

1	2	3	4	5
Not at All		To Some Extent		To a Great Extent

10. Innovation is something that our leaders make prominent through their passion and actions.

1	2	3	4	5
Not at All		To Some Extent		To a Great Extent

11. Staff meetings or other team meetings spend time to focus explicitly on innovation.

1	2	3	4	5
Not at All		To Some Extent		To a Great Extent

12. Our customers and competitors think of us as an innovative company.

1	2	3	4	5
Not at All		To Some Extent		To a Great Extent

13. We have a vision for innovation that is widely accepted and agreed on.

1	2	3	4	5
Not at All		To Some Extent		To a Great Extent

Interpreting Your Results

Each category for the embedment wheel is addressed by one or more questions above. Use the following guide to determine the areas of the embedment wheel on which your firm might need more work. A score of 3 in more than two areas means you have considerably more work to do to become embedment ready.

Question Number	Embedment Wheel Category
1	*Infrastructure:* Systems Alignment
2	*Capability development*: Tools and Processes
3	*Infrastructure:* Knowledge Management and Learning Systems
4	*Infrastructure:* Resources
5	*Infrastructure:* Leader Accountability and Development
6	*Infrastructure:* Measurement and Reporting Systems
7	*Infrastructure:* Rewards and Recognition
8	*Vision and goals:* Vision and Goals
9	*Infrastructure:* Culture and Values
10	*Infrastructure:* Leaders Accountability and Development
11	*Infrastructure:* Change Management and Strategic Communications
12	*Vision and goals:* Vision and Goals
13	*Vision and goals:* Vision and Goals

CHAPTER THREE

Vision and Goals

We found that the keystone to innovation embedment was, without doubt, a clear vision and set of goals. A well-constructed vision provided an emotive description of the desired dream state and made it come alive to recipients. Our vision was powerful in that it connoted a common message to a diverse audience, while at the same time motivating and stirring their imagination.

While tapping into the emotions and passions of people, our vision was also bolstered by a set of goals that added clarity and specific direction. Both vision creation and goal setting were the accountability of our leaders. Goals delimited the vision to options that the leaders selected as the best methods for vision deployment. They also helped us monitor progress at interim steps along the way so that leaders could make midcourse corrections. Together, vision and goals were the first steps to creating an embedment plan.

We were fortunate to have started our innovation embedment effort with just such an imaginative vision statement from the CEO: "Innovation from Everyone and Everywhere." He created it to communicate Whirlpool's unique philosophy toward innovation and to send a message of inclusion to sixty thousand Whirlpool people: innovation at Whirlpool is not by a select few but by everyone. As you will see in this chapter, we then worked to deploy our vision and goals so that innovation embedment would ultimately encompass everyone.

ALIGNING VISIONS

We need to clarify an important point about Whirlpool's visions. We already had an overall enterprise vision, so we needed to make sure it was aligned with our vision for innovation. Just as much as we didn't want our innovation embedment to become a program of the month, we didn't want our innovation vision to become a vision of the month.

Organizations have different views about whether it is appropriate to have more than one vision in the company. Some organizations have an overall vision, sometimes called an enterprise-wide vision, with subordinate statements that they refer to as purpose or mission statements. Other organizations find that multiple visions are acceptable. There is no right or wrong answer. We have worked with visions in many organizations and within Whirlpool, and we have concluded that the culture and leadership of each enterprise will determine what is right for it. What matters is that there is alignment between the multiple visions and that people can picture themselves in the vision description.

Given this background, it is important to understand that Whirlpool had such an enterprise-wide vision, as shown in Exhibit 3.1. This vision was created in early 1998 by the CEO and the Executive Committee in an effort to fundamentally redefine our business. It challenged our long-held orthodoxies about the appliance industry and forced us to question how we thought about ourselves. Whirlpool's enterprise-wide vision was enormously successful because it was memorable, simple, and compelling. It accomplished two important tasks: it freed us from our dominant mental model of an old-line manufacturing company and set us on the path toward innovation.

In 1999, Jim Collins discussed the need to have catalytic mechanisms. Catalytic mechanisms are tied to the enterprise-wide vision, but adopt a shorter time frame than the vision. They describe something that every person in the organization can directly contribute to, whereas enterprise-wide visions are often lofty and too grandiose for one person to feel as if they can have any influence.

In Whirlpool's case, our embedment vision, "Innovation from Everyone and Everywhere," became our catalytic mechanism, while also directly linking our

---

Exhibit 3.1. Whirlpool's Enterprise-Wide Vision

Every Home, Everywhere . . .
with Pride, Passion and Performance.

Exhibit 3.2. Whirlpool's Enterprise-Wide and Innovation Visions

Whirlpool's Enterprise-Wide Vision		*Whirlpool's Innovation Embedment Vision*
Every Home, Everywhere . . . with Pride, Passion and Performance	➡	Innovation from Everyone and Everywhere

innovation vision to our enterprise-wide vision. Where the enterprise-wide vision connoted expansion into unknown areas of the world and the home, the embedment vision connoted expansion to an unbounded community of people, both inside and outside the company. We took great care to ensure that these two visions were mutually reinforcing, as shown in Exhibit 3.2.

VISION AND CORE COMPETENCE

We realized that our vision for innovation could not be tied to any one product, customer, or service. The minute we focused too much on innovation as a single product, service, or business process, we would fall into precisely a trap that we wanted to avoid: thinking about innovation too narrowly or living off the latest product or service idea. Instead, our vision for innovation needed to center on the larger issue of embedding innovation as a core competence.

Constantinos Markides (1997) makes the point that strategic innovation must redefine the actual business of the company. Strategic innovation is targeted at the strategy of the company and the overall business model or economic engine. Markides lays out five ways that organizations can kick-start strategic innovation:

- Redefining the business
- Redefining the customer
- Redefining the products and services offered
- Redefining how they do business
- Redefining how they think about their business

For Whirlpool, innovation embedment addressed all of these elements. We innovated our products, services, and, to some extent, how we do business.

But the embedment vision also redefined something that we did not predict. Because it reached out to all employees, it redefined how people thought about their jobs and their relationship with Whirlpool. As we will discuss in Chapter Five, it also changed our culture. To this extent, our innovation vision truly seemed to form the basis for innovation to become a core competency.

VISION EXTENSION:
THE VISION STATEMENT WAS NOT ENOUGH

As the embedment work began, our innovation vision statement became a sort of blueprint for the environment we needed to create in order to embed innovation. However, in the early months of embedment, our senior leaders—the Executive Committee and the next level of twenty-five leaders, the Chairman's Council—expanded the vision by creating a set of forward-looking statements about the Whirlpool of the future.

It soon became clear through several meetings and venues, as we hammered out additional descriptions of what our environment needed to evolve to: these statements needed to become an equal part of the embedment vision. We realized that the statements painted a vivid picture of the environment that we needed to create inside Whirlpool for the strategy to succeed. They were effectively extensions of both the innovation and enterprise-wide visions themselves. We now consider these additional statements to be integral parts of the visioning process for innovation embedment.

Specifically, the leadership created eleven aspirational statements of how Whirlpool had to operate. The statements included the already created enterprise-wide vision and the business strategy, as well as new statements about customers, innovation, resource creation (moving and creating resources to fund the innovation), leadership, operational excellence, change management, decision making, and performance management. The eleven statements were combined into a document that we named the "Customer-Focused Performance Model." Naturally, we shortened it to an acronym: CFPM.

CFPM became an important extension to the enterprise-wide and the innovation embedment visions. If you come to Whirlpool, chances are you will not hear it discussed in the halls. However, it has become a valued touchstone that many people in Whirlpool use to remind themselves of what we are trying to create with innovation. CFPM accurately describes the profound changes that will be required to fulfill the embedment vision and to reach our specific global and regional embedment goals.

DUCT TAPE VERSION:
Our Ugly Baby: CFPM

If you were a Whirlpool leader exposed to CFPM in its early formative months but you had not been in the group that created it and understood its context, it appeared to be a verbose and complicated document. Moreover, even if you were in the senior group of twenty-five people who created it, you were not sure exactly what to do with it or who needed to see it.

As the leadership team who created it, we even spent several months trying to explain the document and determine what to do with it. One group of leaders used it as a teaching tool, drawing on it to talk to the people of Whirlpool about the vision and the changes that it would take to achieve it.

One regional leadership group decided that there was too much to tackle all at once. The group prioritized the eleven categories into bite-sized chucks and determined to work on two categories one year, then two the next year, and so on, as if the statements and the work they represented could be prioritized and slowly metered out. One Executive Committee member became so tired of being accused of not supporting CFPM that in an impromptu light moment, he got up and sang the acronym to the tune of the Village People's famous song "YMCA," arm-signing the letters "C-F-P-M." Even our internal communications department shortened the document to the title and subtitles of each category and created a visual graphic of a house that made it more palatable than the longer text. Many other leaders simply thought that we should deemphasize and quietly put it away.

Something like this duct tape story might happen in your company. Your leadership takes great pains to articulate a vision statement and descriptions of the future state of your company, and no one knows exactly what to do with them.

Fortunately, the end of this story is proof of the power of well-articulated visions. The senior leaders thought that we might have made a mistake by writing and distributing the CFPM to the larger Whirlpool audience. We were hearing

Although all the CFPM statements are related to innovation embedment, five relate most directly: vision, innovation, strategy, resource creation, and structure and decision making. We present these five statements in Exhibit 3.3.

BEHIND AND AROUND THE EMBEDMENT VISION

What happens behind and around the process of crafting a vision for innovation embedment is as important as the vision itself. The top leadership team behind embedment has to create the vision; human resources or communi-

lots of criticism and getting lots of negative comments and questions: It was too long. What does it mean? Why was it too complicated? What can we do with it? And so on. Dismay set in, so our Executive Committee began to deemphasize it.

Then a funny thing happened. In 2002, two years after CFPM's difficult birth, the CEO was on a plant tour in Brazil and saw it hanging on the wall of one of our plants, in the graphic house form. He asked about it, and the plant manager proudly said that it was an important way to communicate the culture that we were trying to create. Seeing it being used in the factory starkly contrasted with the discussions that the senior leadership had been having about what to do with it. We had already started to rewrite, rename, and shorten it.

But the more we talked to people about the changes we were making, the more they protested. It had become an ingrained part of our culture. Thoughts of changing it caused a concerned reaction; it no longer belonged to the twenty-five senior leaders. It had been accepted and internalized.

CFPM began its life with difficulty. Our senior leaders created it and then launched it into the organization. It created a stir. People pushed back, debated it, even rejected it. But through that process of dialogue and debate, they affectionately made it their own. We did not realize the extent to which the people of Whirlpool had made CFPM part of our culture until we tried to change it.

At the time of this writing, we are in the process of carefully and lovingly updating it and changing the name to "The Culture and Enduring Values of Whirlpool." However, we understand now that it has a following inside the company. Nonetheless, when we show it to anyone outside Whirlpool, they smile and look at it the way you would look at someone's ugly baby, respectfully but with few comments. We hesitated to add CFPM to this chapter because just to read it without context or without living through its short life, it clearly sounds like an ugly baby. However, we have learned to love it, and it has become a valued part of our visioning process for innovation embedment. We add it because CFPM was an important lesson for us.

cations cannot do it for them. It is not about writing a cute statement or propaganda documents. The leaders must own the innovation embedment vision in the same way they own the vision for the enterprise. They must be personally committed to the vision before they can ask others to do the same.

In addition, keep in mind that whatever happens around the vision statement occurs over a series of months and years and likely involves resignations, job movements, and newly hired employees. There can be a constant struggle between the perfect boardroom vision and how it is played out in the day-to-day dealings of the company.

Exhibit 3.3. The Five CFPM Whirlpool Statements

Enterprise-Wide Vision
Every Home . . . Everywhere

Our vision proposes a higher order of purpose: Every home is our domain . . . every consumer and consumer activity our opportunity. This vision will fuel the passion that we will develop for our consumers. This means not just building white boxes . . . but rather providing a wide range of innovative solutions that uniquely meet our customers' needs.

Innovation
Value Ideas from Everyone and Everywhere

Innovation will become a core competency of the enterprise. Innovation will come from everyone, from everywhere, and in everything that we do. Our heroes will be the people who seize opportunities, not just the people who solve internal problems. We will rid ourselves of processes and practices that hamper risk-taking and innovation. We will view falling short of risk-taking goals as learning, not failure. All of this will allow us to continuously win consumer loyalty. We will value the diversity of our people and their ideas, as only significant diversity at our company will lead to great innovation. Innovation will allow us to win customer loyalty and create value.

Strategy
Branded Solutions That Build Consumer Loyalty

Branded solutions represent an immense transformation for our company. These strategies will change our jobs and how we work with each other and it will force a personal connection with the consumer. They will create mindset changes, actions and outcomes that will build exceptional consumer loyalty to our brands . . . thus continually expanding our opportunities. This will lead to the growth and performance that we must deliver.

Resource Creation
Investments in Great Ideas

We will understand that the focus and beneficiaries of our resource decisions must be the consumer and shareholder. This will require us to look at all of our activities with a new perspective. We will create purposeful investments around great ideas. We will stop feeding the status quo and underperforming activities and fund those activities that contribute to our success with our consumers and value for our shareholders. We will put our money and talent behind innovative consumer solutions and invest in doing this faster than anyone else.

Organization Structure and Decision Making
Open. Flat. Fast.

We will organize around our brands as our key connection to the consumer. We will be open, flat and consumer-centered. We will drive decision-making close to the markets and at the appropriate level. We will spell out clear accountabilities for every job that, in turn, will propel us to have a sense of urgency for what is important. We will create great jobs that challenge our spirit. We will create well-defined "decision space" where people know their decision-making accountabilities, and then we will get out of the way and let our people do their jobs. We will move faster internally than the external world.

At Whirlpool, we encountered several situations of this behind-and-around phenomenon during and after creating the innovation vision statements. There were times when the top leadership team did not notice what was really happening to their embedment efforts because of the day-to-day demands of their business units. They were so busy running the business that they had little time to assess how well their innovation embedment efforts were going. In most cases, our leaders worked on embedment episodically; on some days, they could pay a lot of attention to embedment, but their attention was punctuated with short-term business issues that took their mind away.

We also found that it was easy to be lulled into a false sense of comfort when it was quiet and calm: "I'm okay. You're okay. Embedment is okay." This false comfort especially lingered if leaders did not have an ongoing opportunity to think and talk about the vision. It required constant monitoring. Our regular I-Board meetings often filled this need for us.

We learned that to keep on top of the ebbs and flows in the embedment process, the top team must discuss the embedment vision regularly and take corrective actions to keep it on track. The key to success is that the top team is wrestling with the vision rather than with each other.

CREATING GOALS OUT OF THE EMBEDMENT VISION

Goals are the second and equally vital part of the preparatory process in embedment. Once the vision is created, the leadership team needs to articulate a set of goals that will drive the behaviors required to fulfill the vision. Vision is the right-brained emotive dream state, while goals offer the left-brained, rational milestones to realize the vision.

For Whirlpool, creating the right goals may have been the most difficult part of the embedment process to date. From the beginning, Whirlpool conceived of only two types of goals around innovation: results and embedment. As discussed earlier, results are destination goals, while embedment engenders journey or learning goals. This distinction handed us a valuable lesson in hubris. From the onset, we had a very hard time differentiating between the two types of goals.

In addition, we were two years or so into embedment before we identified a third type of goal: individual goals. As we write this now, this third type of goal seems obvious, but at the time we missed it. We were embedding innovation exclusively at the organizational level. Indeed, after much trial and error, we discovered that until we ensured that innovation was occurring at the individual level, we had not embedded anything.

GOALS THAT BITE AND GOOD GOAL GENES

Results goals are the tangible outcome that you want from embedment. In most projects and initiatives, results goals are relatively easy to articulate. They coincide with the vision by answering the question: If we are successful at the end, what will we have? The amount of revenue generated, the number of patents secured, and the numbers of new products created are all examples of reasonable results goals from innovation.

However, the goals of the embedment process are as important as the results goals. They drive near-term behavior and provide tangible issues to debate, measure, and assess. Embedment goals represent a path to the overall outcome of changing the actual way you do business and provide guidance on where to focus your energy, resources, and attention. However, for us, embedment goals were not easy to identify. We did not have experience in working with embedment goals. Although we had frequently defined process or start-up types of goals, embedment goals presented a new challenge.

We discovered that setting embedment goals was one of the most difficult aspects of embedding innovation. This is where we learned that these goals can bite. Embedment goals tend to be illusive, hard to pin down, and difficult to quantify. It is easy to mix up embedment goals with the results of the innovation effort. What is worse is that once you inadvertently set the "wrong" goals, you and the senior team might quickly see your mistake, but changing the goals midstream is not easy or recommended. Goals that are set, agreed on, and communicated become public domain. Changing them takes enormous effort to explain to others and to adopt. You also run the risk of looking as if you do not know what you are doing or what you want.

To avoid setting goals that bite, we recommend that every top team working on embedment needs as least one person with a "good goal gene." This should be someone who can constantly keep a vigilant eye on the difference between embedment goals and results goals. In our case, it was our CEO, Dave Whitwam, who reinforced how embedment and results goals were different but related. He possessed that innate "goal-setting gene" that helped him recognize the difference between the two types of goals that the rest of us were missing or had not developed.

Here is an example of how easy it is not to see the forest for the trees. Early in our process, we believed that we needed a team of experts trained in innovation techniques to help with innovation embedment. We called these experts I-Mentors. I-Mentors were to be trained over two to three weeks and certified using a peer review process so they could help teams through the innovation tools. (I-Mentors were different from I-Consultants: the former were selected ad hoc and worked part time on an innovation project while based in the businesses, while the latter worked full time in their innovation consulting roles and were more highly skilled in innovation tools and processes.)

In our first year, the number of I-Mentors trained was set up to be one measure of embedment. However, once we began our work, we realized that in the first fragile year of embedment, the number of I-Mentors trained may not really serve as a good embedment measure. Furthermore, two or three years into embedment, the number of I-Mentors trained became even less meaningful.

We then understood that truly meaningful goals are those that drive substantive changes. For example, better embedment goals for us would have been things like:

- The creation and use of a knowledge management system for innovation
- The level of disruptive changes in systems like resource creation where resources are redirected from old ways of doing things to innovation
- The quality of redirected processes that drive behavior such as compensation or talent pool
- The depth of our penetration down into the workforce in terms of successful innovation projects

In addition to our confusion between embedment and results goals, we realized that we had also missed a critical aspect of embedment: a third type of goal, the embedment of innovation at the individual level. Having results and embedment goals without ensuring that individuals understand embedment is like figuring out how to do the world's most beautiful golf swing and then missing the ball.

We uncovered the need for individual goals only after a long spell that missed the true essence of the outcome we were looking for: change at the individual level. Real embedment, especially in the context of having a vision of innovation from everyone and everywhere, required change and learning at the individual level.

THE EMBEDMENT GOAL TRILOGY

After much trial and error and a few wrong turns, we finally pinned down the three types of goals critical to innovation embedment (see Exhibit 3.4). All three sets of goals had to be driven by the vision for innovation embedment.

This portfolio of goals is an ever-changing landscape that needs to be refined and tinkered with constantly—daily, weekly, and monthly. The challenge is that because these goals are likely communicated to large groups of people who use them as a touchstone, their formal rate of change needs to appear constant. Although they may be discussed and debated at the executive level on a continuing basis, they should be communicated in a more stable manner.

Results Goals

Results goals are the predominant set of goals for embedment efforts: they represent the business outcomes. They need to be tied to the enterprise-wide vision and to the long-term business outcomes for innovation. To the extent that results goals are part of the balanced scorecard or highest organization goals, they will drive long-term organization behavior. When embedment matures, the results goals are generally all that remain. Results goals are tangible, the real deal. Following are some examples of results goals:

- The amount of new revenue generated from innovation
- The number of projects in the innovation pipeline
- The number of intellectual property rights generated
- The number of people in the process
- The number of new customers as a result of innovation
- The number of new methods of distribution and doing business

Results goals can be both means and ends. For example, some of the means goals listed above are the number of projects in the pipeline and the number of intellectual property rights generated. These don't create revenue themselves but rather lead to it.

One important point to consider also is that you need to be careful in setting revenue goals. While these are the holy grail of business, in a long-life-cycle

Exhibit 3.4. The Goal Trilogy

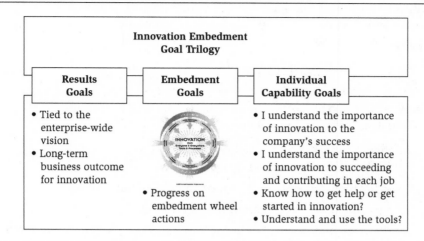

business such as appliances, it sometimes takes more than an annual business cycle to realize revenue from an innovation.

Embedment Goals

Embedment goals are a new set of goals that most of us are not used to setting. They are journey goals. They represent broad-based learning activities that lead to the innovation vision. Embedment goals focus on how robust the set of activities is in each element of the embedment wheel. They examine how balanced your approach is to innovation, how well the embedment strategy addresses all the elements of the wheel, and how robust your set of embedment activities is—for example:

- The amount in seed funds set aside and used to fund innovation projects
- The number of or diversity of people certified in levels of innovation expertise
- The number of change management projects defined to drive innovation
- The number of key barriers removed to allow innovation to thrive
- The number of jobs changed due to innovation

Embedment goals are tollgates along the way. They acknowledge the areas of change and transformation required. They focus at the organization level. As implied above, embedment goals should develop and change more frequently than results or individual goals because they need to measure the moving progress of embedment, while results and individuals look to a fixed end state, albeit at different levels.

Individual Capability Goals

Individual capability goals articulate the changes that you want to happen at the individual level and represent the point in time when the change is evident. For example, as a leader, you might have as goals the following:

- Number or percentage of people in your work group who can describe how innovation has changed their job
- Number of job descriptions rewritten to include innovation
- Ways in which people use innovation in their day-to-day job
- Identification and removal of barriers to innovation in your work group
- Written statements about how each person has used innovation tools
- Number of performance appraisals that have listed innovation goals for individuals

To help Whirlpool adopt the individual level of goal setting and achievement, we identified some example actions that leaders could take to ensure embedment at the individual level, as shown in Exhibit 3.5. Many leaders found this list helpful to get started, but soon outperformed the list with their own ideas to ensure that innovation was embedded in the people who worked for them.

Although not every leader at Whirlpool has yet accomplished this, there are increasing numbers of highly motivated leaders who are involving their people. They are doing this at all levels and seeking feedback by focusing on people as individuals and asking them what they have learned and how they understand and use innovation. Focusing this lens on the individual level has made and continues to make a significant difference in the rate and pace of innovation embedment in our company.

WHAT WE LEARNED

- Creating an embedment vision is a critical first step around the embedment wheel.
- The embedment vision must be closely aligned with and linked to the enterprise vision. There cannot be confusion between the two.
- The embedment vision statement may not be enough for the leadership

Exhibit 3.5. Measures and Examples of Individual Goals

Goal Area Required	Goal Measure	Examples of Short-Term Actions
1. I understand the importance of innovation to Whirlpool.	Ability to link innovation to the company's success in: increasing customer loyalty, revenue growth, and EVA growth Ability to link success innovation to my personal success	Staff meetings to explain the connections Personal one-on-one sessions with supervisor to related innovation to each person Other communications Include in all goal setting or personal appraisal
2. I can apply the innovation tools.	Documented list of required skills and capabilities for innovation Documented list of innovation tools and processes that I use to do my job Documented connection of my work to innovation	Skills and capability inventory listing Personalized statement of my work in innovation completed at year end as part of appraisal Statements collected and analyzed to understand progress
3. Has my job changed as a result of innovation?	Job description indicating role of innovation	Begin systematic job description overhauls (two paragraphs)
4. Do I understand innovation?	Ability to articulate my role in innovation	See goal areas 2 and 3 above
5. Are the barriers removed so that I can participate in innovation?	Change management survey results indicate barriers are removed Asking individuals if they feel as if they have the opportunity to join the innovation effort	Change management survey oriented to innovation Top leadership monitors barriers and helps remove them
6. Do I know how to get help to get started?	Demonstrated use of knowledge management site for innovation assistance Survey I-Mentors to see how many and what type of calls they are getting for help Supervisors training and/or orientation material Ask individuals if they know how to get help	Education started broadly in knowledge management site Create supervisor packets to address how to take the first step to join the innovation effort Communicate five steps and names or numbers of people to call to get help
7. Do I understand its importance in getting my job done?	Ability to articulate my role in innovation Practical use of innovation tools on the job	See goal area 2 above
8. All of the above	Employee engagement initiative addressed in a larger way Employee engagement survey (Pulse) continually administered to a sample	Employee Engagement Survey created Baseline administered

to ensure a common understanding. You may need additional statements that define your future state.

- One set of goals to measure the outcome or result is insufficient. You need to measure and monitor results and embedment goals, as well as individual goals.

- Embedment goals are a new type of goal setting. These goals are harder to establish. It may take several iterations before you feel you have them right.

- You cannot change goals too frequently while maintaining credibility.

- Any transformation or change has to occur within individuals, not just at the organizational level. It is not until individuals change that a transformation will occur.

- The embedment wheel has many categories that embedment practitioners and leaders can misread as organization-level interventions. Instead, each category must be thought about in terms of both the organization changes required and the individual ones.

- There are many ways to determine if a core competency has been embedded, but one of the most important is to ask the people and listen to how they describe the change in their terms. The most important part of embedment is getting to the individual level.

SELF-ASSESSMENT: GOALS

This self-assessment contains two worksheets. Use Worksheet 3.1 to assess where your organization stands relative to setting goals for innovation and embedment. Then use Worksheet 3.2 to help you think about developing a balance of the three types of goals.

Worksheet 3.1. Embedment Vision Development

Check as many of the following statements as apply to your organization:

_____ We have a vision for the enterprise.

_____ We have a vision for embedment of innovation.

_____ The vision for embedment was created by our top team.

_____ Our vision for embedment targets a shorter term than for the enterprise.

_____ Our vision for embedment is imaginable.

_____ Our vision for embedment is accessible to all levels of the organization.

_____ Our vision for embedment is feasible.

_____ Our vision for embedment is flexible.

_____ Our vision for embedment can guide decision making.

_____ Our vision for innovation can be easily communicated.

Scoring: How many checks do you have?

0–3   Your organization has more work to do on your embedment vision.

4–6   Not bad. Be sure that you have the basics of the first four items in the checklist covered.

7–10   Excellent.

Worksheet 3.2. Goals Balance

Use the following checklists to ensure that your approach to goals is balanced among the trilogy of results, embedment, and individual goals.

Results Goals

Make sure you have checked at least three to five from this list:

_____ Revenue from new products or services

_____ Number of new products or services

_____ Number of new business opportunities generated

_____ Number of ideas in the pipeline

_____ Number of new patents

_____ Number of new products in the pipeline

_____ Types of new customers or customer segmentation

_____ Recognition by outsiders as in a new business area

Embedment Goals

Make sure that you have checked at least three to five from this list:

_____ Actionable and observable activities under each element of the embedment wheel

_____ Two or more sets of strategies and actions under each element of the embedment wheel

_____ Management attention and resources applied to all elements of embedment

_____ Measures of organizational learning or culture change from embedment efforts such as changes in culture or systems or processes

_____ Change management projects at the organizational level targeted at innovation embedment

_____ Systems and processes adapted to reinforce innovation

Individual Goals

Make sure that you have checked at least three to five from this list:

_____ Awareness and understanding of innovation vision and strategy

_____ Awareness of current and past innovation efforts

_____ Awareness of how all individuals fit into the innovation process

_____ Use of innovation tools by members of the workforce

_____ Penetration of knowledge and skills about innovation through out the workforce

_____ Participation of the workforce in innovation projects

CHAPTER FOUR

Leader Accountability and Development

At our 2000 Leadership Conference outside Washington, D.C., Whirlpool's top three hundred leaders first heard the phrase "Innovation from Everyone and Everywhere." This was the moment that we communicated that innovation would become one of our most critical strategies to move toward our enterprise-wide vision of Every Home, Everywhere. We usually invite only eighty of the top leaders to this yearly conference, but engaging Whirlpool's leadership in innovation was so critical that we almost tripled our list of those invited.

This conference will go down in Whirlpool history as one of the most interesting and motivating. Attendees literally began to embody the spirit of innovation. Our last night consisted of a spontaneous talent show where participants sang, danced, and played instruments (that we had to rent on the spot). It became one of the most uplifting times we can recall at a leadership conference.

The admirable news about leaders at Whirlpool is that they have long been accustomed to taking ownership of organizational change initiatives. In the past ten years, Whirlpool has been quite aggressive about change initiatives in many areas: culture and values transformation, quality, and Six Sigma, to name a few. Each of these has left the organization with a new capability and perspective and, perhaps more important, a group of senior leaders who understand their role in leading change at the enterprise level.

This history provided us a level of openness in our leadership population that we believe has been critical to our success in implementing change at

Whirlpool. In the case of innovation, the leadership group was more than ready; they were eager to lead an initiative that they perceived as freeing, not constrictive, and that would capture the hearts and minds of their employees and customers.

OVERCOMING THE LEADER-AS-VILLAIN MENTALITY

Not all organizations may find it as easy to get their leadership involved in innovation. Often we don't envision our leaders as being innovators.

In recent years, Hewlett-Packard ran a series of print ads with the tag line "Invent." In one of the most appealing of the series, the ad showed a garage that most people would not want anywhere near their property: old, wooden, and falling down. In front of the garage were two professorial-looking men, both with a mischievous, youthful gleam in their eyes. They were the original Hewlett and Packard, two of the greatest American icons of invention, standing in front of their now legendary garage. What was missing in the ad was the stereotypical three-piece-suited business leader standing in the background, smiling paternally at the invention that he or she helped bring into the world by great vision, motivation, or other leadership traits.

Our point is that the standard folklore around invention contains what we believe is a disconnect between leadership and innovation. In most companies, the leader might have been the principal inventor, but as the organization grew and matured and professional managers moved in, the company's current leaders almost always lose their caché as part of the internal innovation culture. The organization's legends are built around the founder or perhaps another innovator who was promoted into management, but rarely does this include large numbers of current management. When we think of innovation and innovators, the lone innovator in his or her laboratory comes to mind.

In our archetype of innovators, leaders are most often portrayed as the villains of innovation: closed-minded supervisors who rebuff brilliant innovators, causing them to break out on their own and follow their dream elsewhere. "Leader as innovation villain" might be the extreme of how most employees have come to view leadership's role in innovation, but it does feed the myth that a lone innovator or team of innovators going at it alone makes the leader seem extraneous.

We believe that this myth might be entrenched in the innovation psyche in many organizations. Worse, we believe that the notion is embedded in the psyche of many leaders themselves. But to have innovation from everyone and everywhere, getting leaders actively involved in the process is clearly one of the keys to success.

We strongly believe that leaders at all levels were—and continue to be—critical to the embedment of innovation in Whirlpool. The question has never been whether to involve our leaders, but how to design their accountabilities in order to develop them as leaders of innovation.

EXPECTATIONS, ACCOUNTABILITIES, AND BEHAVIORS

Given this view, we consciously designed our embedment activities to ensure that all leaders not only owned but actively promoted innovation. We considered that the work of our leaders at all levels was to embed innovation in Whirlpool's very fabric. Those at the top of our organization had the power to make the mega-changes in the structure, systems, culture, and environment that were required to embed innovation. Similarly, the succeeding levels of leaders also had significant accountabilities to lead execution of the day-to-day work that allows for embedment.

We found that the new accountabilities we were creating for innovation embedment needed to be spelled out and made explicit so leaders at all levels would be fully informed and in control of their goals. Innovation embedment, although grounded in a systematic approach, required accountability to empower.

Our philosophy was that we needed to clarify the role of leaders up front and then work with them to move beyond their orthodoxies, that is, their established patterns of behavior. We wanted them to support innovation and use their judgment to know when to get out of the way. We were intentionally clear about the role of leaders in innovation embedment, figuring that clarity would save us months, if not years, of wasted time, and thousands, if not millions, of dollars in wasted effort.

We offer you an outline of the accountabilities and expectations we created for our leaders. These were fashioned through extensive debate and discussion at the Executive Committee level. Some accountabilities flow from what is well known about managing innovation, such as the importance of creating an environment where risk taking is tolerated. Other accountabilities were drawn more specifically from our knowledge and experience with Whirlpool's culture concerning what areas would need the most leadership attention. For example, we targeted a larger need for mobility among employees to work on innovation projects. In the past, employee mobility in Whirlpool was controlled exclusively by direct supervisors. Now, with our mandate of innovation from everyone and everywhere, employees who initiated job moves to work on projects clearly needed the support of their direct supervisors.

INNOVATION AT THE TOP LEADERSHIP LEVEL

In any organization, the top-level leadership teams need to be accountable as chief architects for innovation embedment. Our CEO was therefore very active in creating and communicating new accountabilities for his top leadership team. He immediately established a set of goals and objectives for each member that included specific, targeted accountabilities for some aspect of the innovation embedment effort. For example, one person was held accountable to work with us on establishing a definition for innovation success; another top leader helped with the effort to embed a common change management system that supported embedment. Whitwam wanted to ensure that each member was on point and accountable for a key aspect of embedment. Embedment had to be line driven, not led by staff functions. Leaders had to be visibly engaged in embedment.

In addition, Whitwam and his team created a double set of embedment accountabilities for each member of the Executive Committee: each had the shared accountability of ensuring that the embedment wheel was implemented for the entire enterprise and leading embedment within their own business, region, or function. Not surprisingly, the two sets of accountabilities were highly aligned and linked. A description of these accountabilities follows, along with a summary in Exhibit 4.1.

Leaders' Enterprise-Wide Accountabilities

- Communicate through action that there is a critical role for leaders in innovation embedment. Each senior leader was expected to be active and visibly involved in embedment.

- Leading embedment was not to be delegated to a staff function.

- Describe the desired outcome for overall innovation embedment at the enterprise level. This meant being involved in visioning and goal setting for embedment as well as for innovation results within Whirlpool.

- Establish the infrastructure for embedment by ensuring that proper systems, processes, and capability-building mechanisms are in place. Critics of existing processes and systems were not allowed. If the process or system didn't align with the intent of innovation, then the accountability was to change the system or process. This accountability especially applied to people who owned enterprise-wide processes, such as product development, sales, and human resources, that needed to be adapted to meet the demands of innovation embedment.

- Ensure that embedment was pushed down to the individual level, as well as to the enterprise or strategic business unit level. We asked our leaders not to forget that each person at Whirlpool shared accountability for changing what he or she does at work to make innovation a success.

Exhibit 4.1. Summary of Accountabilities

Enterprise Accountabilities	Functional or Regional Accountabilities
Deeply understand that there is a critical role for leaders in innovation embedment.	Understand their role in innovation embedment within their unit or function.
Describe the desired outcome for overall innovation embedment at the enterprise and the individual levels.	Describe the desired outcome for overall innovation embedment for their business or unit.
Establish the processes and systems for embedment by populating the embedment wheel and ensuring the proper infrastructure and capabilities building mechanisms are in place.	Employ the processes and systems designed to the embedment wheel and build capabilities in their business or unit.
Ensure that embedment is designed to the individual level, as well as to the enterprise or strategic business unit level.	Personally engage each individual on their staff and ensure that every individual in the entire business or unit is personally engaged by their manager.
Engage in personal learning and embrace the innovation tools and processes.	Reprioritize and set direction to ensure that appropriate timing and attention is given to innovation.
Reprioritize and set direction to ensure appropriate timing and attention is given to innovation.	Monitor and report on progress to business or unit to leadership.
Monitor progress.	Model the change in behavior required to embed innovation.

As leaders, we could not afford to live in an ivory tower; we needed to make sure that embedment reached every person in Whirlpool in a meaningful way. Systems and process change were necessary, but the energy for change comes from people.

- Learn and embrace innovation tools and processes. Each leader was required not only to ask that others learn innovation tools, but to understand and apply them. Senior leaders needed to take classes and learn, just as lower-level leaders and employees did.

- Reprioritize and set direction to ensure appropriate timing and attention was given to innovation. As always, the focus needed to be the currency of leadership. Others do what leaders pay attention to. Leaders were accountable for keeping innovation top of mind through communication, expectation setting, measurement, and reward and recognition.

- Monitor progress. We get what we pay attention to. If the focus is the currency of leadership, then active monitoring of the progress of embedment became the way to reinforce it. Embedment progress was a topic at each Executive Committee meeting. We always kept progress top of mind through activities at our weekly meetings, ranging from simple discussions about progress to more formal measurement and monitoring systems (described in Chapter Ten).

Leaders' Business Unit, Regional, and Functional Accountabilities

- Understand their role in innovation embedment within their own unit. In essence, each organization needed to have its own mini-version of the embedment wheel, interpreting it according to its own business unit or function. Leaders were accountable to lead embedment activities in their function or region and to adapt activities to meet their needs.

- Describe the desired outcome for overall innovation embedment for their business or unit. Just as with the visions created for the enterprise level, each function or region needed a vision for embedment that would guide it appropriately for its business situation and workforce. The vision created for India, for example, might not be appropriate for Europe.

- Employ the processes and systems in the embedment wheel to build the right capabilities in their business or unit. Embedment needed to adapt to the realities of the organization and emphasize those activities that were right for each region or function. For example, in Latin America, there was a strong focus on building innovation awareness and communicating it to the hourly workforce. In other regions, the target of embedment was aimed more at the functional or work team level.

- Personally engage each individual on his or her staff and require that every person in the entire business or unit be personally engaged by their direct manager. Each Executive Committee member had the accountability for ensuring that learning about innovation, creating an environment ripe for innovation, and employing the tools and methods of innovation rippled down the organization in a personal manner. We asked each senior leader to talk to each of his or her direct reports about these accountabilities and to facilitate this type of discussion throughout the organization.

- Reprioritize and set direction to ensure appropriate timing and attention given to innovation. Business realities change. We asked leaders to be the grounding mechanism to ensure that innovation was not lost in the realities of short-term or midterm business demands. We also asked them to balance work on innovation with meeting short-term and midterm business goals.

- Monitor and report on progress at the business or regional level. At the enterprise level, we created methods to measure and monitor progress of innovation embedment. We asked each functional or regional leader to do the same for his or her organization.

- Model the change in behavior required to embed innovation. We all know the saying, "Walk the talk." Each leader was asked to model some of the critical behaviors necessary to create an innovation-ripe environment, such as being open to mistakes, taking risks, and learning about and trying out new innovation techniques.

CHANGING THE CULTURE: INNOVATION BEHAVIORS FOR ALL LEADERS

In addition to accountabilities created for senior leaders, we established a more general set of accountabilities or behaviors required of all leaders. Whitwam and his Executive Committee believed that if all leaders at Whirlpool—from supervisors and directors to vice presidents and Executive Committee members—acted in concert, we could move innovation embedment more smoothly and quickly to the level of success we expected. If we were going to create a culture where innovation could thrive, we needed to address those cultural characteristics that might inhibit innovation.

We wanted to transform these characteristics:

- Decisions were made top down. We wanted a culture where there was co-creation of programs and initiatives.

- There was little tolerance for ambiguity. We wanted a culture where you could admit that some situations were ambiguous, messy, and challenging.

- Short-term to midterm operational focus was valued. We wanted to focus equally on a longer-term perspective.

- People worried about making mistakes or saying the wrong thing. We wanted a culture where employees could think creatively, make errors, and learn from them.

- People worked within their own function. We wanted people to move freely to work on interesting projects.

The best way to accomplish this culture change was to ask all leaders to engage in behaviors designed to create the new culture we desired. We chose to target a set of five behaviors that in our view created an environment rich for innovation embedment:

1. Co-creation

2. Time and space for involvement

3. Out-of-the-box thinking

4. A balance of day-to-day pressures with innovation embedment

5. An innovation-rich environment

Here's an overview of how we described and fashioned each of these behaviors for our leaders.

Co-Creation

At Whirlpool, the first accountability for leaders was to set aside time to learn about, discuss, and debate innovation. Leaders could not be a thumbs-up or thumbs-down tollgate at the end of the innovation process for a new product, service, or market. They needed to remain involved at every major point. Call it sweat equity or co-creation; we believed that leaders had to be partners in the innovation process.

For this reason, we made I-Board meetings (the top-level innovation councils involved in the innovation process, explained in Chapter One) one of our co-creation strategies. In I-Board meetings, each strategic business unit head and his or her staff segmented time each month to learn and guide the innovation embedment.

For many leaders, adopting this behavior of co-creation became the jumping-off point between talking about the change and ambiguity of innovation, and actually living it. In order to co-create, leaders were forced to struggle firsthand with ambiguous issues and complex problems that innovation from everyone and everywhere raised. Many basic questions had to be answered and so were placed squarely under leadership accountability: Can innovation really come from everyone? How does innovation fit with the strategies of brand building and customer loyalty? What types of innovations might fit into what we have traditionally thought of as our sandbox (our business), or should we still think in terms of having a sandbox at all?

At lower levels of management, co-creation meant finding ways to adapt innovation tools for use in their own work unit or environment. We encouraged leaders at the first line or middle levels to use and adapt innovation tools to meet their needs, especially in helping their people see situations in novel ways. One example was the use of an innovation tool to examine what we called orthodoxies, referring to those taken-for-granted ways of operating that often

DUCT TAPE VERSION
Churning and Gut Checking
in I-Board Meetings

In the ideal world, we expected our leaders to spend time in I-Board meetings learning the tools of innovation, removing barriers, and setting up the infrastructure to drive embedment. But in the real world of these honest duct tape versions, we need to admit that in the beginning, our leaders spent rather large amounts of time in huddles, wondering if they were doing the right thing and second-guessing certain aspects of the innovation effort.

Nevertheless, it is important to recognize that there was a value to these huddles. Our leaders at least felt safe in bringing out doubts in this forum. This churn and gut checking turned out to initiate some of the most meaningful dialogues in I-Board meetings. Grappling with questions such as whether a new product innovation fit or did not fit into our existing brands created a forum for leaders to engage in dialogue and debate the path of innovation for them. Without it, we might have created a hollow shell that would never be questioned or bounced against reality. Inadvertently, the I-Board meetings became a vital forum for struggling with the realities of embedment and for reinforcing a new culture where ambiguity and complexity were not only acceptable but valuable new feelings for our business leaders.

have outlived their usefulness. Another tool managers learned to use were various lenses or perspectives to ensure that a problem was being considered from a number of different points of view, such as from the customer, trade, or employee view rather than just from one narrow position. The idea behind both tools was to increase the complexity of discussion and debate rather than just jumping to a traditional answer.

Time and Space for Involvement

A second behavior we asked from all leaders was to carve out the time and space needed for people from everywhere to innovate. We made leaders accountable for helping potential innovators find the time to work on their ideas. Given that our vision was that innovation should come from everyone, ideas needed to start from all people, not just those who were inside the usual internal R&D think-tank department or skunkworks. This became particularly challenging because innovation was new to our company, and people's work still entailed jobs left over from the last strategy, or they were focused on the usual urgency for short-term results. But we reasoned that if innovators could find only discretionary time of their own to work on their ideas, then the future of embedding innovation as a core competency would surely suffer. We therefore insisted on this accountability of leadership to create time and space during regular work hours to allow potential innovators time to innovate.

An excellent example of this behavior occurred with one factory manager in North America who cut loose a small team of employees to work on an idea for a product not just new to our customers but new to the world. As of this writing, this product is one of the top innovations to have moved forward into a full-fledged product line as part of a new brand for Whirlpool. The product line, called Gator Pak, consists of appliances for tailgate parties and was developed from this small team. The bet is that it will be a great hit in the marketplace.

In calling for this behavior, we did not ask for strong or firm requirements for time allocation for innovation. We asked leaders to allow people time for rotational assignments to innovation teams or to provide some time during regular work to attend to innovation activities. If a person rotated to an innovation team, it might require the leader to backfill their position, understanding that when the person returned, he or she would come back reinvigorated and ready to share new information with others. Time for innovation might also mean that some of the people in their work unit did not work full time on an innovation team, but rather spent some portion of their time working alone on innovation. We found that this varied from 10 to 15 percent for many people in some work units.

Out-of-the-Box Thinking

One of the cultural characteristics we were trying to create was an environment where people would feel free to use their imaginations, or as the trendy expression goes, to think out of the box. We wanted leaders who practiced and encouraged out-of-the-box thinking, not leaders who second-guessed new ideas in advance of their development and were prone to naysay ("It can't be done"). This requirement was so paramount to creating innovation from everyone in Whirlpool that it became a primary criterion for the selection and development of people on leadership teams.

We also found that promoting new ways of thinking required leaders to expand their environments and increase their sense of inclusion and diversity. We wanted everyone's idea to be heard and valued. Every shred of evidence clearly suggested that innovation is fueled by diversity of thought, not groupthink. We therefore asked leaders to set the example by both valuing ideas that were different and ensuring that ideas from people who were different were fully considered. Our leaders had to model the valuing of ideas from sources that they were not used to accepting, such as marketing listening to ideas from engineering or North America considering a product idea from India.

DUCT TAPE VERSION
Out-of-the-Box Thinking

After our first year in innovation embedment, the leaders at Whirlpool measured themselves on their innovation journey goals in a 360-degree feedback process. One of the lowest-scoring items was progress in out-of-the-box thinking. This became a challenge for how far we had to go to embed innovation and revealed to us how much we had become too similar to one another. We realized that this requirement was so critical to creating innovation from everyone in Whirlpool that it became a criterion for the selection and development of our leaders and a major development target. We made it a centerpiece in our week-long leader development programs, as well as a prominent part of our interviewing and hiring process.

Balancing Day-to-Day Pressures with Innovation Embedment

Leaders obviously have ongoing accountabilities to run the business, and in times of crisis, running the business needs to take precedence over everything else. We admittedly had a constant struggle to keep this dual focus, especially when innovation embedment was new. We realized, however, that if we did not make long-term innovation as much of a priority as short-term results, we would find ourselves in a never-ending catch-22. The revolving dilemma of innovation embedment is that leaders must protect innovation from the day-to-day, month-to-month, and quarter-to-quarter pressures while integrating it into the day-to-day, month-to-month, and quarter-to-quarter business.

We did not have a hard-and-fast formula for leaders to follow. But we asked them to take stock during their review of daily, weekly, and monthly activities, and in our longer-term work planning sessions, of two important questions:

- Am I doing enough to balance the short-term and midterm with the long term?
- Are we using the pressures of the present as an excuse not to do the hard work of innovation embedment?

Our CEO modeled this often by describing the long-term perspective that he would use to redirect executive attention when business situations were challenging.

An Innovation-Rich Environment

For embedment to work, leaders needed to create the right environment so that all innovators have the opportunity to raise their hand and not fear embarrassment or ridicule. However, we also saw that the lure that leaders had to cast needed to invite innovators gently, not capture them with too much fervor or with bureaucracy and hierarchy. To do this, the environment had to be broad and welcoming to everyone who had ideas—regardless how odd those ideas might be, because innovators might come from where you least expect them. An innovation-rich environment encourages people to be self-motivated and to move about freely, often clustering in informal "hierarchy-be-damned" networks. But this type of innovation-rich environment changed the demands on our leaders from one of control to one of encouragement.

For example, the group that developed the Gator Pak set of products was strongly encouraged to work on their idea, and not just focus on their day-to-day jobs. Without that encouragement, the innovation project might have never got off the ground.

THE BIG SURPRISE ABOUT LEADERSHIP ACCOUNTABILITIES

We expected that senior leaders would fulfill their accountabilities in a direct and timely manner, while leaders at first and middle levels would be harder to convince. After all, these were the people who had lived through many different initiatives that had been pushed down on them over the past ten years. We figured that since they were not involved in the creation of the innovation effort, they would be harder to engage.

What we learned was surprising. We incorrectly assumed that because people were at higher levels, they would be more engaged, interested, or motivated than first- or middle-level managers.

A great example of our error was a factory plant manager in Latin America who involved 100 percent of his employees in learning about innovation tools and processes. He made it so exciting, mostly through his own enthusiasm about including everyone, that even the hourly employees came in on their own time, without pay, to participate in innovation.

In contrast, it proved not as easy as we thought to keep the focus of top leaders on innovation embedment. Clearly, these are people who have a lot to risk by diverting their attention away from their short- or midterm business results. We knew this from the start, but we sometimes had difficulty executing. We were inundated with business realities, as well as with embedment issues that focused on the deployment of new systems and processes related to innovation. It was a struggle to keep our attention on top leadership accountabilities. Sometimes it was easier to let things go by than to address them.

For example, early on, we had set up I-Boards, the groups of senior managers in each region who were to meet regularly to discuss and guide innovation activities and experiments, review innovation ideas, and approve large allocations of funds for innovation experiments. However, we found that the leaders involved in the I-Boards were often too busy to attend the meetings. We let many meetings go by before we had to make attendance as mandatory as it was for their other operations meetings. In short, the senior leaders realized that they needed to continuously reinforce the role of all leaders in innovation embedment.

Although these lapses did not cause our overall effort to sputter, they did cost time and money. We had to reassess and reinforce leadership accountabilities regularly. One or two times were not enough. The lesson is clear: nothing of significance will change in an organization without top-level leadership. Innovation embedment is no exception.

DEVELOPING INNOVATION SKILLS IN LEADERS

Once the accountabilities and expectations were established, we designed a variety of development mechanisms to help all leaders learn the new skills required to lead innovation. One of our surprises (though it shouldn't have been) was that after a year of communicating expectations around accountabilities during leadership workshops and events, some people still didn't seem to get it. We decided that if innovation embedment was important, we needed to begin a full court press. We needed to ensure that everyone understood their accountabilities, had the requisite skills and knowledge, and had a plan for how they were going to use these new skills and support back on the job.

We therefore created a massive strategy that targeted development of all levels of leaders, starting with the top. We believed that experience is the best teacher, so we designed the development efforts to combine classroom-type activities with on-the-job activities that would reinforce the book learning and facilitate the adoption of practices to embed innovation. We inaugurated these efforts following a waterfall approach, beginning with top leaders, then moving down to the next level, and so on.

Finally, we reinforced learning with changes in our systems and processes that assess leader performance and potential, such as performance reviews, talent pool assessments, and bonus criteria (explained in Chapter Ten). This allowed us to add some bite to people's motivation for attending development programs and for trying out new behaviors back on the job. Our focus was on rewarding not only innovative ideas but also leaders who were trying to embed.

What we did to develop our leaders falls into three categories: leadership education and training, on-the-job activities, and developmental feedback.

Leadership Education and Training

We wanted our leadership education program to be robust yet interesting. Learning about innovation needed to be fun and exciting. As a result, our education programs were designed to be interactive and fresh in order to mimic the cultural characteristics of innovation that we were trying to embed, such as openness to new ideas, learning from others, and freedom to experiment, risk, and make mistakes.

Embedment Immersion Workshops. We decided to kick-start the process to train Whirlpool's leaders with a deep experiential immersion in innovation tools and techniques. This occurred about six months after we kicked off the innovation effort. In January 2000, we asked Whirlpool's most senior twenty-five leaders from around the world (those composing our Chairman's Council) to join us in the first week in January in Chicago for a three-day immersion session. Now, everyone knows that Chicago in January is not an ideal place for a relaxing retreat, so it was perfect for our immersion experience: it got people's attention, and they knew that this was important.

Because we had not yet created the embedment wheel, our agenda focused heavily on teaching the tools around our approach to innovation, such as how to challenge orthodoxies, review global trends for the business, use lens crashing, conduct hundred-day experiments (short, quick proofs of theory in the marketplace), and develop criteria for good business plan writing that our innovators would need to follow. At this time, we believed that such tools would play an important role and tended to be "sexy" enough to get our leaders excited about what was ahead. The agenda would at least start their thinking process about how innovation would unfold.

What our meeting did not do, however, was to engage the leadership in their role in embedding innovation. In retrospect, we do not recommend that you start so pronouncedly with innovation tools, but at the time, it was really all we had. We recommend instead that you focus on some of the tools but that you also target leader accountabilities. A good agenda might be better spent on promoting deep understanding of how leaders need to create the context and environment for innovation embedment, as well as on the specific tools. In hindsight, we would recommend focusing on the following items on an immersion agenda:

- The business challenge and strategy behind the innovation effort and how it fits with the overall strategy and other initiatives
- Co-creation of the plan to roll out the effort on a global basis
- How the mind-set and behaviors of leaders play a critical role in the suc-

cess of the effort, including an assessment of the organization and its potential for change

- The challenges inherent in this effort, such as culture change; time, focus, and short-term demands; resource allocation; and measurement
- The resources—people and dollars—that might be necessary for success
- Leader accountabilities in the roll-out process, now and in the future
- Space for dialogue around what it will take to embed and time for discussion of the challenges that impede success
- Time for all leaders to plan or create an immersion session like this one that their own regional or functional leadership teams can use to launch the regional innovation embedment efforts

We also recommend that this type of workshop be repeated in every major region, function, or business unit. We did this and found that it provided the momentum needed to get everyone's attention about the importance of this new effort.

Regular Leadership Events. One of Whirlpool's existing cultural characteristics that proved useful in embedment were our regular leadership workshops in every region and function. We began to use these as opportunities to get innovation on the agenda.

In the first year, we focused on teaching leaders innovation tools and concepts. Remember that this is all we had at this point, since we did not come up with the idea of the embedment wheel until later in the process. These meetings offered many good opportunities for leaders to begin learning innovation tools as participants. It also provided the seventy-five I-Team members an opportunity to act as teachers for the management population in these events. In other words, we were using our internal people to present these tools, not our outside consultant, Strategos. This provided exposure and visibility for these individuals.

In the second year, we migrated to a focus on embedment in these conferences. We worked with regional and functional leadership to design workshop events that targeted various elements of the embedment process, always focusing on the accountability of the participants in the process. In most of these types of meetings, we did not "teach" anything. Rather we designed and helped facilitate discussion, debate, and planning about an aspect of embedment.

Inviting Leaders from Other Companies to Share. Another useful educational method we employed was peer exposure. Tapping into our Strategos partner, we made contact with a number of its larger clients that, like us, were struggling with innovation. Strategos invited executives from some of these companies at well-timed moments to come in to share where they were on the learning curve for innovation. Often these were middle- to upper-middle-management leaders who came to address our I-Board meetings around innovation topics or lessons learned. We also used these visitors to act as evaluators of innovation ideas. For example, before an innovator moved into the experiment phase with an idea, this person was required to write a business plan and have it evaluated by a mini–venture capital board, and so we used some of these outside visitors as part of this board.

These shared exposures proved to be extremely valuable for our leaders. They were a nonthreatening and highly personal way to learn from other leaders facing the same or similar situations. Interestingly, it was often true that the primary learning from these meetings was not a new technique or method but rather a confirmation that the struggles and challenges we were facing were natural and normal. Leaders confessed to their difficulties in finding the time for innovation activities, balancing short- and long-term efforts, and challenges in resource allocation. The visitors seldom provided hard-and-fast answers that we could adopt wholesale for Whirlpool, but they gave us a sense that we were not alone, and that always helps.

Later in our own embedment process, Strategos asked some of our Whirlpool leaders to meet with their other clients on targeted subjects. Attending other company's events became a valuable development mechanism for Whirlpool leaders as they were required to articulate their decisions about what they were going through and why. As it is often said, teaching others is the best way to get your arms around a topic. Preparing for and presenting the Whirlpool embedment story turned out to be an excellent way to begin codifying and reinforcing our own learnings.

Leadership Training. For senior and midlevel leaders, Whirlpool leadership training has always been linked to strategy. Training agendas always focused on ensuring a complete understanding of strategy, the leader's role in executing it, and an action learning component where leaders worked on a strategic project with colleagues. Leaders at Whirlpool therefore expected to attend development sessions that expanded on strategy.

We kept in line with this expectation for our leadership trainings in innovation and designed a series of training events that we cascaded down into the organization to target Whirlpool strategy. We focused on embedment activities around the embedment wheel, particularly regarding the role of leadership. We provided time for lessons learned from others and the sharing of experiences. One noteworthy set of activities we designed asked participants to put themselves in senior management's shoes and recommend how to take innovation to the next level. We received many good recommendations from participants.

More important, the exercise clued us into the participants' understanding of strategy, and thus it helped guide us in creating other developmental activities to leverage what they already knew while addressing their deficits.

On-the-Job Experience

We were acutely aware that people learn from experience, so we insisted on leader participation in on-the-job activities designed to embed innovation. Of course, not every leader could do every activity, but most of our leaders had the chance to participate several times if they desired. Listed below are some of the mechanisms we used to facilitate this type of experiential learning.

I-Boards. We set up early in the process a number of steering and learning councils for innovation. Each major business had an I-Board, composed of the most senior leaders from that business unit. Some also had an I-Team member (from one of the seventy-five original innovation team members appointed from our three major regions) on the board.

The I-Boards met monthly for a minimum of a half-day to a full day. Their agenda had to focus solely on innovation topics. Over the course of the first year, the topics ranged from how to set up innovation teams, to selection criteria and process for prioritizing ideas, to updates on major innovation projects, to portfolio analysis of ideas, to general ongoing innovation issues. I-Board meetings served as a valuable development activity. The agendas often included some innovation action-learning component, such as an innovation tool. But most often, the agenda was filled with accountabilities that the senior leadership on the I-Board had to discharge in order to embed innovation. For example, they often had to make decisions on resource allocation for an experiment or decide if the idea portfolio was too focused on existing products and services rather than new-to-the-world products.

I-Boards became a valuable space for debate and dialogue about leading the innovation effort. The meetings carved out innovation from the normal workday and became the only place where innovation took center stage away from the day-to-day demands of the business. The I-Boards were a learning lab of sorts, where leaders could take the time to reflect on and discuss the best way to proceed. The process of co-creation became a valuable part of the learning experience.

We offer the following advice to anyone thinking about innovation embedment: create a similar forum to our I-Boards. Your forum should become the place where your leaders can get real innovation work done of approving, rejecting, and tinkering with ideas and where they can learn from their peers and participate in co-creating the path to innovation embedment. For Whirlpool, the I-Boards created an important clearing for people to reflect, debate, and act on ambiguous and complex situations. We have no doubt that these meetings will ultimately take us further toward embedding innovation than will any tool in the classroom.

Participation on Innovation Teams and Projects. The most obvious developmental experience was to participate on an I-Team or project. We encouraged leaders and people from all levels to do this. We also used our talent pool process to select high-potential individuals to work on or lead these teams. We wanted participation in innovation to become an integral part of the leader development process at Whirlpool. We also wanted to make a clear cultural statement: participation on an I-Team was the path to success.

What we found was that mid- and first-line-level leaders often jumped at the opportunity to lead or participate on an innovation project. It was not hard to talk people into participation. For some people, their participation led to a new role of leading a new business area; for others, it provided a valuable learning experience that they could take back and share. For all of them, it offered a significant opportunity to learn about and contribute to something creative and strategic.

Developmental Feedback

Targeted feedback is the fodder for growth. Given this, 360-degree feedback has been part of the leadership development culture at Whirlpool since the mid-1990s. We slightly revamped the process to provide leaders specific feedback about how others saw them in their role as leaders of innovation embedment and other strategic initiatives. Our feedback process also provided us with important aggregate data about our leadership population that we could use to craft new development experiences. We incorporated a coaching component into development to provide individual attention for leaders who wanted to make changes or reinforce what they were doing well.

360-Degree Feedback and Development Planning. In the second year of our work, we set up a 360-degree feedback process to give leaders feedback on general leadership behaviors and how others perceived they were doing around the five innovation embedment behaviors discussed earlier in this chapter.

The 360-degree feedback process was first applied to the top leadership team. The feedback reports went only to the leader, who was asked to compile the results and share them with his or her supervisor. Based on the feedback, the leader and supervisor then created a development plan focusing on the person's leadership in total, but also including his or her role in innovation embedment.

We then cascaded the 360-degree process down through the leadership population over a two-year time frame. Most leaders reported that they found this to be highly valuable in providing them with specific feedback about where they could improve in innovation embedment.

The important lesson we learned was that we needed to wait until we were relatively sure that leaders at each level had enough exposure to innovation in order to get them a fair assessment from others. We were tempted to move too quickly and conduct a 360-degree assessment right away. However, we held back because we knew that leaders needed a chance to learn about innovation and discharge their duties around embedment, and that the people rating them needed time to see this happen. This was a wise decision, as the 360 feedback gained credibility in helping people see themselves as others saw them.

One-on-One Coaching. We provided leaders with outside coaches to help them plan and execute development actions in innovation. This provided an external perspective in addition to their supervisor's coaching following the 360-degree feedback process. Some people felt safer trying the new behaviors from their external coaches, while others did not seem to need this. In any event, it was a potentially useful form of development that we made available to all leaders.

We also used senior leaders as coaches to help other leaders learn about their role in innovation embedment. We believed that this was perhaps the most powerful and targeted coaching that leaders could receive. Although not as formalized as external coaches, leaders in each region and function met on a regular basis (about once a quarter) with their direct reports to discuss how innovation embedment was progressing. This forum provided mid- and lower-level leaders with valuable feedback, not only innovation tools themselves, on how the embedment process was progressing in their function or region and how they were executing their accountabilities. Such one-on-one meetings were often valuable in helping leaders to converge on their philosophy of innovation, or to work through trouble spots that would have been otherwise difficult to resolve in the larger group setting. The one-on-one experiences helped establish a strong pattern of personal two-way communications about embedment.

WHAT WE LEARNED

- Senior leaders must share enterprise-wide accountability for embedment as well as be individually accountable for embedment in their own functional or regional areas.
- You need to be almost too explicit in laying out accountabilities for leaders at all levels around embedment.
- Senior leaders need accountabilities laid out and access to development experience just as much as mid- and lower-level leaders do.
- You cannot assume that mid- and lower-level leaders will have less readiness to learn about and act on embedment than more senior leaders.

- You need to explicitly describe culture-changing behaviors for all levels of leaders.

- You need a robust innovation development process for all leaders that includes training events and workshops, on-the-job experience, and feedback. Development reinforces the commitment that you are serious about innovation embedment.

- You need to time development activities to match the pace of embedment activities. The learner will be motivated when there is a purpose to learn.

SELF-ASSESSMENT: LEADERSHIP IN YOUR COMPANY

Leader accountabilities and development hold an essential place on the embedment wheel. Use Worksheet 4.1 to assess the health of your leadership accountability and development system for innovation embedment.

Worksheet 4.1. Leadership Accountability and Development Assessment

Check as many of the following statements as apply to your organization:

_____ We have outlined and communicated embedment accountabilities for our senior leaders.

_____ We have outlined and communicated embedment accountabilities for midlevel leaders.

_____ We have outlined and communicated embedment accountabilities for first-line leaders.

_____ Senior leaders have enterprise-wide accountability for embedment.

_____ We have asked senior leaders to communicate leader accountabilities down through their organizations.

_____ We check on how people are acting on their embedment accountabilities in senior staff, regional, and other staff meetings on a regular basis.

_____ We have added leadership accountabilities for innovation embedment to the performance management system.

_____ We are using the talent pool process to develop people around their accountabilities for innovation embedment.

_____ We have provided a robust set of development activities for senior leaders: training, on-the-job experience, and feedback.

_____ We have provided a robust set of development activities for mid- and first-level leaders: training, on-the-job experience, and feedback.

_____ We time development activities to match the timing of embedment activities.

_____ Leaders get informal time with senior leaders to discuss how embedment is going on a regular basis.

Scoring: How many checks do you have?

1–4   You run the risk that lack of leadership focus will get in the way of embedment.

5–8   You are doing well but need to strengthen your strategy.

9–12   You are exemplary!

CHAPTER FIVE

Culture and Values

Understanding the culture and values of your organization is critical to the embedment process. Culture and values reside in the every fold of an enterprise, influencing the dynamics of how people perform, relate, and perceive the organization's impact on their lives. The noted organizational psychologist Edward Schein defined organizational culture as "a pattern of shared basic assumptions that the group learned as it solved its problems of external adaptation and internal integration, that has worked well enough to be considered valid and, therefore, to be taught to new members as the correct way to perceive, think, and feel in relation to those problems" (1992, p. 12).

We like this definition. It begins with shared assumptions, which we believe are the heart of any culture. It references problem solving and adaptation, which differentiate organizational culture from other types of cultures not bound to business. Finally, it highlights the generational nature of culture, recognizing that succeeding groups of employees learn about culture from the current generation. All of these characteristics of culture are critical to innovation embedment.

Given the importance of culture, we believed from the start that having access to a robust view of Whirlpool's culture and values would help us understand how to approach innovation embedment. We were fortunate to be able to pull recurring characteristics, values, and traits from a variety of interventions and studies Whirlpool had made during past years in examining its culture. As result, over the years, we had developed an in-depth understanding of our culture and its values, which became an enormously valuable platform on which to build innovation embedment. We present you with some of our analysis and learnings about culture in this chapter, because we think it informs how deeply we had considered it and how serious we were about transforming it to create the right environment for innovation.

A SHORT HISTORY OF CULTURE AT WHIRLPOOL

The year 1995 proved to be very difficult at Whirlpool: from all indicators, our business was under stress. If that were not enough, like a gothic creature that becomes visible only in bad times, the culture of Whirlpool came out of the shadows and began menacing our social interactions. We began seeing and experiencing actions by leaders in the organization that were antithetical to what Whirlpool holds dear. There was a silo mentality that developed into infighting between work units. In addition, there was a lack of dialogue and debate to get to the right answers.

During this period, there were a series of stories going around our water coolers throughout the world that were shocking—stories of disrespect, distrust, and cynicism. It soon became clear to Dave Whitwam, CEO and chairman at that time, that the company's culture needed attention. In late 1995, he chartered an intervention to learn about and repair our culture and values. His goal was to create what he called High Performance Culture, or HPC for short.

Nancy was appointed to a global strategic organization development position reporting to the head of global human resources and later to the Executive Committee to work on HPC. (This work predated her role as global vice president of innovation.) Nancy was the lead internal consultant on the project. At key points, Deb worked for us as an external consultant on numerous projects within the culture initiative. The workshops and interventions we describe were designed by Nancy and the Executive Committee. At certain key points, she brought in outside expertise such as Robert Quinn a culture expert from the University of Michigan, and Jim Channon, a business artist, as the visual recorder of what happened in a series of culture workshops and as a storyteller.

Getting Started: The Culture Audit

We began to design our intervention with a culture audit aimed at developing a vivid picture of the current culture. Employees in twenty countries, from senior leaders to blue-collar workers, were interviewed face to face. From these employee focus groups, we distilled a list of descriptive statements that reflected how the interviewees (and probably many other people) thought about Whirlpool culture.

As we suspected, the results depicted a global culture that was, paradoxically, at the same time enabling and out of alignment with our strategies of globalization, growth, leveraging synergies, and learning. Our findings are presented in Exhibit 5.1.

This audit not only helped us craft the direction for change, but prepared us to begin to address culture as a business enabler. It also became critical to embedding innovation into our culture in later years.

Senior Leadership Culture Workshop

To begin to change the culture in 1996 (still during our pre-innovation period), we conducted a series of workshops consisting of eight work groups and four hundred senior leaders over the course of one year. The first workshop, with the Executive Committee, was followed by a Chairman's Council workshop, held for the next twenty-five to thirty officers. Following these workshops, we conducted regional business unit workshops at Whirlpool's business headquarters in the United States, Brazil, Italy, Hong Kong, India, and Thailand. These workshops were designed to engage each leader in the HPC process and to emphasize the need for personal change.

In all of these workshops, the central focus was a simple, clean premise: culture change starts by telling the truth. The workshops culminated in an exercise that forced leaders to look at their personal behavior and engage in a rich dialogue about their cultural attitudes. Such extensive interchanges about culture had not happened in the past at Whirlpool. As a result of one of these workshops, one participant recommended that each leader keep a journal to reflect on his or her personal change process, and many began to do just that. Their journals became symbols of a broad cultural transformation in the company. Arising out of these workshops, a legacy of truth telling, candid dialogue, and discussion began that became critical in the innovation embedment effort.

In Search of Values Past

As part of this workshop series, a museum of artifacts was created from around the Whirlpool world. The museum's exhibit time line started in 1911, when Whirlpool was founded. On display were vintage washers, documents from as far back as the 1940s, pictures and portraits of many Whirlpool employees from as early as 1911, the founder's personal journal recording washer sales in 1914 in his turn-of-the century handwriting, letters to employees from management starting a vacation policy in 1917, and a myriad of other artifacts that represented the history of Whirlpool's rich culture. As we took the core museum around the world, we added artifacts from the local Whirlpool cultures. The museum became an inspiring centerpiece for each workshop whose participants experienced it. It reminded us in concrete ways of what was precious and noteworthy about the organization, and it set the stage for what we knew we needed to protect and honor going forward with innovation.

Exhibit 5.1. Cultural Descriptions for Whirlpool, Circa 1995

"Employees are very committed to Whirlpool."

"We have too much change."

"We have focused on globalization, quality, and performance, but we have forgotten the values."

"We are a 'PowerPoint' culture with no real dialogue. We are too polite."

"We have no real discussion or communication."

"There is no one single Whirlpool culture."

"We are too hierarchical."

"Our global strategy is well accepted and understood, but we have questions about the implementation."

"Whirlpool has exceptional ethics, but this is more about the legal external ethics. We are not as strong on ethics when it comes to how we treat each other."

"We have unclear priorities and accountabilities."

"Whirlpool focuses only on short-term financial results."

"We place little value on diversity."

"Pretense and formality abound at Whirlpool."

"The quality of work/life balance has eroded over the years."

The Values Book: Touchstone and Signpost

Another element of the HPC work that played a role in our innovation embedment work on culture actually began in 1990, when the leadership team articulated a set of organization-wide values, the first such effort for Whirlpool. It was, however, purely an intellectual exercise. These leaders took a list of generic values and, using a mathematical formula and a spreadsheet, asked the senior leadership group to vote on the values that best described our culture. The result was a value set that had all the right corporate buzzwords but lacked commitment and emotion. The values were articulated without dialogue, debate, and interaction.

During the HPC leadership forums in 1996, we pulled these sterile values off the wall and discussed and debated them, allowing them to be touched, challenged, and internalized. The result was a set of values that the senior leaders felt deeply committed to and began to discuss with other people. From this exercise, a Values Book was created and handed out for the purpose of successive discussions in the workforce. Exhibit 5.2 shows one value, respect, from the Values Book.

We wanted to understand how these values would play out around the world and if they could connect with the entire workforce. To do this, we conducted a series of focus groups to get reactions to the new values. One person in a focus group read the book and said: "Who is this company? I'd like to work for them." In the end, a product emerged that had great pride of authorship from employees. One employee, while thinking about the ups and downs of any business, said that the values were a touchstone to help us find our way in bad times.

Exhibit 5.2. Respect Value Description from the Values Book

RESPECT

We do our best work when we trust one another as individuals,
encourage diversity in our workplace, value the capabilities and contributions
of each person, and recognize that work is but one part of a full and rewarding life.

You can expect Whirlpool to:
* Create a global high performance company culture built on these enduring shared values and strengthened by the richness of local differences.
* Foster an environment that promotes trust, individual dignity, and an open exchange of opinions and ideas.
* Seek and manage diversity in our workforce.
* Provide a safe and healthy work environment.
* Treat people fairly and consistently in good times and bad.
* Provide work that is challenging, rewarding, and respectful of each person's potential.

Whirlpool expects you to:
* Treat others as you think they would like to be treated.
* Challenge opinions and ideas to ensure the best decisions and solutions.
* Encourage open discussion and debate of issues.
* Focus your competitive drive on competitors, not on colleagues or partners.
* Understand and accept the challenges of our global business and work to your full potential to meet those challenges.

1996 © Whirlpool Corporation.
All rights reserved.

As a result of this intense effort, the values have been and continue to be an extremely important aspect of our culture and strategic direction. We have continued to adapt them over the years to focus on areas that need the most attention and to foster new strategic initiatives such as innovation. For example, the values of inclusion and diversity are central to innovation embedment and so are now being enriched and reframed. We'll return to discussing how the values document influenced our efforts for innovation embedment.

Values Challenge Meetings: The Power of Moral Statement

Following the leadership workshops and focus group sessions, we felt a need to bring the discussions about values to the wider audience of employees. To accomplish this, we asked leaders to hold values discussions in a safe and "off-line" setting. We believed that this setting was the best way to discuss and ingrain the values so that when and if a crisis or moral dilemma occurred, people would already have a history with grappling with values.

Each senior-level and midlevel leader at Whirlpool was asked to hold meetings on each value contained in the Values Book with a multilevel group. These "Values Challenge Meetings" became a place where people could discuss, debate, and internalize the values. These were, without question, one of the most successful aspects of our work in realigning culture and values. They allowed all Whirlpool people to understand the values, particularly how the values needed to be relevant their day-to-day work. The summary in Exhibit 5.3 presents some of the feedback from the meetings on the value of respect that we received from the leaders who conducted these meetings.

Exhibit 5.3. Leaders' Summary of Values Challenge Meeting Results on "Respect"

"It was a very lively and fruitful meeting. Participants exchanged ideas freely, and they really got down to think about what this value of respect means in the workplace."

"The most important message I can derive from this meeting is that employees welcome this kind of challenge meeting. It is in itself a sign of 'respect.'"

"HPC means a lot to the employees. They want this type of company."

"On the whole, the meeting proved to be very positive. Each participant had the opportunity to discuss issues of the heart in a candid manner without compromise."

"There is still a strong reluctance for people to speak out and criticize the sacred cows. It is expected that they will be viewed negatively or perhaps undergo negative consequences in their careers."

"Key theme: We create artificial barriers that get in the way of respecting each other."

The Values Challenge sessions generated candid and frank dialogue and set the stage for creating a culture where all people were involved in values creation and everyone could be open with one another and speak freely. In retrospect, they also helped Whirlpool get ready for the cultural changes we would need to make for embedding innovation.

360-Degree Feedback on the Values

One last key element of our culture change process we should mention was the 360-degree feedback process we used for leaders. As part of the HPC effort, employees were asked to give confidential feedback to their leaders in terms of their conduct around the values. This too proved to be a successful element of the culture change process because it provided a way to allow managers to get feedback from others in a safe forum. It also set the stage for 360-degree feedback on innovation embedment behaviors that we found very useful in leader development.

STARTING INNOVATION EMBEDMENT: WHIRLPOOL'S CULTURE AND VALUES

The extensive efforts to analyze, codify, and repair our culture and values described above predated innovation embedment. However, they proved invaluable to the embedment practitioners and top leadership in preparing us for innovation. Almost unknowingly, we had been assessing and addressing the Whirlpool culture over the years, and as a result, we had already analyzed what aspects of our culture were enablers and which created barriers. Through that earlier work, we already had a sense of what in our culture would positively or negatively affect our innovation embedment process. Indeed, after reviewing the workshops, focus groups, and internal studies of Whirlpool culture, we were able to generate a list of enablers and barriers without even breaking into a sweat. Exhibit 5.4 lists some of our findings.

CULTURAL ASSESSMENT FOR INNOVATION READINESS

To begin our work in aligning our culture with embedment, in 2000, shortly after our innovation effort began, we asked our senior leaders to conduct culture audits in their organizations in an effort to describe the cultural characteristics that represented their readiness for innovation. This activity was our first crack at the embedment wheel category of culture as it related to innovation embedment. The findings were not surprising given what we already knew

Exhibit 5.4. Cultural Descriptions of Whirlpool Before Innovation Embedment, Circa 1999

Potential Cultural Enablers for Innovation	Potential Cultural Barriers for Innovation
Midwest or "small town" like	Everyone can say no-risk averse
Friendly	Lack of alignment and consistency
Ethical	Too many programs and projects
Deterministic	Not-invented-here syndrome
Integrity	Change averse
Respect	Not customer centered
Team decision making	Silo mentality
Cost containment and quality centered	Internal or trade only focused

about our culture, but the work helped the leaders focus their thinking on how culture can be a barrier to innovation in their organization. In particular, it provided us with a specific set of statements about how the culture was a barrier to innovation, as shown in Exhibit 5.5. From this, we could now begin to develop a specific plan for what we had to address culture change in the area of embedment.

CULTURAL CHANGE AND THE EMBEDMENT WHEEL

Before we continue the story of what happened at Whirlpool, it is worthwhile to comment on the process of changing culture for embedment and what exactly can be expected.

First, once you complete a culture and values description, the findings can be used to understand what, if any, areas of the embedment wheel need to be altered or adapted to ensure that your culture becomes an enabler of, not a barrier to, innovation. In this way, the embedment wheel helps you focus on the areas of your culture that are not consistent with the overall direction of innovation embedment. Your observations should be viewed as useful insights, but weighed according to how powerful they are in contributing to or derailing the innovation embedment process.

Exhibit 5.5. Leaders' Assessment of Cultural Barriers for Innovation Embedment, Circa 2000

Many new ideas, few new businesses: "Our renewal rate [the percentage of new business revenues] is too low across all regions and products."

No sense of a "burning platform": "We define our required pace of innovations by looking at other (slow) industry players, not by newcomers who are not part of the current competitive landscape."

Narrow focus of innovation: "When we think about innovation, we think primarily about product platforms or product features. We see innovation primarily as a result of applying a new technology, not as a combination of user needs, brand promise, and technology."

Inside-out view on innovation: "We look for innovations inside our organization instead of extracting ideas from our external environment [for example, customers, suppliers, and universities]."

Slow innovation means no innovation: "We seem to be caught in a trade-off between speed and quality, leading us to miss market time windows."

Killing ideas with the wrong measures: "We evaluate new business opportunities with the same measures as established business, primarily financial measures, thereby killing many ideas too early."

Risk adversity: "Because of our fear of failure and mistakes, we tend to be overly risk averse."

Innovation pipeline versus portfolio: "We end up having too few innovations in the pipeline, which then must succeed, instead of managing our innovation options in a strong portfolio."

Lack of diversity: "We often view diversity as a human resource requirement, as opposed to a fertile ground on which innovation can flourish."

Here's a rundown of how culture can have an impact on selected elements of the embedment wheel. For each element, we discuss only one aspect of the connection between embedment and culture. Of course, many more may need to be considered.

Vision

The culture must closely match the vision statement. For example, if an organization has a strong hierarchical culture but innovation is supposed to be more team- or self-led, then the embedment practitioners and top leadership team need to make a calculated judgment about whether the strong hierarchical factor can be changed. If not, it could doom innovation embedment.

Leader Systems

Leader systems must address the way the culture views leadership. If, for example, the cultural description indicates that there is a deep-seated belief that everyone, at any level, can be a leader, then the approach such as the one Whirlpool took of innovation from everyone is consistent. If the enterprise views leadership as a select group of people who control, organize, and set direction, then innovation from everyone will be stymied by the culture. The embedment practitioner and top leadership team must make a calculated judgment about how cultural factors around leadership will affect progress.

Resources

At first pass, it may seem counterintuitive to think of culture in terms of resources, but each organization has basic assumptions about resource allocation. For example, an organization's resources can be centralized or decentralized. If supervisors control all resources of any magnitude, innovation embedment may not succeed. Instead, resources need to be dispersed lower in the organization, and some of the traditional power that supervisors have needs to be examined closely. The embedment practitioner and top leadership team need to address these culture aspects of resources to ensure success.

Knowledge Management and Learning Systems

The enterprise's orientation toward being a learning culture will influence any embedment effort. For example, if there is a strong "not-invented-here" trait in the culture, it will be hard for people to be open-minded and learn from best practices, a necessary characteristic for innovation. Furthermore, knowledge management can be a cultural powder keg if those who possess knowledge see sharing it as eroding their personal power.

If knowledge is not broadly shared, innovation from everyone will not succeed. This cultural attitude must be overturned to provide incentives for people to contribute to shared knowledge systems.

Change Management and Strategic Communications

Culture and values are critical to understand in the change management process for core competency embedment. At every step of change, culture and values not only guide the embedment process, but also serve as a check for what fits within the bounds of work and how people in the enterprise interact and treat each other. Culture and values, although tacit, are a critical construct to consider when creating and deploying a change plan for innovation embedment.

Culture and values are the foundation for strategic communications. If you are seeking major change, the culture and values can be positively represented as a departure, a break with the past, especially if the past is negative. If innovation embedment is part of an existing overall strategic architecture, strategic communications can use culture and values as a platform or springboard to give comfort that this is not a new program of the month or a modification of the previous initiatives.

Rewards and Recognition

Rewards and recognition are another aspect of the wheel that has great dependence on culture and values. The types of rewards and recognition handed out must fit the embedment activities and yet be based on the culture and values of the enterprise. For example, if the organization is very team oriented, rewards and recognition for innovation embedment should be structured to align with this characteristic. If the organization values community activities and gift giving, rewards and recognition could be in the form of honorariums or gifts to charities of the innovators' choice.

Measurement and Reporting Systems and Systems Alignment

Ideally, these systems need to be pliable enough to align and adapt to innovation embedment. Culture may play a role in their flexibility and the speed (or slowness) at which these systems can be changed. This is where hidden culture can kill embedment, particularly with regard to the potential for one or several of these systems being considered sacred or protected from people who want to change or adapt it.

CULTURAL CHANGE AT WHIRLPOOL: DIGGING DEEPER INTO RISK TAKING

Let's come back now to what happened at Whirlpool. To our surprise, embedment changed our culture. During the innovation effort, we experienced a combination of positive changes in our culture. Some of these were surprising because efforts in the past to adapt or change these aspects of Whirlpool's culture had been met with mixed reviews. At best, many of the culture change efforts described above became a series of events that moved the needle but largely did not result in deep change. This time, some culture changes that had been tried without much change before were more successful, because they were undertaken as part of innovation embedment.

We want to take one aspect of culture and do a deep dive to show how it changed as a result of embedment. For this illustration, we selected risk taking at Whirlpool. It is not the only aspect of our culture that changed as a result of innovation embedment, but we believe that risk taking presents a robust example of how embedment can change the culture.

Before the innovation process, Whirlpool's culture generally held that risk taking was best left to the few people at the top of the organization. There was, and to some extent still is, a deep-seated belief that risk takers are fired or derailed. Although real examples of such treatment were hard to find, the belief was stronger than the reality, and so risk taking was not viewed positively. This belief was continually cited in the culture audits.

As a result, there were underlying myths that we had to debunk about risk taking in Whirlpool. It is important to note that risk taking was most affected in the areas where innovation embedment was occurring. (Even today, these changes are not yet completely pervasive within Whirlpool.)

We will consider risk taking in terms of experimentation. Experiments are an integral part of our innovation process. Innovation requires people to take risks through experiments. Innovation is by its very nature risky business, so we use experimentation to mitigate risk in an innovation project.

With innovation embedment, experiments became part of the subtext of innovators and leaders. New standards for risk taking through experimentation were quietly adopted. In the past, people who took risks believed that all risks had to be big. There was no mind-set of taking small, progressive risks to test a concept. Innovation embedment, however, introduced a variety of planning and experimentation tools that made risk taking more common.

There was also a belief that testing ideas had to be expensive. But the new thinking in innovation considered that experiments are best when they are small and progressive toward an end, where small means $25,000, not $100,000. With this construct, innovators developed a new understanding of how far $25,000 could take a potential innovator if he or she were resourceful. A lot happened for $25,000: a whole informal network sprang up within the company to help these passionate innovators experiment on the cheap. This made risk taking more palatable.

Next, we wanted innovators to see that experiments needed to exist in the context of being the biggest idea in the space. For example, an experiment on a washer should be conceived in terms of a bigger space, like the fabric care business. Innovation requires that although experiments can be small, they should not stand alone but should be evaluated within this bigger, richer space. Innovation embedment forced people to start with the biggest idea and put risk taking and experimentation into that context. It made risks more strategic and part of the normal business reality.

Last, if we were to sustain innovation, innovators had to think of failure as learning. Even if an innovation was stopped, we wanted people to capture the learning and extract the maximum value from each innovation project.

Although this is not completely true today at Whirlpool, we have made a good start. For example, we keep track of shelved projects (innovations that are put on hold or stopped). In the long run, our hope is that innovators can still learn from shelved ideas and someday leapfrog that learning to create similar innovation at a higher level. In addition, by leveraging our global platform, these learnings can be translated from one market to another. In fact, Whirlpool India routinely looks through shelved ideas from other parts of the world to see if they can apply something from them in their unique marketplace. We have effectively created an after-market for shelved ideas, thus extending the intrinsic value of the first innovation. Realizing this reset our basic assumption about how much risk we were really taking since we continued to extract value after the innovation was shelved.

TWEAKING WHIRLPOOL'S CULTURE FOR THE REST OF THE EMBEDMENT WHEEL

Given that culture is so intertwined with embedment, it was important to look at the interdependencies between culture and every category of the wheel for Whirlpool. Below are a few examples of the categories of the embedment wheel and how innovation ended up changing the culture at Whirlpool.

Vision

Our vision statement, "Innovation from Everyone and Everywhere," matched the preexisting cultural factor of determinism: everyone could contribute. But it did not match the strong hierarchical factor that existed within Whirlpool's culture. As we discovered, the top leadership team and the embedment practitioners needed to make a calculated judgment about whether the strong hierarchical factor could be addressed or changed. Our decision was that if this factor could not be changed, it would doom innovation embedment. Our vision statement made a bold statement about where we wanted the culture to head.

Leader Accountability and Development Systems

When we started innovation embedment, we were implementing a concurrent renewed focus on leadership assessment and development. Our culture already had a strong foundation for leadership involvement in change initiatives. We built on this and augmented it, which helped renew the basic assumption that leadership had to drive innovation embedment. We used the momentum of past and currently planned leadership assessment and development systems to fold in the innovation accountabilities and development required for leaders. In addition, we used this opportunity to clearly define what leaders were expected to

DUCT TAPE VERSION
One Size Does Not Fit All Cultures

Whirlpool found that in some of its factories located in countries where hierarchy was deeply ingrained, innovation participants had a strong deference to their boss. This was antithetical to the innovative environment that we needed to create, where ideas could come from anyone at any level.

One example was Brazil. It took our local leaders only a short time to discern why they were not getting as many ideas and up-front innovations as some of their colleagues in other parts of the world. They quickly attributed this to their closed border history, the resulting lack of familiarity of potential innovators with open market constructs, coupled with a strong paternalistic national culture where the boss is, first and foremost, the "boss."

Behind the scenes, however, Brazil's innovation embedment was creating a buzz with factory workers who truly wanted to learn more about innovation and had great interest and passion in joining the effort. The local leaders took a few extra steps to open up the flow of ideas and practice of challenging each other, no matter what level. For example, when one team of innovators would not move forward without affirmation from their bosses, the I-Consultant respectfully put them in a room and asked them not to come out until they worked through it for themselves—tough love, but it worked. They first had to understand that their boss did not have the right answer and was not going to tell them what to do. As a result, Brazil generated hundreds of ideas and exhibited great passion to think outside the box.

In another part of the world with a history of closed borders, Slovakia, the opposite happened. Their history of a tightly closed border made the people burst with ideas and quick starts. They did not wait for their bosses to comment or set a direction. These teams were also very successful in the innovation effort, but in a very different way.

These two examples illustrate how essential local leaders are in adapting the innovation process to the local culture. Although innovation embedment can follow a template for global consistency, you need to account for how national culture and history can change how it is received and how successful it will be. Leaders and I-Consultants who understand local cultures and engaging in day-to-day interaction can best gauge how to adapt approaches to national culture.

One size does not fit all.

do in innovation. Also, leaders rethought their long-held beliefs about how leaders lead in an innovative environment. They no longer could be involved at every step in the innovation process. Their role shifted from knowing every answer to creating the right environment and using the values to drive innovation embedment.

Resources

The embedment effort caused us to shift our beliefs about how funds should be distributed in an innovative environment. Whereas we had believed that funds should be allocated from the top down, we created seed funds and moved them closer to the innovators. Although we have not yet completed this shift, we are making progress.

Another part of resources is people. When we looked at our basic assumptions about how people were assigned to jobs, we saw that we needed to switch our culture to one in which people assign themselves. We have not made as much progress as we would like on this aspect, but with some of our successful innovation projects, we have quickly moved the right people to these projects.

Knowledge Management and Learning Systems

The CEO stated from the onset that he did not have the innovation skills required by the embedment plan and that he must learn these like everyone else. His frank honesty set the stage and modeled the type of learning organization that Whirlpool needed to become, from the CEO down through every level of the organization. Fortunately, Whirlpool people had a legacy of learning, so training and education in innovation were quickly accepted and valued. However, knowledge sharing across organizational boundaries was not a strong part of our culture. People did not naturally share across organizational boundaries. As a result, we knew that we needed to address sharing through intense focus on knowledge management and sharing mechanisms.

Change Management and Strategic Communications

The fact that Whirlpool has a history and process for change management helped us greatly. We leveraged our skills learned from the HPC and other efforts to innovation. In addition, one of the most widely articulated values from our previous HPC effort was diversity. This value helped us introduce the notion that diversity of thinking was to be respected and recognized for its relationship to innovation. This set the stage for the acceptance of many innovation tools that were built on diversity of thinking and created the foundation for the major change: Innovation from Everyone and Everywhere—regardless of origin of idea.

One example of strategic communications at Whirlpool represented how culture can foster innovation. After the North American region had two years of solid innovation under its belt, it hosted a communication event called Innovation Days. The event was held at the local shopping mall. The organizers invited each I-Team and their innovation to the event. Each I-Team pitched its ideas to the Whirlpool people who came to learn more about innovation. The community and the media were also invited. It was a hugely successful event. It motivated many people to get more involved in innovation because not only did we get to see the many innovations that were under development, we got to see people just like us pitching them. This was also a great example of how building on the cultural aspect of community orientation was helpful in embedment.

Rewards and Recognition

Our cultural trait of being "nice people" created an environment where people were hesitant to be in the spotlight for achievements. For the most part, our recognition system showcased teams of innovators rather than individuals. Rewards, on the other hand, could more easily focus on individuals. For example, certification as an I-Mentor became an individual reward that the people at Whirlpool felt comfortable with. Our culture fostered a pleasant environment for I-Teams but worked against us for individuals to come forward and be individually recognized for ideas.

Measurement and Reporting Systems and Systems Alignment

Our culture was slow to change systems and processes but at the same time was process focused. We learned that these systems are the visible artifacts of an unstated culture, critical to making innovation work: they can speed up, slow down, or stop embedment. Because our systems were traditionally slow to adapt and change, we needed to make their change explicit and part of the embedment process. One region identified the top systems it needed to adapt and assigned them to senior leaders to change. For one year, the redesign of these systems was one of their embedment goals.

OUR VALUES TODAY

The Whirlpool Values are continually updated. Exhibit 5.6 sets out the values during the period of innovation embedment, from 1999 to 2002. These values are used extensively by Whirlpool people to guide behavior. They are an incredibly important component of our strategic architecture and the culture of Whirlpool. They have also played a critical role in helping us design innovation embedment actions. The fact that we had taken the time to create and embed many of them before we began the innovation effort most likely took us a long way toward embedment in the first place. If a company does not have a strong cultural assessment and set of values, we strongly suggest addressing this before beginning an embedment process.

Exhibit 5.6. Whirlpool's Enduring Values

Values	Description
Respect	We do our best work when we trust one another as individuals, encourage diversity in our workplace, value the capabilities and contributions of each person, and recognize that work is but one part of a full and rewarding life.
Integrity	We conduct all aspects of our business in an honorable way, recognizing that there is no right way to do a wrong thing.
Teamwork	Pride results in our working together to unleash the potential of every person. By working together, we will achieve exceptional results.
Inclusion & Diversity	The broad diversity of our people and their ideas is the fundamental foundation for the future success of our company. Differences create value. Inclusion allows everyone to contribute to her or his fullest potential.

WHAT WE LEARNED

- Culture and values shape how you approach innovation embedment. What might be right in one culture may not work in another.

- Be aware that much of culture is unarticulated and may not be visible. A culture assessment or a keen understanding of your culture before you start embedment planning will help you counteract the invisible hand of culture. Also, the more you can make culture part of the open discussions during embedment planning, the greater are the chances you will have success.

- Your culture will not be overturned as a result of innovation embedment, but if you are successful, your culture will change and be shaped.

- Use the best of your culture to drive and enable embedment. All cultures have positive and negative traits for innovation embedment. Pick and expand the ones that will help.

- Cultures live in local settings at each country or location in your company. Local managers are the best judges of how to address barriers to innovation or how to use enabling culture traits to drive innovation. You can still have a global or central template, but do make plans for local deployment.

- Your culture will never be "right." You will always have barriers to embedment. If you wait to start embedment when the culture is in place, you will never start. Get started, and use embedment to address the barriers.

SELF-ASSESSMENT:
BRINGING INNOVATION TO YOUR ORGANIZATION

Given the overarching importance of culture, the embedment practitioner needs to have a candid description of the culture and which aspects will be enabling to innovation embedment. The more you understand your culture, the more successful the embedment plan will be to create the changes required by innovation embedment. One way is to create a simple description of your culture using Worksheet 5.1.

It can be a challenge to describe your organization's culture and to see which aspects affect performance if much of your culture is taken for granted. In fact, it is possible to overlook culture and values as a critical performance factor because culture and values by their nature are taken-for-granted invisible assumptions. Cameron and Quinn (1996) write that organizations are not aware of their culture until something happens that puts the culture under stress, thereby making it visible and explicit. Most of the time, it is ignored.

In your embedment work, you have to make these basic assumptions explicit. The basic assumptions of culture can even affect the way you approach embedment planning. Consider as an example that your company culture has a history of being risk averse. This risk aversion is taken for granted or is invisible. As a result, you approach embedment in small, incremental ways instead of taking or recommending the large risks required for embedment. In this case, culture is invisibly controlling you and the embedment process itself.

In contrast, consider a company whose risk aversion is also a characteristic of its culture, but it is explicit and talked about. As a result, this organization's embedment plan will be constructed with this in mind. Its leaders will have a more realistic approach to how much risk taking they are willing to take on without shutting down the embedment process.

The embedment effort can and should drive culture shifts within the organization. This is especially true when you are trying to embed innovation. However, keep in mind that all organizations will have some cultural incongruencies with innovation goals. It is a natural tension. Take it as a given that you'll have to focus on culture when embedding innovation and that you can do this by working on innovation competencies rather than rushing into a head-on "culture change" effort. Building an innovation capability can be used as a culture-shifting mechanism. Whether an organization uses it to deliberately drive culture shifts, there is a bit of a "pill in the apple" effect regardless.

Given the organization's culture as your starting premise, the top leadership team and embedment practitioner should make an assessment to describe its existing culture and values. The description should be broad enough to cover the overall culture of the enterprise, not just one area, function, region, or the headquarters.

Worksheet 5.1. Simple Culture and Values Embedment Description

Using key initiatives or business practices as the basis of evaluation, describe your culture in terms of shared values, beliefs, behaviors, heroes, systems, stories, and symbols.

Validating the description will entail taking additional steps to conduct a more detailed culture and values audit or assessment. There are many culture and values instrument available. One instrument is the Quinn and Cameron Competing Values Assessment (1996).

1. Describe five or six shared values of your organization. How do people in the organization describe what is important? What values would be additive to embed innovation?

2. Describe the key beliefs in terms of how things are accomplished. What beliefs would be additive to embed innovation?

3. Name three people in the organization who are seen as heroes. Describe why they are viewed in that way. What values and beliefs do they portray?

4. What are the key shared systems, processes, and procedures in the organization primarily designed to do (for example, simplify, align, codify, expedite, diversify, count, measure, control, create)?

5. What are the top three most frequently told stories, folklore, or myths in the organization? Why? What is the purpose of these stories? Why are they told? What values, beliefs, or behaviors do they portray?

6. What are the primary symbols or artifacts that best represent the organization? Think in terms of logos, buildings, physical spaces, accepted or usual dress, reserved parking spaces or other benefits by position, colors, songs, and sayings. What do they represent? What values, beliefs, or behaviors do they portray?

CHAPTER SIX

Resource Creation

Open Markets for Funds, Ideas, and Talent

The process of creating and allocating resources to fuel innovation is critical to the innovation embedment process. Many enterprise-wide initiatives starve and wither due to lack of resources. This often occurs because leaders underestimate the amount of resources necessary during start-up, or they underfund it from the beginning thinking they will just "wait to see what happens." Clearly, it is difficult to foresee the amount of resources required at the onset of an initiative. It also takes incredible courage to set the resources aside before they are actually needed and extreme discipline not to redeploy them when things look grim in other parts of the business. Consequently, for many new innovation initiatives, the flow of resources sputters like a poorly tuned engine, ready to stop at any time.

As we were exploring how to define and find the right resources for Whirlpool, we clearly needed to avoid these resource problems. One of our best insights into how to do so came from Gary Hamel (1999). Hamel suggested that large and established organizations need to develop three key internal "markets" in order to emulate the innovative developments of Silicon Valley. According to his paradigm, organizations need to set up markets for capital, ideas, and talent, which allow resources to flow freely, unencumbered by the bureaucracy of the hierarchy.

We readily adopted this position. We liked the notion of free-flowing resources and people. We knew that the innovation tools and processes portion of the embedment wheel would provide the ideas, as long as we could ensure the other two components of Hamel's recommendation: funding and people.

TWO MIND-SETS: CREATION VERSUS ALLOCATION

Before we review what Whirlpool did to manage our resources for innovation, it is important to understand a fundamental distinction between resource allocation and resource creation. A disciplined resource allocation process is a central operating process for most firms, but it is not generally innovation friendly in the same way as resource creation is, for three reasons. First, most resource allocation processes begin with strategic planning and annual budgeting. However, innovation usually does not happen once a year or on a schedule, and it cannot be controlled or predicted. Second, resource allocation, except for zero-based approaches, usually starts with the amount of money that the department had last year. This leaves little room for new funding required for ad hoc innovation or innovation that does not fit nicely into a single departmental budget. Finally, the resource allocation mind-set often establishes controls to limit risk, not encourage it.

In contrast, resource creation implies a different cultural mind-set from resource allocation. Resource creation does not begin with the amount you had last year. Rather, it begins with a small amount of funding available to innovators, allowing them to prove their case through experimentation and then receive additional levels of funds as their idea pays for itself. Whereas allocation suggests entitlement—something someone "gives" you once you clear certain business return and control hurdles—creation is determined through an assessment of the idea and can have multiple sources inside and outside the organization. There is no precedent for the funding, no automatic home that it starts from as in allocation. In a resource creation environment, innovators get resources by qualifying for them and attracting them based on the business potential of their ideas, not on an annual process.

We have summarized the differences between resource allocation and creation in Exhibit 6.1.

FUNDING INNOVATION BY SEED FUNDS

Under Hamel's Silicon Valley paradigm, funding is the first key internal market that organizations need to emulate. Research shows consistently that one of the primary factors behind innovation failure is the lack of ample funding for ideas. Financial systems in most companies are not set up to fund innovations that by

Exhibit 6.1. Resource Allocation Versus Resource Creation

Resource Allocation	Resource Creation
Annual or scheduled funding through the planning calendar	Funding as needed
Triggered by a traditional profit planning process; starts with the precedent from last cycle	Triggered by an innovation process, but within the profit planning process; no precedent exists, so each is a one-off judgment
Generally manages downside risk	Seeks out and funds upside potential
Entitlement based, meeting certain thresholds or history of spending	Determinist based, by the assessment of the potential innovation
Trigger: An allowance where everyone gets something	Trigger: A creation where only those with innovation ideas attract funding
Dispersed from the top of the hierarchy	Dispersed close to the ideas
Sources: Internal—funded by the pockets of the enterprise	Sources: Internal, partnerships, venture capitalists, and others, that is, funded by potential investors and the pockets of the enterprise

their nature create risk. Quite the contrary, the typical financial system is dedicated to managing, if not reducing, risk. Even if risks are funded, they are generally big "bet-the-farm" kind of risks that only the people at the top of the organization can take.

For innovation embedment to succeed, leaders must set a much lower threshold for risk. They need to think in terms of small, successive risks instead of one or two large, monumental risks. This requires a different approach to funding innovation: the innovation seed fund. Seed funds set aside monies and make them accessible to innovators everywhere. The first goal of seed funds is to distribute bite-sized increments of the monies close to the ideas, rather than distribute large amounts of money from the top of an extensive hierarchy. Seed funds aim to provide resources to small experiments concerning one aspect of the innovation, and those experiments exist on a migration path of successive experiments, ultimately leading to the launch of a product or service as a new business.

A second goal of seed funds is to change the organizational mind-set that it takes multimillion-dollar risks to innovate. We call this derisking; the organization derisks large experiments, funding smaller ones instead. This approach differs extensively from large R&D budgeting, where budgets are typically set in three- to five-year increments and commit millions of dollars to future actions, leaving little or no funding for on-the-spot or midcourse innovations.

Even when finding the money is easy, it is often the actual process of fund assessment and disbursement that gets in the way. Think about the situation in which a cross-section of department supervisors wants to create a midcourse innovation, and they try to get numerous managers of their collective departments to contribute funds to a pot to start the innovation. The amount of energy spent on gathering funds for this type of situation in a traditional profit planning system is usually more than the amount of energy it would have taken to launch the actual innovation. In such traditional non-innovation-friendly environments, innovators are always swimming upstream looking for funds, and their enthusiasm dies.

The last goal of seed funds is to reduce or eliminate traditional barriers to getting resources, such as having one supervisor stop an idea because he or she controls all the funds. This aspect of a resource creation mind-set is essential to driving the money closer to innovations. However, this does not imply that seed funds should remove every barrier to receiving the funds. Innovators still need to put hard work into their ideas to prove them. However, the criteria used to evaluate ideas and the process of applying for money are always made far easier in an innovation environment that employs seed funds.

Changing the Control Game

Seed funds are not just about money; they also reflect a cultural change that needs to occur around the control and distribution of money. Successful innovation funding is a result of the totality of the embedment wheel converting the financial control mechanisms to boost innovation. A resource structure needs to be established that fits the innovation environment while meeting the finance standards required in a company to ensure fiscal responsibility and create value.

To ensure fiscal responsibility while avoiding a control battle, it is useful to operate the seed fund according to clear rules and guidelines. No matter how the seed fund is established and who makes the decision to fund the innovation, those in charge of disbursement should keep the following six rules in mind at all times:

1. The disbursers have to track and account for the money. Innovation embedment does not change the fiscal responsibility that every leader has to control and disburse funds. It only changes the way that this is accomplished.

2. The disbursers cannot feel that this is their money; it belongs to the innovation embedment effort. They cannot forget the purpose of the seed fund in the first place.

3. A ceiling amount should be placed on each individual idea and be perceptively small, such as a range from $25,000 to $100,000. As innovation progresses, larger amounts can be dispersed and tracked through more traditional systems of resource funding.

4. The money is to be used for real experiments in the marketplace with real customers.

5. Innovators must complete a business plan that discusses the innovation and its potential as a new business idea, but they should *not* be required to provide the detailed analyses that the organization may be accustomed to receiving for projects. Innovators should be allowed to focus on their innovations, not on verbose proposals and detailed financial projections that should not be required in the early formulation of an idea.

6. The thinking should be that a small amount of money from the seed fund is a big amount to a potential innovator, and each amount, even if totally lost, will not break the bank.

David Campbell, the Smith Richardson Senior Fellow at the Center for Creative Leadership in Greensboro, North Carolina, has a helpful analogy for implementing the last rule in the list above. He suggests that leaders need not do anything that is career ending in terms of risk to engender new breakthrough innovations in their people. He has a simple test to help us understand how to assess this.

First, think of an amount of money in your personal life that if you risked on a hot stock tip and lost it all, it would not be a wrenching loss to you. And if you won, the gain would not change your lifestyle in any extreme way. Regardless of the outcome, you would essentially remain in the same financial status.

Next, take that amount of money and pass it down to your teenager who has been asking you to fund something that he or she wants to try. The multiplier effect is enormous because to your son or daughter, the same amount that you can lose and not change your lifestyle is a fortune to him or her. Success in this endeavor would be a huge upside to your teenager.

Now, Campbell says, take that same scenario and bring it inside the workplace. The $25,000 or $30,000 that you might risk on an innovation should not break your bank, but it is an enormous amount of money for a potential innovator to use in experimenting with an idea that could pay off big for the organization.

No Jumping Through Hoops for Approval

The seed fund approach is also valuable for the innovators themselves in that it greatly facilitates the process by which they can obtain funds. Innovation is stymied if potential innovators must jump through numerous approval processes and layers of management before they receive funding. You do not want innovators encountering endless managers or accountants who control the funds and might be tempted to turn down funding for innovative ideas. The best scenario for a seed fund is that it brings the funds as close to people as possible, literally enticing them to innovate.

Whirlpool used middle managers, boards of managers, and internal innovation consultants to disperse the seed funds based on the business potential of the idea. We developed our model from several other companies' successes that we were familiar with, as well as from the literature on seed funds and talking to consultants.

One interesting example cited by Hamel (1999) is Royal Dutch Shell, which developed a resource creation process called GameChanger. The company gave a panel of particularly free-spirited employees the authority to allocate $20 million to new innovation ideas submitted from employees throughout company. To qualify for the finding, innovators had only to propose their ideas in a ten-minute pitch to the panel, followed by a fifteen-minute question-and-answer session. After a few months, the innovators had to return for a proof of concept review. This example of a company that took the resource creation decision closer to the idea generators, using a panel of employees to evaluate and disperse funds for innovation, inspired us.

We set up our seed fund with this same framework in mind. To receive seed money at Whirlpool, innovators were required only to describe the economic engine for their idea and the specific customer benefits of their innovation. If they could not do this on their own (and most innovators could not), they were invited to work with an I-Consultant or an I-Mentor to write up an application summarizing their innovation and its potential market.

To facilitate innovators in understanding the application process, Whirlpool developed an on-line tool, the Resource Creation Primer, that explained the process and supplemented the assistance of the I-Boards or I-Consultants. The primer provided innovators with the necessary background context and supplied the actual forms to use when applying for funds. (You will find an adapted version of our primer at the end of this chapter to use as a worksheet for creating your own resource creation primer.)

Once the application was ready, the innovator had to present the plan to the I-Board or one of the I-Consultants, depending on how much money he or she was seeking. As a general rule, I-Boards reviewed ideas that cost more than $25,000 to bring the experiment to the marketplace, and I-Consultants reviewed ideas that required less than $25,000.

If the application was approved and funded, innovators were then required to participate in ongoing reviews with their I-Board or an I-Consultant. Experiments were to take one hundred or fewer days. Once the innovator reached this final milestone, an automatic review was held to determine the status and next steps.

Determining the Initial Amount to Set Aside

In setting up our seed fund, the most difficult issue to predict was the level of total onset funding to set aside. Should we allocate $200,000 or $2 million? After many rounds of discussion, we settled on two important criteria that determined the amount of seed fund money to commit: our anticipated start-up levels for innovation projects and an amount that would get people's attention.

In the end, each geographical region was asked to set aside between $1 million and $3 million. In addition, the CEO set aside $5 million at headquarters to be used for any innovator who was turned down in his or her region. These amounts were a minuscule fraction of the total Whirlpool operating budget, but they were enough to draw people's attention.

Reinforcing Embedment Behaviors

The seed fund also needs to create an environment that reinforces the entire embedment process and the values of innovation from everyone and everywhere. To do this, leaders must establish in advance the behaviors that the organization is trying to embed. There should be a link between the innovation behaviors and the embedment goals. If a lone innovator can receive funds but is not required to use the established embedment mechanisms that have been set up for innovation, the funds will not reinforce the overall embedment goals.

For example, one of the areas that innovation embedment targets is an understanding of the customer benefit from direct customer experiments. To get seed funding, innovators must show that they have used the customer benefit tools and the details of how they will set up an experiment with customers to prove their hypothesis.

SHOW ME THE MONEY

How you communicate the existence of your seed fund is critical to the start of your embedment process. The birth of the seed fund may be the first encounter most employees have with the innovation embedment plan. If the outcome of embedment is innovation from everyone, it is critical to get the word out that money exists to help all innovators. Here are some guidelines we created on how to announce the availability of seed money for everyone and everywhere.

The First Communiqué

We recommend that your first communications be very broad in order to reach as many people as possible. It should introduce, or reintroduce, the innovation embedment initiative and the planned outcomes. You should provide an overview of how potential innovators can access the seed fund. These communications are

DUCT TAPE VERSION
Embarrassed to Yes

Whirlpool took the idea of a seed fund to heart from the start. The CEO set up two levels of seed funds in the first two years of innovation embedment. The first level was at the strategic business unit (SBU) level, headed by a regional vice president of innovation. The CEO asked each region or SBU head to fund its seed fund with $1 to $3 million from existing budgets.

Our CEO then took an additional action: he set up his own seed fund of $5 million. He announced this separate fund by publicly issuing the following statement: "If any innovator goes to their regional innovation head with an idea that the SBU head will not fund, they can come to me, and I will consider it for funding."

Although he believed his separate fund was a useful backup to inspiring innovation, his announcement engendered unexpected indignant reactions from some of our business leaders. These leaders tried to convince the CEO that his idea was foolhardy for several wide-ranging (and often conflicting) reasons. One rationale argued that potential innovators would not come to the CEO because they would be too awestruck to come in and ask him for money, especially after already having been turned down. Another claimed that the CEO's seed fund would send the message that he wanted to get involved in the details of innovation, micromanaging the process over his managers. A related argument was that the CEO's decision would publicly undermine senior leaders' decisions. Even leaders who accepted the CEO's seed fund cautioned him not to say he would fund any innovation out of hand. They wanted his criteria to be harder than theirs.

This debate went on and on, but each reaction was met with a steely CEO grin. Throughout the turmoil on this issue, we did not know what Dave Whitwam had in mind when he established his seed fund, but the ultimate outcome was astonishing: not a single innovator came to him for funding. When we probed to find out if all ideas that came into the SBUs had been funded, we found that not one had been turned down.

So what really happened? Our hypothesis is that our local leaders in the business units would have been too embarrassed if they had turned down an idea that the CEO later funded. It therefore put the regions in a "just say yes" mind-set. This changed the culture from "everyone can say no" to "just say yes."

Is it possible that the CEO set up his own seed fund more to guide the senior leaders to new behaviors than for actual innovations? We think he had both things in mind. As it turned out, this one symbolic leadership action by the CEO had as much to do with overturning the "everyone can say no culture" as anything else that we all did to overcome this barrier. Because the risks were controlled to small amounts and leaders felt accountable to encourage ideas from innovation, we effectively chipped away at "everyone can say no."

best when you add a context that is brief and consistent with your innovation vision. The tenor of your first set of communiqués should be positive and inviting, imparting a feeling that this is an exciting initiative; anyone can get involved and there are positive benefits to individuals and the company.

This first series of communications can be done through your company newsletter or Web site, but it is most effectively transmitted through senior leaders' using the communications to help them talk about innovation in day-to-day settings like staff meetings. We discuss this in greater detail in Chapter Eight.

The Second Communiqué

The second time to communicate the potential of seed funds occurs the moment your first innovator has successfully received the funds and is out in the marketplace, experimenting with his or her ideas. This is an opportune time to create a second communiqué focused on that person and what he or she is innovating. You can then reexplain the seed fund process and the availability of I-Mentors or your I-Board to help other innovators. Be sure everyone understands through this communication how they can get involved in innovation and how to obtain the seed fund money for their ideas.

Further Communications

Establishing the fund is the first step to move innovation embedment along, but communicating it well and continuously catapults innovation embedment. It simultaneously helps you find more lone innovators who have not yet surfaced, while getting the message out that innovation from everyone and everywhere is valued.

It is important to continue discussing and sending messages that reinforce your innovation embedment efforts. You want to be sure that everyone understands that the seed fund is available to fund all ideas that are central to the strategy, without prejudging whether they will succeed or fail. Innovators need to know that there is a value associated with the innovation experience, whether it achieves success or failure. However, innovators should clearly understand that a prerequisite of funding is that they are expected to extract the value of what they learned so that others can benefit if failure occurs. Your sequential communications can reinforce this fact by disseminating the knowledge learned. If an innovator's idea has been shelved, be sure that the innovator is thanked and praised, not denigrated.

These messages should reinforce that the criteria for receiving funds are based on two qualities that the innovator brought to the table:

- The innovator's passion for an idea, along with the person's research and backup information that convinced the I-Board or I-Consultant that the innovator could take the idea to the next level.

- Despite success or failure, the innovator's willingness to capture and share what he or she learned from the experience. These learnings are critical to the ongoing success of innovation throughout the organization.

GOT TALENT?

In the formative years of innovation embedment, getting the right people to join the innovation effort is by far the hardest part of the resource equation. Indeed, no matter how complicated or hopeless it seems, the money is the easy part. An open market for resources, talent, and ideas is required to embed innovation. Ideas will come about from the process and tools you establish to create the innovation. But, ultimately, they come about only by having the right talent to innovate, as well as talent to move fluidly toward the ideas of other innovators.

When we began our efforts, we believed that with our provocative and inclusive vision of innovation from everyone, and the enormous energy spent in announcing the process and establishing the seed funds, we would have no problems signing up talent. We were right, but only to a certain extent. Many people expressed an interest. But something happened between their willingness to be involved and their actual participation. They were excited, they walked the hallways talking about the excitement at Whirlpool, but many never knocked at the door of innovation.

Our initial reaction was to try harder to build involvement. With three large businesses in three regions of the world concurrently struggling with this issue, we adopted a variety of methods to spur involvement and even had many initiatives happening simultaneously. We were becoming increasingly frustrated at our inability to lure talent into the process and away from their everyday work. It was like throwing the most exquisite, sumptuous, one-of-a-kind dinner party, only to find out at the last minute that all your invitees were already booked and no one could make it.

In the end, the ordeal to get talent involved became what we called a head-scratcher puzzle to those of us in charge of the embedment process. It is useful to present some of our head-scratching problems, along with our proposed solutions and a brief description of the results we were able to achieve. As you will see, in some cases, we were able to turn the situation around, but in others, our solutions had little effect.

Head scratcher problem:
People do not have time to get involved.
Proposed solution: What if we could manufacture time?

After reading about 3M and other companies that set aside time to innovate, one of our business heads decided that mandating a percentage of people's time to innovate might help build participation. That group therefore implemented what they called the "5% Solution," in which every department had to make 5 percent of its people available every month to join innovation projects.

Actual result: Mandated time did not work very well. Managing it took more energy than the innovation results obtained. We concluded that this was an artificial attempt to get people started in innovation. Many of the "5%" participants did not want to think about innovations or did not have the interest or skill set needed to join an existing innovation team, while others not in the 5% group proved more successful. In addition, the timing never seemed optimal to free up the right people at the right time. Their existing responsibilities did not go away when they joined an innovation project. It became too much of a "push" method of marketing innovation. We finally stopped this approach. Our conclusion was that you can't manufacture time for innovation. Fortunately, we learned this early on and were therefore able to try a variety of other methods that helped us address this issue with greater success.

Head scratcher problem:
Innovators are unable to find and attract the person with the right skills at the right time to help them.

Proposed solution: What if we used our talent placement system to assign people to innovations?

Almost like matchmaking, we decided to do a trial in which we used our existing human resource "people selection system" and talent pool system to assign people to innovations.

Actual result: Although the intent seemed to be well founded, it proved to be a logistical nightmare. Innovation logistics require that when a fast-moving idea needs certain resources, people need to be ready at the drop of a hat. Although we were able to use the talent system to move people, we realized that it was an inadequate stand-alone solution for all but specific assignments such as formal positions in innovation or visible innovation team assignments. Innovations were happening at a quicker rate than the talent pool committee could meet and select individuals. In addition, we were not always clear, nor were the innovators, on what skills we were looking for. To use the talent pool system effectively, we had to get better at defining the requirements at any one point for an innovation team.

Ultimately, we learned a very valuable lesson in this: for most assignments, it is better to work from people's passions. You need to allow people to "vote with their feet" about their involvement in innovation rather than assign them. The locus of control needs to be on the individual, not from a forced talent pool system. We became better at anticipating innovation talent needs.

We also learned another valuable lesson from this effort. What helped this process as much as anything else was an informal system that we refer to as "who you know." As innovators advanced to points where they needed help and as the formal talent pool system failed them, they reached out on their own to colleagues. There are great heroic stories of individuals with a full plate who managed their personal workload to help a passionate innovator colleague who personally asked for help. The informal system of talent worked better than any system that we could design. Nevertheless, we will say that an informal system alone is not enough. We keep experimenting with talent pool solutions to assist innovators and especially to assign talent to high-visibility projects.

We also modified this method by having shorter-term assignments, using a broader range of people (rather than the same people over and over), and, most important, not focusing on moving people as much as changing their jobs so they didn't have to move. This combination of remedies is working to address getting the right talent to innovation.

Head scratcher problem:
Supervisors won't free up their talent to get involved in innovations.

Proposed solution: What if we bring innovation directly to the people?

In conjunction with our entire innovation embedment process, we developed a knowledge management (KM) system (explained in greater detail in Chapter Seven) that enabled anyone to log on to the company's intranet site to learn about or get involved in innovation. As part of our KM system, we created a section called MyPage, which was an on-line space for individual contributors to create a vita or resumé and to volunteer for innovation projects. The MyPage site was to be "the place" in our talent system where everyone could describe themselves and their interests outside their current job. Our hope was that more and more people would start to use the KM system and thereby participate in innovations that were under way.

We did this because in addition to the top-down approach, we wanted to go directly to potential innovators. This set the stage for an approach that allowed people to control their career at Whirlpool. It asked individuals to volunteer for innovation projects instead of waiting for the human resource systems to move them to a new full- or part-time assignment.

Actual result: Over time, this solution generated some success, but it took roughly a year to begin to see results. In the beginning, it seemed difficult to get people to post their vita or resumé. One reason appeared to be that they were not used to a self-directed talent pool process. It was a new concept and so took a while for people to learn about it and trust it. To compensate for this, we started a push for all senior leaders to post their vitas on-line. An example of a MyPage is shown in Exhibit 6.2.

Exhibit 6.2. MyPage Example

Name: XXXXXX, Ali M
Region: North American Region
Country: USA
Location: XXXX   **Other:**
Office Phone: 269-XXX-XXXX
Cell Phone:
Fax: 269-XXX-XXXX
Current Job Level:
Manager
Current Job Position:
GCD—User Experience Group—Manager

Mission of My Job (Position):
Design for human use: simplify complexity & humanize technology.

Professional Background:
2001–Present: Whirlpool Global Consumer Design—Manager, User Experience Group.
1998–2001: Founder/President of XXXX Inc. (design consulting firm).
1990–1998: XXXX Corporation—User Interface design team manager.

Educational Background:
1984–1990: BS with honors in Cognitive Science from XXXX; minor in computer science.

Languages:

English:	First Language
Italian:	
German:	
French:	
Portuguese:	
Spanish:	
Others: Farsi	Intermediate

Additional Info: Trainings
Public speaking; I-Mentor training

Skills, competencies, expertise: *(ex. interpersonal relationship, change management, use of specific software)*

Product research, design, simulation, evaluation, and strategy. User-centered design philosophy and techniques. User needs & requirements gathering. Driving user needs into product designs. Creative & analytical problem solving. Designing user interfaces and interactions. Digital prototyping.

About Me: *(personal and professional expectations, hobbies, sports, interests, community memberships, etc.)*
Passions: Movies, home electronics, audio-video entertainment systems, video games.
Sports: Tennis, volleyball, soccer, cycling, hiking, camping, swimming.
Memberships: XXXX.

NOW: If you would like to contribute some of your time to a new business opportunity (maximum 20% without Supervisor approval), please continue by filling out the next three questions for I-Volunteer. This is completely voluntary and it does not commit you to immediate participation. Consideration is based on your time availability and year plans.

1. Area of Interest:	Strategic Direction
2. To what kind of opportunity do you want to contribute?	Smarter homes of the future. Smart devices (e.g., PDAs).
3. In which function do you want to contribute?	Brainstorming, conceptualization, consumer immersion, consumer needs & requirements gathering, translating needs and requirements into design solutions, consumer validation and evaluations.

Used with permission from Whirlpool employee and Whirlpool Corporation

Ironically, curiosity drove many people to the MyPage site to see what their senior leaders put on their vitae. Then, slowly, we began receiving a burgeoning flow of MyPages from many employees. However, it took another six months to learn how best to use the MyPage for "just-in-time" innovation help.

Subsequently, the MyPage site took on even greater importance than we expected, as it was used not just for innovation but for many other purposes within Whirlpool. It became a living database of people from around the world in the organization. For example, as new people joined the company, they used the MyPage to learn about their new colleagues before they met them. It also became a recruiting tool for employment, not just innovation. MyPage is now a key component to the innovation embedment process.

Head scratcher problem: People don't know enough about the innovation effort to want to get involved.
Proposed solution: What if people knew more?
This was purely a question of communication, so we doubled our communication efforts about innovation and the process of how to get involved. We used internal publications, Web sites, and other methods.

Actual result: One communication effort succeeded tremendously, the event that one region held called Innovation Days, in which we showcased innovators and their work. We don't know precisely how many potential innovators this event sparked, but we know that as a result of this event, many people expressed interest in learning more about how they could get involved. This one effort gave us great hope that along with more embedment wheel communication activities, there would be a proportional payoff to making more people aware of the innovation effort. We went on to design more events and communications that captured people's attention. Currently, we are succeeding at getting the word out to people and gaining their interest.

Head scratcher problem:
People at Whirlpool are too busy working on other things.
Proposed solution: What if went outside Whirlpool?

Many innovation regions went outside to find greater involvement. This included getting suppliers, universities, groups of potential customers, and trade partners involved in our innovation teams. In one example, a key trade partner joined the innovation process. We used our I-Mentors to conduct an innovation workshop between Whirlpool people and employees from the trade partner company. In another example, Whirlpool Europe selected college students from a local university and seeded them into the process.

Actual result: This effort had many positive outputs, though facilitating involvement from people inside Whirlpool was not one of them. However, it was a case of hoping for A and obtaining a surprisingly better result with B. Although it did not free up more inside people to innovate, it greatly expanded the diversity of participation and developed several innovative ideas to pursue. In the case of the trade partner mentioned above, they have now started their own innovation process using some of our learnings, and we expect that their innovation efforts will eventually affect Whirlpool positively.

More important, it helped perpetuate a new image of Whirlpool as a leader in innovation in the outside world, such as among our suppliers and customers. It brought into the process many different voices than we were getting from only our internal Whirlpool employees. Going outside was one of the most successful additions to our innovation process.

Head scratcher problem:
Many people at Whirlpool are busy working on other things and are simply not motivated to innovate.
Proposed solution: If we gave a reward, would more people get involved? Does money buy innovation?

Various divisions of Whirlpool tried several experiments that provided rewards for people to join the innovation team. One group created a reward that gave people $500 to join an innovation team or to become an innovation mentor, a process that required them to go through the innovation tools training process and then get certified as an I-Mentor. Another group had special recognition ceremonies for people who became I-Mentors or took an idea through the experimentation phase.

Actual result: These efforts had a positive effect on innovation. The recognition efforts generated great pride in personal as well as work group innovation. They all moved the innovation needle, but none spiked the results to the degree we expected. In fact, not one reward effort seemed to be enough to get masses of people to innovate. Moreover, the rewards or money did not guarantee that people would see the innovation through to its natural conclusion in the experimentation phase. Again, the best conclusion to draw is that self-motivation and passion about an idea are better motivators than money. Money helps, but it does not buy innovation embedment.

Head scratcher problem:
Anyone can get inspired to innovate if they have time and energy.

Proposed solution: What if people could see the results of their peers' successful innovations? Will success breed more success?

Most of us do not see ourselves as innovators. However, holding the view that one is an innovator is critical to the success of embedment: everyone has to believe that "they can do it too." We therefore believed that if more people could hear about their peers as innovators, they would begin seeing themselves as capable of doing the same. Consequently, after about one year into the innovation effort, we began to get out the stories of the "common" people at Whirlpool who joined the innovation process and became innovators. We published their stories in a variety of ways and in a number of venues.

Actual result: The stories of innovators were very motivational and succeeded in making others aware and getting them excited about joining innovation. We believe, but do not have proof, that additional people joined the innovation efforts because of these stories. But overall, we came to recognize that it is a huge leap of faith to begin conceiving of yourself as an innovator if you have never done it before. A person who writes does not necessarily see himself or herself as an author. There needs to be some transformation within people that allows them to say to themselves, "I am an author." The same is true for innovation. Many people have to believe that they can do something before they actually try it.

However, over time, we changed the mind-set of who could be an innovator. The concept of innovation became immensely approachable when people saw their peers innovating. We realized that this was a start-up issue: once we had some success stories and communicated them, people could begin to see themselves in the role of innovator.

Head scratcher problem:

People's work has not really changed as a result of innovation; it feels as if innovation is added to existing work.

Proposed solution: Can we make it so that 1 plus 1 seems to equal 1?

Sometimes the key to a problem is where you most expect it. The critical enabler to talent resource creation is not in a mathematical equation of freeing up more talent. It takes the totality of the embedment process to address this question. To get 1 plus 1 to equal 1, there must be a set of job expectations folded into existing ones, not added on. In other words, if innovation looks like an add-on to existing work or more work, no one will enroll in the effort. But if innovation forces outdated work to change or stop, more people will be attracted to innovation.

The goal is that each person must incorporate the new competency into his or her job and do this in a seamless way. This requires a transformation in the work itself. It has to change for every person involved so that innovation is the core of work, not on the edges or added on to daily work.

Actual result: Over the three years that we spent on embedment, we learned a valuable lesson about getting talent. We started out, as the head-scratcher problems imply, wrestling with how to move people to ideas. We wanted to create this open market for talent that Gary Hamel described. The ideal was to have total fluidity for people to move to the best ideas. We spent the first year and a half trying to understand how to do this. However, a concurrent set of activities had to occur. We came to the understanding that we also had to bring innovation to the people, to embed it into their individual jobs. We worked on making the innovation tools relevant to individuals' jobs so people didn't have to move toward innovation; rather, innovation came to them. Innovation embedment is what accomplishes this goal.

WHAT WE LEARNED

- Funds and people are critical to driving innovation embedment. This can be the most political section of the wheel because you are dealing with the organization's pocketbook for both money and people.
- It takes a new mind-set around people and funding to drive innovation embedment. The goal is fluidity of people and funds to the best ideas.
- There is a difference between resource allocation and resource creation. Innovation requires both.
- Resource creation covers both the funding of ideas and enrolling talent.
- Resource creation requires a great deal of experimentation to customize it to your organization's unique characteristics.

- Resource creation must sit alongside a rigorous resource allocation system with all the controls and predictability required in today's world. When created properly, resource creation does not add risk; rather, it derisks innovations toward a goal of revenue creation by doling out resources in small, bite-sized increments across a broader group of people.

- Most of all, what resource creation will accomplish is innovation embedment by funding the best ideas closest to the innovators and with wide-scale visibility so that other innovators will come forward and get involved.

- One of the most symbolic and practical initiatives that you can deploy as leaders and embedment practitioners is to establish a seed fund where the money is moved closest to the ideas.

- Talent movement needs a multifaceted approach. We selected communications, changes in human resource systems, a KM system called MyPage, and other devices to create a pull for people.

- The work itself has to change. You cannot add innovation to someone's job and expect it to succeed. While some innovation can occur by zealot innovators who work in the middle of the night, Innovation from Everyone and Everywhere requires a transformation in the day to day work itself.

SELF-ASSESSMENT: A RESOURCE CREATION WORKSHEET TO CREATE YOUR OWN PRIMER

We developed the Resource Creation Primer within Whirlpool for potential innovators, and we have adapted it here to help you create your own primer. This primer, in Worksheet 6.1, can serve as a template for you to develop your own primer. For each part of the primer, we have provided an example of what we wrote for ourselves in Whirlpool. (The only exception to this is the Business Strategy section: we did not add the Whirlpool example because it is proprietary.) Note that the Discovery Centre referred to in the Whirlpool example is the formal name we gave to the team of I-Consultants and the VP of Innovation in a strategic business unit.

Once you complete your primer, you can use it in many ways. Your leadership team can use it to capture and agree on the funding process for innovation. You can also adapt it and use it as a communication device for your own potential innovators. You are free to lift the language and elements of it for your own communications.

Worksheet 6.1. Developing a Resource Creation Primer

PART 1: HOW TO USE THIS PRIMER

Use this space to give the primer some introductory comments that will help the reader through the resource creation steps.

Whirlpool Example

We designed this Primer for Whirlpool people who wish to apply for resources for innovative ideas through the Resource Creation process. It lays out the fundamentals of the Resource Creation process and provides step-by-step guidance about how to apply for resources. To this end, it provides the application forms and, more important, the thought process that people with great ideas should engage in prior to submitting their ideas to the Innovation Board.

This document first takes you through the fundamentals of the business strategy and the Resource Creation Process. Next, it outlines the roles in the application process and provides step-by-step guidance on completing the actions necessary for submission of an idea. Finally, and most important, it provides a framework for evaluating an idea, given the selection criteria associated with the stage of the innovation process.

It is critical that the application process be viewed as a way to think strategically about the value of an idea or experiment. The process IS NOT an exercise in filling out forms. As a result, we suggest that if you have an idea, you visit the Discovery Centre, local Innovation Circle, or meet with a previous applicant to obtain skills and advice on how to analyze and evaluate the value of your idea using the framework provided later in this document.

Please note that this document provides only general instructions about how to apply for seed money and resources. It is not intended as a primer for innovation tools or business analysis techniques. The Discovery Centre, Innovation Consultants, Mentors, or the Knowledge Management Web site for innovation can supply you with these knowledge and skills.

PART 2: THE BUSINESS STRATEGY

Add a section on your business strategy to help describe why innovation is important to your organization. This gives innovators a context for their innovation and ensures that the innovations you review are in line with strategic intent of the company.

No Whirlpool example is given for proprietary reasons.

PART 3: RESOURCE CREATION

Use this space to introduce resource creation. You can also highlight how it is different from the traditional funding or profit planning process.

Whirlpool Example

Resource creation has to do with investment in great ideas. The focus and beneficiaries of Whirlpool's resource decisions must be the consumer and shareholder. This requires us to look at all of our activities with a new perspective. We create purposeful investments around great ideas. We will fund those activities that contribute to our success with our consumers and value for our shareholders. We put our money and talent behind innovative consumer solutions and invest in doing this faster than anyone else.

The Resource Creation Process provides money and talent for:

- Great ideas from everyone
- Innovative consumer-values solutions
- Speed to market

The Resource Creation Process provides seed money (money and capital) and identifies the talent required for innovators. These innovators may be any person in Whirlpool with a great idea. A special global innovation fund has been established that provides resources for creative and innovative projects outside normal regional resource and corporate approval processes. It can be assessed anytime and outside the normal capital allocation calendar process.

The fundamental criteria for seed money focus on supporting business strategy by meeting the following criteria:

- The idea must create distinctive and innovative solutions valued by the customer.
- The idea creates a sustainable competitive advantage.
- The idea creates exceptional value for our shareholders.

PART 4: HOW RESOURCE CREATION SUPPORTS INNOVATION

Use this section to enlarge your description to show the related innovation processes and how and where resources apply. This is still a conceptual understanding. Later in the document, you will have the opportunity to give the specific details of how to apply.

Whirlpool Example

There are different criteria for obtaining resources at each stage of the innovation pipeline.

The pipeline has four stages: Ideas, Experiments, Prototypes and Scale-Up, as shown here. Each stage has a purpose. Note that at the beginning of the pipeline, there are many projects or innovation ideas with few or modest resources applied to these. As an innovation matures through the pipeline, fewer projects progress with it, but they can gain the support of more cumulative funding.

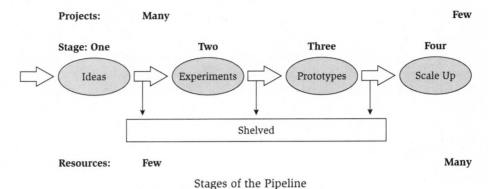

Stages of the Pipeline

For each stage, you should be able to answer specific questions to obtain funds. If you cannot answer these questions, get help from an I-Consultant or an I-Mentor. You can locate these people on the KM site for Innovation.

PART 5: APPLICATION PROCESS

Use this section to be specific about the application process. Start by defining roles and responsibilities. This will help take some of the confusion out of the process and add concreteness to who does what.

Whirlpool Example

The Resource Allocation Process is intended to support creative and innovative projects outside of normal regional or corporate approval processes. The I-Board will review ideas from anywhere in the organization, regionally and globally. I-Board meetings occur once a month to review ideas. Smaller amounts of seed money (up to $30,000) may be approved locally by an the I-Consultant without going to the I-Board.

Roles in the Application Process

Applicant's Role

- Responsible for thinking deeply about the idea, its drivers and value to Whirlpool, and its shareholders

- Responsible for preparing documentation to support the request for resources

- Responsible for obtaining the required knowledge and skills (through the Discovery Centre or local innovation consultant) to create a viable application

- Sending application form prior to the meeting

- Following up on actions suggested to improve the idea
- Updating local knowledge management progress on a monthly basis
- Responsible for ensuring that the idea is submitted into the I-Pipe system (the innovation knowledge management system)

Discovery Centre, Local Innovation Consultant, or Previous Applicant's Role

- Responsible for assisting applicant during the idea evaluation process
- Responsible for assisting in developing skills in innovation
- Maintain I-pipe system for region

I-Board's Role

- Review ideas from all people at all levels.
- Be aware of evaluation criteria for all stages of innovation pipeline.
- Be aware of ideas from their function or region.
- Be active in helping applicants meet with them to review ideas.

The following outlines the steps in the application process.

Steps to Follow

1. Applicant has idea or is moving to Stage Two: Experiment.
2. Applicant analyzes idea and its potential according to the following framework.
3. Applicant visits Discovery Centre or Innovation Consultant to obtain assistance with evaluation as well as the appropriate documentation.
4. Applicant completes evaluation and documentation and reviews with I-Board. Applicant obtains funds from local I-Board or I-Consultant for a Stage One idea OR applicant goes to the Global I-Board (CEO) for funding.

If applicant obtains resources, *then* . . .

5. Applicant reports to knowledge manager and Global Innovation Council on a monthly basis.
6. Applicant evaluates progress and decides whether to apply for next round of resources.

PART 6: TOOLS TO HELP:
HOW TO EVALUATE YOUR IDEA IN PREPARATION FOR THE APPLICATION PROCESS

We added a tool from the Innovation Toolkit to standardize the application process. This tool helped innovators with the required level of detail to get started for an idea. While the tool we used is rigorous, it still did not require a standard business plan

with a detailed cost-benefits ratio of the ideas. **Whirlpool and Strategos developed the tool. Because this tool is proprietary to Whirlpool, we have not reproduced it here exactly, but have adapted it for this worksheet.**

Whirlpool Example

This part guides your thinking around a relevant and relatively complete set of items to think through as you develop your application. If you would like help on completing this section, please contact XYZ [insert the name of the person in your organization who is responsible for helping innovators].

The six-factor framework for evaluating an idea or opportunity looks like what is shown in the exhibit.

Each of these factors contains a number of key questions that must be addressed for each idea. The in-depth analysis of the questions changes slightly depending on the stage of the innovation process. The applicant should think through each of these before submitting the application. The application forms are attached for the innovator to complete and submit.

Six Categories for Innovation Projects

Fill in the boxes for your innovation using the six categories of an innovation project. Each box should be no more than 4 or 5 sentences.

1. Vision/Description	2. Strategic Fit	3. Risk Factors
4. Financial Implications	5. People Resources Needed	6. First Experiment/ Next Steps

CHAPTER SEVEN

Knowledge Management and Learning Systems
Democratizing Innovation

Innovation from everyone and everywhere necessitates believing that all people are inherently creative, engaged, and eager to make a difference. This perspective posits a world where all individuals possess an innate ability and capacity to create and innovate toward the goals of the firm. In adopting this view, two fundamental questions become critical:

- How do we evoke the potential for everyone to be an innovator?
- How do we channel that energy into innovations that drive the economic engine of the corporation?

These questions are clearly complex and their answers multifaceted. From an organizational point of view, they automatically raise issues regarding skill development, opportunity, and rewards for innovation. For example, we asked ourselves whether it was enough to train everyone in the skills of idea generation and the use of innovation tools. If we moved people into innovation roles on a systematic basis, thus giving them more opportunity, would that create more idea generation and innovation? If we devised the right compensation or recognition strategy, would we see a huge rise in idea generation and innovation?

All of these questions were important, but in the end, we discovered one additional issue to be critical over and above all the others: shared knowledge. When we examined what was missing from our ability to channel energy into innovation, we found that the most significant barrier for many people in developing opportunity and motivation to innovate was having open access to information and knowledge about the customer and environmental trends. Actually, let us correct that statement. The barrier begins as soon as people *perceive* that they don't have open access to this information, whether or not that is even true.

Unfortunately, Whirlpool already had a history of some of its people perceiving that they did not have access to information and knowledge about customers, new products, or new ideas. Even worse was the prevailing sense in our culture that information was available but not widely accessible to employees. As we mentioned in Chapter Five, this perception appeared on every cultural audit conducted in Whirlpool over the previous ten years.

As a result, we recognized from the start that we had to find a way to get people the information they needed to innovate in a manner that did not rely on the formal organizational hierarchy and existing systems. We also knew that given a history of little sharing across organizational and regional boundaries, we needed to foster a way for people to share and leverage off each other's ideas and learnings.

DUCT TAPE VERSION
Where KM Leadership Comes From

The happy (but embarrassing) fact for us was that right from the beginning, Whirlpool's CEO understood the importance of knowledge to innovation embedment. One day, we walked into his office and found a stack of knowledge management journals on his desk. We were somewhere between impressed and shocked that he was spending time reading this material. We were also embarrassed that we had not thought of it ourselves sooner.

To harness the power of sixty thousand people, Whitwam believed we needed to find a way to democratize knowledge and data. We also needed to ensure, as many other organizations do, that good ideas raised before their time are not lost forever in the absence of a specific person who can champion them. Knowledge management, even with its sometimes spotty reputation for effectiveness in other organizations, seemed to be, for him at least, a key success factor. The focus was on a specific effort that would give us a universal mechanism to store and share ideas, as well as help us change our culture to one that was inclusive about its knowledge. Our task was to figure out how to make Dave's idea a reality.

Furthermore, we believed that if new and creative configurations of existing knowledge and data were to be the raw materials for innovation, getting those data and information into the hands of all people who could use them, without this information screened by hierarchy, protected by another function or region, or lost or forgotten, was an absolute requirement. Our problem was how to do this in a culture unaccustomed to managing or sharing information and knowledge across functions.

Again, it was our CEO, Dave Whitwam, who seemed to have the "knowledge gene." He was one of the first to recognize that a robust knowledge management (KM) system would add a significant push to our success. Along with chartering and resourcing the innovation effort, he insisted on a parallel KM effort that included and even went beyond a standard information system that stored and made accessible the data needed to innovate.

The goal of KM, based on our extensive research, was simply stated: *Just enough.* We had learned that many companies get into trouble with KM after building huge, unwieldy systems that cannot be maintained, only to outgrow their usefulness. Our vision for KM was to stay ahead of the users just enough to meet their needs. This "just enough" KM approach set the stage for our KM deployment strategy.

THE FIRST KNOWLEDGE MANAGEMENT EFFORT: I-PIPE

We began developing ideas for a KM system immediately. We needed a fast way to integrate all Whirlpool people into the innovation effort and at the same time track what was happening in innovation across the corporation. We developed a vision of a KM system that would let anyone who wanted to have access to current information about innovation activities anywhere in the Whirlpool world. This included information such as the number of ideas generated, listing of ideas being developed or experiments being conducted, reviews of innovation projects in progress, and directions for how to become involved if the KM system user were interested.

For our first effort, we opted to go with the fastest possible implementation: the proverbial "low hanging fruit" solution. Strategos showed us a knowledge management system it had, called I-Pipe (Innovation Pipeline), which it provided to clients to track ideas and projects in their firms. It was not a fancy system, but it provided some good basic technology to track the movement of ideas through the business development process.

We therefore adapted the Strategos version of I-Pipe to kick-start the Whirlpool effort. We basically took this system and placed it on our intranet with little initial modification. We did not want to divert our time from innovation to become information systems experts. Initially, we gave I-Pipe to our innovation teams for their use. As soon as we could, we opened access to the system to any person in Whirlpool who wanted to use it through the employee intranet portal. It was not, of course, accessible to people outside Whirlpool. In addition, for security reasons, detailed financial and company-sensitive information are not kept on this site.

I-Pipe was very useful in that it allowed us to see how many ideas were moving toward a real market launch and how many were shelved in each phase of the process. It tracked four phases of idea movement: business concept, experimental phase, prototype, and scaled-up businesses. I-Pipe's tracking also allowed us to see in real time how many new-to-the-world ideas we were generating and moving through the pipeline, versus how many ideas were just incremental changes in products or services. This helped us measure how well we were making progress toward our new-to-the-world goals.

Exhibit 7.1 shows the summary screen for the portion of I-Pipe that tracks ideas. Note that it allows users to quickly see how many ideas are in which stage of development. The screen can also show the regions associated with the projects and projected revenue by fiscal year, as well as the amount of projected revenue that would be generated from the ideas in the pipeline. (The box in the exhibit that says "risk-weighted revenue" refers to revenue that is adjusted to take into account the probability of success. Revenue from higher-risk projects is projected at lower dollar figures than lower-risk projects.)

I-Pipe quickly became one of the most important tools we had in working with leaders and staff. The site graphically captured everyone's imagination and provided senior leaders with solid business information that they could use to make decisions relative to guiding innovation activities. We eventually modified the graphic to look like a "dashboard" view of innovation activities. The new format made it even easier for senior managers to assess the status of ideas in the pipeline, as well as the balance between incremental improvements and new-to-the-world innovations and the type of revenue streams that might be generated in the coming years.

THE SECOND KNOWLEDGE MANAGEMENT EFFORT: INNOVATION E-SPACE

The first iteration of I-Pipe turned out to be the perfect Trojan horse to break through the KM skepticism. It provided many people with valuable information about the status of innovation efforts. But it was only a beginning. We also realized that we needed to do more to engage the entire Whirlpool population beyond tracking innovation ideas through the pipeline. We wanted a place where people could input suggestions and ideas, obtain feedback, and volunteer for innovation projects.

Exhibit 7.1. I-Pipe Tally

I-Pipeline				Estimated Incremental Revenue ($000)	Risk-Weighted Revenue ($000)
Business Concept	Experiment	Prototype	Scale-Up		
35	7	2	11		

Stage/Project Name	Region	Estimated Date to Complete Stage	Estimated Incremental Revenue ($000)			
			2002	2003	Steady State	Status
Business Concept Stage 35 distinct projects			$	$	$	
Experiment Stage 7 distinct projects			$	$	$	
Prototype Stage 2 distinct projects			$	$	$	
Scale-Up Stage 11 distinct projects			$	$	$	

Within months, we decided to enhance our innovation KM site by building new modules around I-Pipe and creating numerous features to draw in more users. It is important to note that the KM site was not an electronic suggestion box. There was not an option to put an idea into KM and hope that it went somewhere. The innovation KM site was a self-help and exploration system to help innovators get started. We created additional functionality that allowed users to obtain information about the innovation effort itself. This information included newsletters and articles about where to find resources to help with innovation efforts, such as I-Mentors and I-Consultants. The site also allowed people to volunteer for an innovation project.

We renamed the entire site the Innovation E-Space. Our goal was to add some pizzazz to the site and thereby attract more users. It worked: people began to come by droves to the site. Soon we had many people applying for innovation projects and trying to move their ideas forward.

The success of this revised site prompts us to explain here some of its features. First, we called the home page for the site the Innovation E-Space. As you can see in Exhibit 7.2, the leading toolbar on the home page shows at a glance all the attendant pages that innovators and curious onlookers can use. From the

Exhibit 7.2. Innovation E-Space Home Page

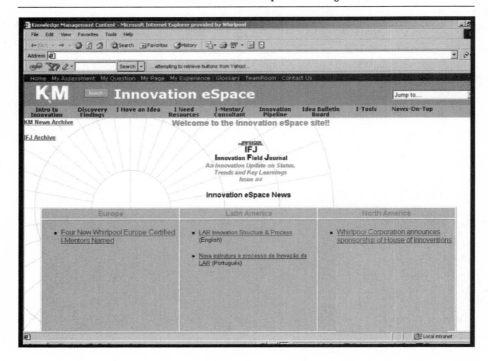

home page, users can also link to our innovation newsletter, the *Innovation Field Journal,* as well as link to individual regional news pages covering our European, Latin American, and North American locations.

The first tab on the home page toolbar, Intro to Innovation (in the upper-right-hand corner), leads to a page, shown in Exhibit 7.3, announcing an extensive tutorial that Whirlpool people can read any time. This tutorial covers three areas of information: an introduction, specifics on the innovation process, and team learnings from other innovators.

We mentioned the development of MyPage in Chapter Six in reference to a solution we implemented to get more people involved in innovation. As you recall, MyPage was a place where any Whirlpool person could input information about themselves, their skills, knowledge, expertise, and interests. The goal of a MyPage entry was to let anyone working on or leading an innovation project know that you might be interested in helping them. It was sort of our version of an electronic job matching service.

We placed the link to all MyPages on the home page of our Innovation E-Space KM site, so that anyone could go on-line and post their resumé in order to

Exhibit 7.3. Innovation E-Space: Introduction to Innovation Page

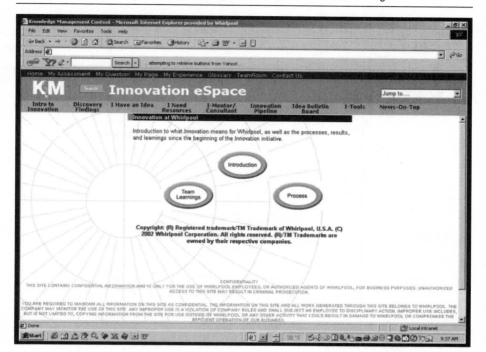

announce that they were available to work on any innovation projects for which their skills were desired. The use of MyPage required no supervisor or human resource approval. It was intended to be a direct link between potential innovators and people who wanted to join an innovation effort. The MyPage main page is shown in Exhibit 7.4.

The final page reproduced from our innovation E-Space is the I Have an Idea link that comes off the home page. This link leads to a page called Developing Your Business Idea, which contained step-by-step information for potential innovators to see how they might turn their ideas into innovations for the organization. This page begins the process for any innovator. It is effectively the electronic support mechanism for starting an innovation and links innovators to the people resources they needed, such as I-Mentors who were available to have one-on-one talks with innovators to get them started in the process. This page is shown in Exhibit 7.5.

As we continued to transform the original I-Pipe on our internal network into this new Innovation E-Space, its functionality grew. At this time, we continue to use it in a number of ways:

Exhibit 7.4. MyPage Introduction Page

- Facilitating the tracking of ideas as they move through the innovation pipeline
- Making certain that ideas are available to everyone who wants to use them in innovation efforts around the company
- Ensuring that ideas generated by innovation teams are not lost if they are not moved immediately into development
- Providing a place to review ongoing innovation projects and volunteer to participate in any project as a team member, subject matter expert, or in some other way
- Providing useful information about how to get involved in an innovation effort, how to access the work that other innovation teams have generated, and how to contact I-Mentors or I-Consultants

The Innovation E-Space is available to any Whirlpool employee around the clock who has intranet access. At the time of this writing, we are still working hard to make sure that all Whirlpool employees know about the site and its

Exhibit 7.5. Developing Your Business Idea Page

potential and that managers encourage its use on a regular basis. To further these goals, we designed a set of meeting agendas that managers can use to prompt their employees to access the Innovation E-Space. These agendas are available for use by every manager in Whirlpool and consist of a set of activities that managers can use with their work unit, such as visiting the site as a group, collecting information about innovation, and figuring out how to begin to use it in their work.

FURTHER STEPS: DEVELOPING KNOWLEDGE MANAGEMENT TO FEED INNOVATION

I-Pipe and its expanded version of Innovation E-Space gave us a great start in making KM a success. We had a good though basic KM system to hold us over for a while, especially in the area of innovation. But it was focused only on innovation. Something was missing.

What we were lacking soon became clear. We were acutely aware that a major characteristic of our history and culture was not sharing information across functional lines. Many people perceived that they did not have proper information about environmental and customer trends, needs, and wants, which were extremely relevant to innovation. Therefore, if we were going to encourage innovation from everyone and everywhere, we needed a way to get that type of information to everyone. We then recognized that we needed to build a comprehensive internal KM system that could hold the requisite information to feed the innovation embedment effort.

The challenge at this point was figuring out how to begin such an extensive KM effort. We needed to build an electronic system that would allow everyone in Whirlpool access to in-depth knowledge about the customer. Meanwhile, our information systems department also advised us that we should make sure that this site could serve as a template or model for future KM sites. We ended up with a dual project: (1) making sure that this site was well constructed and easy to use and could be a model for future efforts and (2) providing people the raw material they needed to innovate. This task was clearly not going to be as easy as buying I-Pipe from our consulting partner and modifying it for our use.

Starting Blocks

Unfortunately, we found no book or manual on KM or organizational learning that told us how to start this type of effort from scratch. We did realize that we could not develop a new KM system using a very narrow group of people. We needed broad support from management and, perhaps more important, the people who held the very knowledge that we were trying to capture and share. Those who managed the knowledge flow about customers and environmental trends had a huge stake in the KM system. As any book article on KM or culture change will tell you, their stake was the potential loss of their power and status as keepers of scarce knowledge and information. We were therefore well aware that we might encounter resistance from this population.

To make matters worse, as we began working on this newest KM site, we discovered that few people understood what we were talking about when we mentioned knowledge management. Most people thought that we were putting together a stand-alone management information system that would replace the people or functions that currently housed that knowledge. Even several consulting firms that we sought out to help us seemed to want to build an information system with little regard for the people side of the equation involving sharing and leveraging knowledge and applying it to innovation.

In our view, KM, even when facilitated with robust user-friendly interfaces, still needed to be augmented by human activities that encouraged the active use of the data in the information system. We did not want a sterile information system that never encouraged people to talk to one another. Instead, we wanted a system that would provide us with a catalyst that facilitated learning and sharing without replacing human interaction.

We began designing an information system that would act as an enabler by fostering a set of practices and behaviors to support the creation, storage, and sharing of information and knowledge. The system was intended to be a stimulus for spawning more interaction and dialogue. We will describe in more detail how this worked after we describe how we developed the concept for this new KM system.

Knowledge Management Team Unplugged

To demonstrate a level of high visibility and support for KM, we started this effort by forming a team made up of senior managers sympathetic to the need for a KM system and for cultural change in the area of knowledge sharing. We brought in one manager from customer service and one from product development, then added representatives from human resources, information technology, and innovation. We also engaged people from different functions who currently collected and stored knowledge, such as employees from market research.

To spearhead the work, we created the position of a global KM director who reported to the global vice president of innovation. The appointment of the global KM director was critical, because it provided legitimacy to the effort to develop a lasting KM capability and facilitate interaction and exchange across the organization. We also made an unusual choice, selecting someone from Europe, rather than from headquarters in North America, in order to make the point that innovation was from everywhere.

Creating a Knowledge Management Primer for the Team

Once we had people in place, we held a project initiation session. This session focused heavily on education about what KM is, what it is not, an analysis of the current environment for knowledge sharing, and what technology could reasonably accomplish and what it could not. One of the points we wanted to drive home was that a technology system alone would not solve the problem of getting information to employees or of leveraging and sharing knowledge. Here are the outcomes we wanted to obtain from this first meeting:

- Agree on a vision and mission statement for KM. We wanted to come out of the session with a vision for KM for Whirlpool overall, and not just about customer knowledge. We wanted to be able to articulate clearly what KM could do for Whirlpool.

- Agree on some common understandings and definitions about KM, such as what knowledge means and what roles were necessary to create and sustain a KM system.

- Identify primary users of a KM system and understand their needs. We wanted to ensure that we had a common understanding of who would use the system so that we could be sure to address their needs.

- Identify units of analysis for pilot KM activities. We wanted to be clear about what data or specific information we needed to include, such as whether we needed all customer information from all regions or a more limited target such as customer preferences for design or colors.

- Identify critical elements of a successful KM system. We needed some measures for knowing what constituted success.

- Generate preliminary requirements for the information system portion of system. This included some very practical issues, such as open access for employees, service capacity, and platform.

- Create a work plan for the KM effort including actions, a schedule, and accountabilities.

Before the session, we also asked that the participants read several articles in a special edition of the *California Management Review* about KM in a manufacturing environment. This provided them with a working framework that showed how such a system was possible.

We also invited a consulting firm that agreed to present its KM system to us. The system consisted of both information systems and face-to-face sharing. This made it possible for our participants to see the potential of a dual-designed KM system. The consultant's system housed detailed electronic information about its clients, future trends relevant to the business, proposals offered to all clients, and deliverables. This information was available to any consultant who needed to use it. This system also facilitated interaction among consultants as they usually called one another to get clarification on the information in the system. The firm also shared the type of effort it took to develop the system and the resources needed to maintain it (a little daunting for us!).

Our "Stake in the Ground"

The meeting was a complete success. We had people calling us offering to be on this KM team. The team created an incredible vision and mission statement out of that kickoff meeting, as shown in Exhibit 7.6.

In addition to the creation of this vision and mission statement, we derived several other useful outputs from the team initiation meeting:

- A set of common definitions around knowledge management

- The selection of a specific unit of analysis to begin a beta test of KM in addition to the innovation site

- A set of guiding principles around the use of KM

Exhibit 7.6. Knowledge Management Vision and Mission Statement

Knowledge Management Vision

Whirlpool will create a knowledge-rich culture with the ability to transform knowledge and expertise into a superior market value.

KM Mission

Build a global knowledge-driven environment which will enable all Whirlpool HR people to spontaneously create, easily capture, and share their knowledge, expertise and skills. This will be accomplished so that we exploit scalable and sustainable innovative opportunities, support faster and effective customer solutions, and ensure a unique competitive advantage that is hard to duplicate.

The set of common definitions was vital for all further efforts. Knowledge management literature is immense and almost impenetrable for those not initiated into the field. We therefore found that we needed to agree on some basic definitions so that we could all work in unison. The following is a subset of the glossary we created as we moved forward:

Knowledge Management (KM)

KM is the ability to acquire, integrate, store and share knowledge in a continual manner using both human and electronic or technical systems. KM systems address:

- What knowledge needs to be managed and shared?
- How do we acquire that knowledge?
- How is that knowledge stored?
- How it is distributed, shared and re-used to create leverage or new knowledge?
- KM has a human as well as the technical side.

Types of Knowledge

There are two types of knowledge: explicit and tacit. Both are critical aspects of a knowledge management system. Often we fail to capture tacit knowledge because it is harder to codify in an information system—it often requires face to face interaction.

- *Explicit* information includes data, records, presentations, and what people report. For us, in the customer knowledge area, this meant hard data about customer satisfaction, preference, needs and wants, often collected from interviews, focus groups, external sources and surveys.
- *Tacit* information is what people cannot easily tell you. Tacit knowledge includes: know-how, judgment, routines, experiences and lessons learned. For

customer knowledge this comes from direct experience with the customer such as service technicians, people in the call center and trade partner sales people. This type of information is harder to collect and share widely than explicit knowledge.

Practice Areas

In our case, practice areas were formal functions or units that have direct accountability for interaction with the customer. Practice areas were one of the primary ways we decided that we could collect and organize knowledge in Whirlpool about the customer. Practice areas for our purposes include marketing, customer service, product development. People in the practice areas became important in targeting the users of the knowledge management system.

Practice Area Head

The person who is accountable for a practice area from a global standpoint. This person is usually one of the main partners (and users) in the creation of knowledge management systems. Often these individuals are also the head of a functional area, such as customer service, marketing, etc. In our knowledge management effort, we asked the head of customer service in each region to act as the practice area head for customer knowledge during the pilot portion of the KM effort.

Experts

People in the organization who have a unique set of skills or knowledge-set in the practice area. These were the people we mentioned earlier that have specific customer information such as people in market research, strategic planning, product development and product design.

Community of Interest

Groups of people who, on an ongoing basis, create and share know-how and knowledge and then put that knowledge into practice. Communities of interest may not even think of themselves as a community or as a formal group, and often the group is not chartered or formally organized. For us, the community of practice for customer knowledge was almost anyone in Whirlpool who had a strong interest in the customer and using data and knowledge for innovation or other purposes.

DEVELOPING THE CUSTOMER KNOWLEDGE SITE

Developing the customer knowledge KM site was invaluable in helping us understand what information existed at Whirlpool, who had access to it, who needed access to it, and how people were going to use it. We did not know the answers to all these questions and therefore engaged our newly formed KM team by having team members interview people in their regions. For consistency, we provided team members with an interview form to use in the process (see Exhibit 7.7). The form essentially covered the following issues:

Exhibit 7.7. Knowledge Management Needs Assessment Interview Protocol

Target Interviewees: About 10 individuals who represent users of knowledge management. You may want to add others who are important to you. You will need to separate your answers based on the target group you are interviewing.

Timing: 45 minutes.

Definitions: Please note that we are using the word information to denote data that have not been systematically "mined" and interpreted and knowledge as data that have been systemically interpreted. You may need to explain this difference to your interviewees.

Suggested Questions

1. In your work (on the Innovation Team/in implementing Brand Strategy, e-commerce) what decisions are most critical to your success (for example, customer needs, product, service)?
2. Right now what data or information do you use to make these decisions?
3. Where do these data reside?
4. How accessible are they to you?
5. What information or knowledge do you wish you had (internal or external)?
6. What other information/knowledge systems are currently available to you that you do not use?
7. What KM systems have you been exposed to? Good? Bad?
8. What ideas do you have about how to ensure that a new knowledge management system is used and is adding value (for example, culture, education, communication system, simplicity)?

Information/Knowledge Management Inventory Systems

Also please bring to the meeting an inventory of the current information and knowledge management systems currently in use in your region.

- What data people need to do their work
- What knowledge or information they already had
- What information they would like to have
- What characteristics of a knowledge management system would be useful to them

Our goal was to learn about the critical decisions these people make in their roles, where they got their data to make decisions, and what they might need in the future in terms of customer data and information. The results were surprisingly consistent and demonstrated how great the need was for a system that stored, shared, and distributed knowledge around the customer.

DUCT TAPE FACT
Nooks and Crannies Made Visible

One day, the CEO walked down to the innovation group's offices and saw the knowledge management person surrounded by stacks of storage boxes. He asked what was in the boxes. The KM person told him that he had been in the marketing department going through files and borrowing documents so that he could scan or find the e-version to put them on the KM site.

This stark picture of how hard loading the system was had a big impact on the CEO. It made visible the fact that knowledge was physically distributed in every nook and cranny of the building and that we were very reliant on people and relationships to find data.

Innovation embedment became the letter of introduction to get people to give up their files because they wanted to help the innovation cause. This was an important milestone for KM and for innovation embedment in total.

Overall, these interviews were very successful and useful. They confirmed our assumption that people had a thirst for such a system, and they enrolled people in getting involved in development of the site.

The actual creation of the final KM customer site took some time. It was heartening, though, to see that the people who had been the biggest keepers of customer knowledge were the most active in creating the system. They truly appreciated the benefits of the system.

The most difficult part of the process was getting all the data loaded into the Web site and deciding on a global platform to use for the site. The data input was such a challenge that in the end, we threw a "party" during which people input data over about four days. After that, it was kept up by knowledge managers in each region, accountable for keeping the data in the system up to date.

The end of the road was the long process of notifying people that the system was born and educating them how to use its functionality. We chose a very labor-intensive strategy to accomplish this. We met with a large number of senior leaders in North America, Latin America, and Europe on a one-on-one basis to show them personally how to use the system. We also offered training sessions to everyone who was interested in using the site. We believe that this face-to-face session was the best way to introduce people to the system and its capability.

The customer knowledge system now has a great deal of functionality. It includes up-to-date information about Whirlpool's customer trends, along with

Exhibit 7.8. Home Page of Customer Loyalty Knowledge Management Site

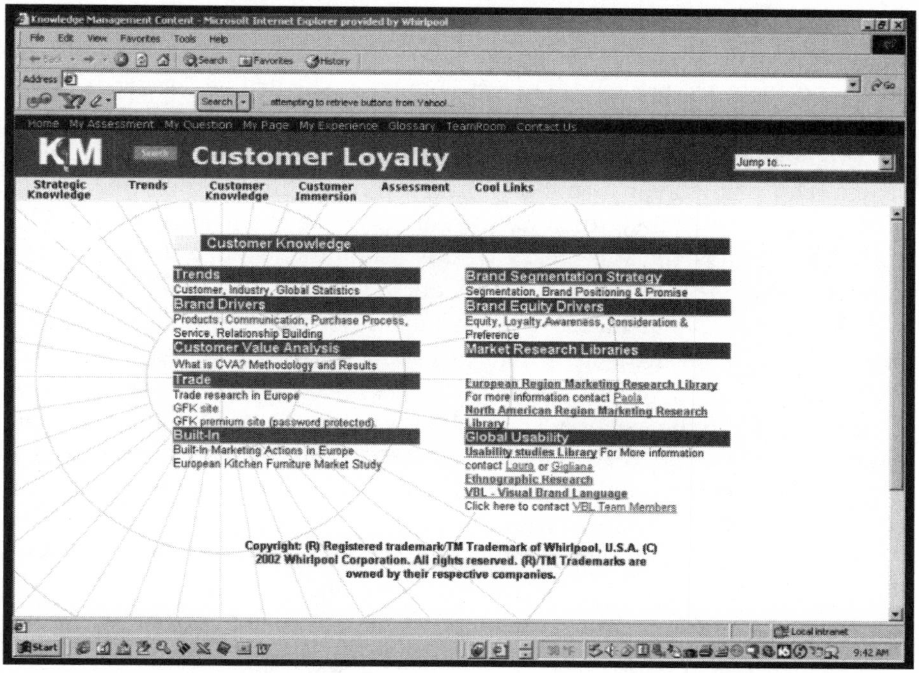

data collected and displayed on both a regional and global basis. The site continuously updates itself with internal reports that are generated by marketing departments on customer preferences and reactions to our products. In addition, the site contains information about new products, services, and features. The information is easily accessible to any employee around the world. The home page for the Customer Loyalty site is shown in Exhibit 7.8.

WHAT WE LEARNED

There is ample literature about how to build and deploy the technical part of a KM system (for example, how to collect data, map the knowledge, and build a usable, accessible system). However, you will seldom find information explaining the real-life unexpected turns that invariably happen in building such a site. Here is what we learned that we wished we knew going in:

• *People will take action when given the basic truth.* People will act to create and deploy the system long before the technical requirements are set. This turned out to be an amazing testimony to how interesting and even alluring KM can be. We saw a dedicated expression of desire spawned in people who wanted to get involved in developing our KM system. We had one person, an innovation team member, in charge of the I-Pipe KM portion of the system, who became so energized by the idea of a customer KM site that he developed a Web site by himself. Unfortunately, the way he developed the site was not compatible with our global information technology system, so we couldn't use it on our system. Our challenge was not to extinguish his energy but to integrate his efforts into our global system. We were finally able to integrate some of his work, but in hindsight, it is clear that it is useful to spell out any constraints early on and to identify the roles for people to play.

• *Data are readily available for the asking.* Data and other information that were appropriate for the system were easy to locate. We thought originally that we would need to dig to find the data we needed to build our KM sites. But we did not. You might be asking then, Why do you need a KM system if the data and information are so easy to find? The reason is that although we could find it, most other people could not, particularly people outside the corporate center and, especially, in remote regions.

• *Information has nooks and crannies.* Information exists distributed in nooks and crannies throughout your organization, and finding it often requires someone who can work the system. Although we did not have to dig and dig, it did take a considerable amount of effort to find things in file cabinets or to get access to individuals' hard drives. It also took quite a bit of effort to get the data into the system and maintain it. We found we needed a formal position in every region, which we called a knowledge manager, to keep the system up to date.

• *Your data donors may need help.* People who had the current data and information could not input the data on their own; they usually needed help. After training people to input their data and information into the system, we waited for data to appear. They did not. After a few months, we designed a "data input party" where administrative help was trained to input data. Using this method, we completed the initial data population of the site within one week.

• *High touch, not high tech, motivates people to tap into the system.* People, especially senior managers, will not find the site by themselves or come to training about the KM site on their own. We underestimated the amount of internal marketing it would take to get people to see the benefits of the system. Our best strategy was for the KM manager in each region to sit down with the executives in their region and show them how to use the system. In most cases, it was difficult even to get an appointment with these managers. In every case, they eventually became converts, but . . . it would have not happened without the one-to-one human interaction from our KM managers.

- *"It's not the system, Stupid."* People invariably will come to think of KM as an information system unless you correct them. The notion of sharing tacit knowledge is often overshadowed by the information on the system. Although we knew that we needed to begin to leverage the information system as a catalyst that fostered the storage and sharing of information and tacit knowledge, this has been harder to get off the ground. If we had it to do over again, we would have heeded advice and built stronger systems from the start that would accommodate better sharing of tacit knowledge. Currently we are trying to integrate sessions into most regional and Whirlpool-wide meetings that focus on face-to-face sharing of knowledge to get people used to sharing information across organizational boundaries.

- *Senior leaders are the last to change.* Although we were gaining traction with innovators, senior leaders were not converted as KM believers until late in the embedment process. This could reflect our strategic decision to start at lower levels of the organization. However, the coup de grace occurred one day when the Executive Committee was in session and happened to be talking about global competitive intelligence. At a "just-in-time moment," we demonstrated our global competitive intelligence site and discovered that many on our Executive Committee were not even aware it existed. They became immediate converts.

SELF-ASSESSMENT: GETTING READY FOR AN EFFECTIVE KNOWLEDGE MANAGEMENT SYSTEM

Use Worksheet 7.1 to determine if you have the pieces in place to create an effective knowledge management system. Check as many as apply to you, and compute your score.

Worksheet 7.1. Are You Ready for an Effective KM System?

Check as many of the following statements as apply to your organization:

_____ We know the impact of our culture on the sharing of knowledge and information.

_____ We have leaders who will use the information in the system for decision making.

_____ We have people in cross-functional organizations who are interested in the concept of knowledge management.

_____ We have senior leaders who are willing to act as champions for knowledge management.

_____ We have resources in our information systems group who can assist in creating a knowledge management system.

_____ We have a common platform for storing and accessing information across our organization.

_____ We have leaders and experts in practice areas who can help locate important information and data.

_____ We have sufficient people resources to assign people to work on creating a knowledge management site and to act as knowledge managers in major regions or functions.

_____ We have a common portal that all employees can access.

_____ We have access to senior managers to meet with them one on one to show them the system and how to use it.

Scoring: How many checks do you have?

1–3   You are not ready at all.

4–6   You might want to strengthen certain aspects of the system.

7–10   You are ready!

CHAPTER EIGHT

Integrating Strategic Communications with Change Management

Change management and communication are usually thought of as two different disciplines and discrete areas of activity. Colleges and universities teach the topics in separate departments and, to our knowledge, communication majors do not have to take business classes and business majors are not required to take organizational communication. In companies, organization charts and reporting relationships usually separate these two functions. Moreover, change and communication are generally planned and executed separately in most organization change efforts.

In the beginning of our embedment effort, we followed this traditional separation of activities. Our embedment strategy did not merge change management with communication, largely because Whirlpool was already in the process of establishing a common change management process for all change initiatives. In addition, our communication practices were targeted, for the most part, at tactical messages such as announcements and personnel changes rather than being focused at the strategic level or at enabling a change process. Therefore, at the beginning of our embedment work, we assumed we would just tap into each set of processes, without being concerned about their integration or alignment with each other.

However, with time, we began to see a strong connection between these two areas. As we delved further into the change management process for embedment, we realized that we needed to integrate strategic communications into the core of change, by which we mean communicating the strategic intent of innovation to all employees in a way that reinforced embedment. This required getting senior leadership involved, obtaining their agreement on key elements of the messages, and then seeding these messages into every communication, training, meeting, project charter, and key event held.

This chapter explains how we came to recognize that the two pathways of change management and strategic communications are better thought of as one road with two lanes. We will explain how we learned to integrate our change management efforts with strategic communications and provide advice for other organizations seeking a smoother ride when it comes to change management.

THE PATH OF CHANGE MANAGEMENT AT WHIRLPOOL

Although embedment is about the last stage in many change management processes, the institutionalization of change—in this case, innovation from everyone and everywhere—requires a strong discipline in change management. As we moved through the embedment process, we realized that many processes, systems, skill sets, assumptions, and behaviors still needed to be modified and adapted to meet our requirements around embedment. Embedment, albeit the codification of just one change process, spawned the need for many other change initiatives.

Whirlpool has long had a history of using specific, focused change management processes. The culture and values change effort described in Chapter Five is one example of several large-scale change processes that we have undertaken. Although we did not have a common methodology for change management, many pockets of Whirlpool used change management to great success.

In the late 1990s, our Latin American region set a leading example for change management. Their passion for change management was so effective that the process they used was elevated to a global best practice and now serves as the template for change management at Whirlpool. The template they followed is based on research from numerous change theorists who contend that people move through eight stages before reaching a state of commitment to change. These stages occur over time and are roughly divided into three larger categories or phases: acceptance, understanding, and commitment.

Exhibit 8.1 graphs the curve indicating people's path to change according to this model. Notice that the curve is parabolic, indicating that the stages progressively accelerate as people come to know and accept change. The more they understand how change will affect them, the more willing or reconciled they become to accept the discomfort that change brings.

The change management process shown in Exhibit 8.1 was accepted and codified across Whirlpool in 2001. As a result, the Executive Committee decided to ask leaders to apply this change management paradigm to innovation embed-

Exhibit 8.1. Change Path Curve

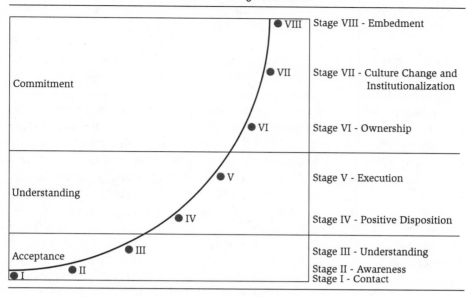

	Stage VIII - Embedment
	Stage VII - Culture Change and Institutionalization
	Stage VI - Ownership
	Stage V - Execution
	Stage IV - Positive Disposition
	Stage III - Understanding
	Stage II - Awareness
	Stage I - Contact

ment. They asked all executive vice presidents to create a specific change plan indicating how they would embed innovation as a core competency in their work units. The committee suggested that each plan be created in accordance with the embedment wheel, describing for each element of the wheel the actions that the executive would take to move his or her people through the main phases of acceptance, understanding, and commitment. The change plans from each executive vice president were then presented to the Executive Committee and updated on a regular basis.

These change plans had to follow the change management model. In order to move people up the commitment curve for innovation embedment, the plans needed to begin with a targeted exposure to innovation, followed by the leader's communicating the business case and the need for innovation, followed by specific actions on the part of the leader to move people up the curve.

For example, in the embedment area of vision and goals, one change plan addressed the phases with the following activities:

1. Communicating the need for innovation in the current business environment (Stages I, II, and III: Contact, Awareness, and Understanding)

2. Asking people to integrate vision and goals into their work unit activities (Stages V and VI: Execution and Ownership)

3. Measuring progress toward goals, sharing best practices, training others in the process, and rewarding outcomes (Stages VII and VIII: Culture Change Institutionalization and Embedment)

However, the Executive Committee decided that the metrics for measuring the change did not have to be uniform across all Whirlpool regions and businesses. Every region was already in a different place in terms of progress in innovation embedment, and each region also had a very different business situation that necessitated a different change plan. For example, the Europe region was having difficulty focusing on embedment due to the departure of its executive vice president and business setbacks. As a result, its embedment process was rolling out at a bit slower pace than other regions. Similarly, when the currency and economic crisis hit Brazil in 2001, the region decided it had to refocus and change to a slower pace for embedment than it had followed in its first year of embedment, though it was still faster than Europe. Meanwhile, India kept on track with its pace and scope of embedment activities, and in North America, the business situation allowed for a more vigorous effort.

Our leaders became very attached to their change plans. The plans provided a way to think about and frame how change would progress in their units. The plans helped them see how innovation fit in with their other initiatives and how they needed to measure progress. In many locations, the change plans literally became the leaders' bible, often including plans for more than just innovation embedment, such as other strategic or operational initiatives that the leaders were deploying. The executives took great care in writing the change plans, updating them for status reports, and modifying them on a regular basis. It was impressive how committed they became to their change plans. In addition to creating a clear path for change, the plans also forced alignment with the disparate parts of the business to ensure that both prioritization and integration were occurring.

These plans were an excellent start for us. However, as time went on, it became clear that we were still missing something. The change strategies were too linear and related overwhelmingly to processes, systems, and operational goals. They all operated under the assumption that reason, communication, education, and training, along with performance management, could move people from acceptance to understanding to commitment.

What was wrong was that the people side of the equation was not moving at the pace that we would have liked. An emotional side to change had been neglected. We realized that we did not have sufficiently strong strategies to have an impact on people's everyday activities, roles, skills, and accountabilities with regard to innovation. Each region had excellent change plans for innovation embedment efforts, including activities aimed at human resource systems change, all-hands meetings about vision and goals, training on innovation methods, and so on. But despite all these activities, we could still not tell how much of a brand director's everyday job was changing. The change plans focused at the regional or department level, rarely hitting the individual level.

Before we complete the story of what we did with change management, it's time to explain what was happening on the communication front.

FINDING THE PATH TO STRATEGIC COMMUNICATIONS

At the same time that our senior leadership group (the members of the Chairman's Council) was developing its change management plans, the Executive Committee began putting a greater emphasis on innovation communications. Committee members were concerned that we needed to begin spreading the word about innovation throughout Whirlpool worldwide. Because communications could be focused at the individual level, we hoped that they might spark the greater emotional reaction to innovation that we desired. The Executive Committee also knew that communication was critical to change management, especially in initiating the first stage in our change model: acceptance. If people were not made aware of our innovation efforts, we could never hope to move them up into the higher phases of the change curve: understanding and commitment.

Corporate Communications

The first major effort in strategic communications was to create articles about the innovation effort that could be regularly placed into our existing internal Whirlpool communication publications. A central corporate group created the key messages or themes to ensure consistency and alignment with the Executive Committee's intent. Next, local communicators, working with the regional innovation vice president, created point-in-time communications for their employees using the approved themes. Articles about innovation were inserted into our regular newsletters and magazines.

Our second major effort focused on starting two new strategic communications publications devoted to innovation embedment. These were both worldwide publications, but each had a unique purpose. The first publication, a magazine we named *Connect!* was intended to establish the business and environmental context for innovation, as well as to discuss other strategic initiatives within Whirlpool. The magazine was conceived and written by one author of this book (Nancy), along with help from outside editors and a graphics designer. Our goal was to make it look distinctive and different from other publications within Whirlpool through a provocative graphic design and an edgy writing

Exhibit 8.2. Cover of *Connect!*

New Passions. New Rules. Great Achievements.

Connect!

A *Revolution*

is underway, and it's changing EVERYTHING.
We're in an explosion of activity that's unlike anything we've seen before. New processes and procedures are being established. Weird acronyms and new buzz-words are being used more and more. Many people are working harder than ever before. We're surrounded by chaos. Fatigue. Energy. Excitement.

Vol. 1 Issue 2000

Whirlpool

style that screamed, *This is not traditional corporate-speak!* Exhibit 8.2 shows the cover from the first issue of *Connect!*

We intended to publish the magazine quarterly, but we published only one issue before we needed to reframe and redesign *Connect!* into a magazine that covered two other new core competencies that Whirlpool was trying to embed (operational excellence and customer excellence). (The Epilogue provides more detail about these efforts.)

Our second new publication was more highly focused on innovation and was designed exclusively for our intranet site rather than print. Its purpose was to capture everyone's imagination about how innovation could be relevant to him or her personally and to motivate people to take concrete actions to embrace innovation. We wanted this publication to remind people to visit the innovation knowledge management site, attend innovation activities, and join innovation teams. We named the magazine the *Innovation Field Journal* (see Exhibit 8.3 for a sample page). This publication was written closer to the action, in that we had innovators from around the world submit their stories, which were then edited and pushed out quarterly on our KM site. This e-magazine became one of the most visited sites on our KM site. We terminated it after publishing six issues over eighteen months, believing that it had served its purpose of introducing innovation.

Innovation Days and Road Shows

We used several additional communications strategies to spread the word about innovation. The most interesting of these was a three-day event that the North America region conceptualized and deployed, called "Innovation Days." The event was designed to share with our employees and the entire local community what was happening in innovation in Whirlpool North America.

We took over space in a local mall in Benton Harbor, Michigan, setting up displays to show our new products, services, and innovative ideas. This event was an enormous success, both internally and externally. Not only did Whirlpool employees and people from the local community attend, but so did reporters and Wall Street analysts. The event provided an exciting hands-on way to communicate the extent of innovation happening within Whirlpool. The company benefited enormously from numerous press opportunities and news reports that aired or were printed following the event.

Another major activity that we used to communicate innovation were road shows, in which our innovation vice presidents from each region took their message out to Whirlpool people using various formats. Some of these were open forums in which people came to learn innovation tools. These proved to be fun and informative. Another approach was to conduct leadership conferences in which people experienced innovation in a firsthand way. Even Whirlpool's

Exhibit 8.3. Page from *Innovation Field Journal*

Highlights

- Popcorn Opportunity Generation
- "My Page"
- Experiment Overview from North America

Inside

Page 1: Popcorn Process
Page 3: My Page
Page 4: Local Heroes
Page 6: NAR Experiment Overview

The Innovation Field Journal

*A Quarterly Update on
Status, Trends, and Key
Learnings
Issue #3
October 2001*

Popcorn Opportunity Generation

Embedment Update from Latin America

The Latin American Region has come up with an innovative approach to innovation. They have developed an exciting new strategy for innovation embedment, born out of the belief that there should be more people involved in the embedment effort, as well as a need to reduce the cycle time and cost of the embedment process. The "Popcorn Opportunity Generation Process" was designed to replace the Compressed Double Diamond and BOP concepts initially developed to embed innovation within an organization.

Highlights of the Popcorn concept include "making it happen at the sites," allowing for maximum participation in the process and maximum commitment to innovation. The Popcorn Opportunity Generation Process is of shorter duration than the CDD and BOP processes, and can be carried out more frequently. Additionally, Latin America will use the Popcorn mechanism to certify I-Mentors and I-Consultants.

Participants in the Popcorn process will learn and use various innovation tools and will have the chance to pursue innovation opportunities with the support of I-Consultants. As these business opportunities develop,

incremental resources will be made available, reinforcing commitment around a good idea. Owners of an idea will move forward with the opportunity; and if the idea turns into a new business (prototype/scale up), the participants may be invited to be part of the implementation effort.

The Popcorn methodology can be customized according to the hierarchical level or the needs of an organization. This means that if a specific area asks for innovation support, a customized approach can be designed that fulfills the specific requirement.

Behind the Popcorn name is a belief that the best ideas that "pop up" will be the ones in which the company will invest time, resources and money. Whirlpool Latin America has found an exciting approach to ensure that those ideas will pop up in many corners of the organization.

BOP Update:
The Latest from Europe

The *Access Side-by-Side Washer and Dryer* is an exciting, super-premium niche product about to be launched in various European markets. The launch of this new product category presented several challenges for the marketing team, particularly since the European market is not used to the American style and size of appliances. As the marketing group sought ways to prove the benefits of these products to its customers, they realized they needed to come up with a new and innovative communication approach. The team turned to their I-Consultant, Katrien Saveyn, to help them find a creative solution.

During one team meeting, they tried looking at the problem from a different point of view. According to Katrien, "Each member of the team took turns playing a role: trade partner, customer, sales person. It was a fun, educational and informative experience that could become a best business practice." The team is currently in the divergent phase, but will soon begin cross-stream sharing.

board of directors experienced innovation embedment by visiting the North America region to see and feel the excitement from people working on actual innovation projects.

THE BIG REVELATION ABOUT CHANGE AND STRATEGIC COMMUNICATIONS

After two years of effort with completely separate change management and communication strategies, we had some successes, but we also had some major questions. How could we move people up the commitment curve faster? How could we lessen the confusion or complexity that we were creating by approaching these two areas separately? Would there be a difference in change management if strategic communications could be integrated formally into the system?

During one of our long discussions about these issues at an off-site meeting, one of the members of our Executive Committee, Mike Thieneman, chief technology officer, had a brilliant revelation. With the help of his team, he was reflecting back on the three levels of goals that we had set: business results, embedment results, and individual results. He suddenly realized that we were thinking of the change process and our efforts around innovation using an exclusively *rational* mind-set. To achieve discontinuous change that embedment required, we needed to pay attention to both the rational and the emotional aspects of embedment. He postulated that we would never get the type of change we desired at the individual level if we continued to focus on only the two rational areas of change: business results and embedment. We needed to target more robustly the individual level of change and develop strategies that would connect with individuals.

As a result of these insights, we understood that an effective change management process must link the emotional dimensions of change with the rational process. We also saw that while all three levels of outcomes need to be addressed both emotionally and rationally, it is the individual level that offers the most bang for the buck in relating emotional issues to embedding innovation. In a sense, each type of desired embedment result required a different embedment focus. Exhibit 8.4 shows how each goal responds best to a different focus.

Exhibit 8.5 expresses this concept that each of the three levels of change requires its own approach. This exhibit is our adaptation of the Executive Committee members' work. Using this graphic device at the Executive Committee and senior leader level finally helped us align the many concepts we had developed about embedment with the three results we sought. We now had a visual way to address the notion of rational and emotional aspects of change.

Exhibit 8.4. The Three Levels of Change and Their Focus

Desired Outcome	Change Focus
Business Results	Outside layer of the embedment wheel: Vision and Goals. Written in terms of the desired final state, as well as transitional goals at an organization level. Requires use of measurement and reporting systems.
Embedment	Second layer of the embedment wheel: Review of all categories of the inner layer at the organization level.
Individual change	Strategic communications and change management: Measurement is accomplished using the commitment curve and review of leadership accountabilities and development.

Exhibit 8.5. How Change Management Addresses the Three Outcomes

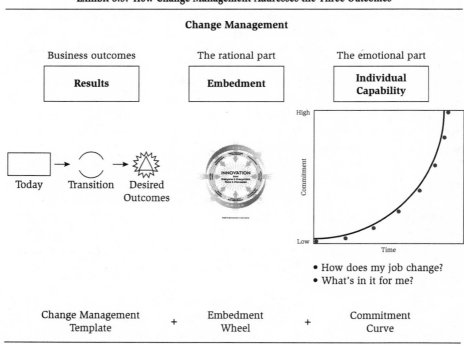

Change Management

Business outcomes / The rational part / The emotional part

Results + Embedment + Individual Capability

Today → Transition → Desired Outcomes

• How does my job change?
• What's in it for me?

Change Management Template + Embedment Wheel + Commitment Curve

BUILDING A NEW CHANGE MODEL

As a result of the work and new realizations we had on the change model, we modified our change management framework to encompass three distinct components and outcomes.

The *business results component* describes the change in terms of the vision and the goals using the change process that describes today, the desired outcome (vision), and the transition. In this case, the results refer to the business opportunities that occur from the innovation effort, including products that are new to the world, increased customer loyalty and commitment, increased revenue, and the number of new products in the pipeline. Business results need to be part of your vision and goals, and they should also be an integral part of your change plan framework.

The *embedment process component* describes change in terms of how to institutionalize innovation as a core competence in the business. This includes ensuring that all the elements of the embedment wheel—vision and goals, leadership, resources, learning and knowledge management, rewards and recognition, and communications—align so that innovation becomes part of the genetic structure of the business. Measures of change for embedment need not be focused on business results, but rather on the progress you make to implement each of the elements of the embedment wheel.

The *individual change component* focuses on creating commitment, capability, and skill at the individual level for innovation. Success in this regard is best expressed according to the commitment curve (see Exhibit 8.1), which involves change at the individual level and moves people from contact to awareness to understanding to commitment.

FOCUSING AT THE INDIVIDUAL LEVEL: DEEP DIVE INTO CHANGE

Given our new understanding and a new change model, we were ready to reinvigorate our focus on individuals to change and accept innovation. We understood that we needed to go deeper into this level to accelerate the change process in terms of individuals.

We turned to one of the best frameworks for addressing change at the individual level, created by Paul Strebel (1996). He suggests that individual change involves addressing three types of questions that people have about how change affects them. The questions are grouped into three categories: formal, psychological, and social. The questions themselves represent areas that individuals

DUCT TAPE VERSION
Floor Plan Versus Blueprint

In terms of using the embedment wheel to measure the outcomes of embedment change, we do need to admit something. We learned a hard communication lesson about our embedment wheel: in and of itself, the wheel does not communicate well. We found that using the wheel as a communications tool is not helpful when communicating to large groups of people, because it is too hard to explain in five minutes.

Nevertheless, the wheel has some value, particularly for leaders designing an embedment plan. For them, the wheel is enormously helpful in that it provides guidance for the areas that need to be addressed to ensure embedment. It shows the interdependence of the embedment categories and provides a systemic way to plan the embedment.

Admittedly, for participants in embedment, the wheel is another matter. In fact, we found that the wheel contains more detail that they want to know. We learned the hard way. We devised it as a communications device to share the overall plan for embedment, but it was more than people wanted to know.

Think about a house that you just purchased. Most home owners' knowledge needs of their new home do not go beyond the floor plan. The blueprints of the house are useful to the contractor who may need to move a wall, but for the people who are living in the house, a floor plan suffices just fine (most of the time). In short, the wheel has more use as a planning device than a communications message. This is exponentially true as you move from the top to the succeeding layers in the organization.

explore as they move up the commitment curve from understanding, to positive perception, to implementation and adoption, to high commitment. The questions are a way to help people relate to what is happening in the change caused by innovation embedment as they move up the commitment curve.

Formal Dimension

This dimension and the questions encompass the most traditional change concerns that people have. It reflects the basic tasks and performance requirements for a new role or job, such as performance agreements and budgets—for example:

- How am I supposed to change what I work on?
- Do my responsibilities change?

- Does my role change?
- Do I need to change my skills?
- What help will I get to make the change work?
- How will my performance be evaluated, and what form will the feedback take?
- How will pay relate to my performance during this change?
- How will I be rewarded if I change?

Psychological Dimension

These concerns address implicit aspects of the organization's relationship to the employee during any change process. Psychological impacts target mutual expectations and reciprocal commitments that arise during the change process. These commitments are often not written or explicit but need to be addressed. To feel comfortable with this dimension, people need to understand a number of aspects of it:

- How will my life at work change if I work on innovation?
- How will I have to change the way I work?
- How much more effort will I have to put on the job?
- What recognition or other personal satisfaction will I get from my efforts?
- How will the change affect my status or power?
- What is the organization's commitment to me if I make this change?

Social Dimension

This dimension involves noting what the company says about change in relation to its values and mission. It involves employees' observing the interplay between practices and management attitude. We think this could be more appropriately labeled the cultural dimension, since it effectively reflects an organization's culture.

As noted in Chapter Five, this dimension takes on heightened significance. Perceptions are tested when people evaluate the conflicts and benefits associated with change. Tensions may be created that reflect disconnects between people and value issues, decisions that value business over people, or about unspoken rules on how the culture of the company really works regarding such matters as career development, promotions, decision making, and resource allocation. This dimension concerns the following questions:

- What are the signs that the organization is serious about this change?
- How does this change align with the organizational-level values?

- Who wins and who loses from this change (groups, individuals, levels)?
- Does everyone really have to change? Does this include management?
- Do management practices and behaviors align with stated organizational values?

THE ROLE OF STRATEGIC COMMUNICATIONS IN THE THREE LEVELS OF OUTCOMES

We finally understood that for each of these three levels of change processes, strategic communications can play a key role. This was precisely the marriage that we were lacking at the onset of our embedment process. Exhibit 8.6 therefore adds these communications dimensions to the outcomes and embedment change focus.

The three levels require different communications strategies.

The *business results level* requires a strategic communications plan that addresses change in terms of the strategic intent, the components of the strategy, and how innovation embedment fits in this change. It should continuously use the same three to five themes in order to reinforce a consistent intent and outcomes for innovation embedment. The messages should be used in all types of written communications, as well as group interventions like staff meetings, innovation workshops, and leadership conferences.

The *embedment process level* requires strategic communications that are customized to the group or region. This communication should be both information sharing and interactive. The key here is that your strategic communications aim to simplify and align rather than complicate. This communication should target what organizational changes are being considered or have been put in place. For example, if the performance appraisal system has changed in order to drive embedment, not only should the changes themselves be communicated but also why the changes were made. All changes made around the embedment wheel should be communicated as they occur, always tying them into and reinforcing innovation embedment. In addition, some two-way communication vehicles need to be established to solicit feedback on the changes and to see if the explanations are clear.

The *individual change level* is very different from the other two. One-to-one customized communications are the backbone of this level. While some of these communications may occur in small groups, what distinguishes this level is that communications are driven by the position that individuals are at on the commitment curve. For example, you would communicate very differently to someone at the first point, Contact, than you would to someone who is on the last

Exhibit 8.6. Strategic Communications Focus for Each Level of Change Outcome

Desired Outcomes	Change Focus	Suggested Strategic Communications Focus
Business results	Outside layer of embedment wheel: Vision and Goals. Written in terms of the desired final state, as well as transitional goals at an organization level. Requires use of measurement and reporting systems.	Three to five strategic recurring themes, to be used in all major communications for all employees.
Embedment	Second layer of the embedment wheel: Review of all categories of the inner layer at the organization level.	Customized to groups or strategic business units. Information sharing and interactive. Continually ties changes from the embedment wheel to the overall outcome.
Individual change	Strategic communications and change management: Measurement is done using the commitment curve and review of leadership accountabilities and development.	One-on-one communications, customized by where each person is situated on the commitment curve.

point, Internalization. All leaders must assess the level of communications for themselves; they cannot rely on an internal communications group to do this type of one-on-one individual communications. And, frankly, a lot of this type of communication happens at the water cooler, person to person.

WHAT WE LEARNED

The intertwined areas of strategic communications and change management are critical to the success of embedment. They are effectively a catalyst to the embedment process. Although we did not start with having these processes integrated, we learned that putting them together creates a powerful driver to embedment. We learned that:

- Traditional communication vehicles can only go so far in creating awareness. Strategic communications targets a large-scale change like innovation embedment and puts it into the context of the vision and strategy of the enterprise.

- Overall, embedment requires both emotive and rational approaches. It is largely through the commitment curve that you can focus on individuals with the emotional element to embedment.

- The staff functions that represent communications on the wheel are incredibly important to embedment. Having leaders who share the vision and align their people is invaluable.

- Business results, embedment, and individual commitment are interrelated but need to be addressed in a change management process that uses appropriate and different communications strategies for each.

- The emotional component of change needs to be addressed in a multi-faceted manner that answers questions such as, "What is in it for me?" and "How will my life change?"

- The embedment wheel itself is not a good communication device in and of itself, but it serves a purpose for leaders in providing guidance in change management.

SELF-ASSESSMENT: CHANGE MANAGEMENT AND STRATEGIC COMMUNICATIONS PLAN

Worksheet 8.1 will help you assess your readiness for change management.

Worksheet 8.1. Creating a Change and Strategic Communications Plan

Instructions: Using the embedment wheel as a framework, create a change and strategic communications plan by answering the questions in each category. Transfer the key points to your company's change management process, or use the process discussed in the chapter. When you are finished, create a strategic communications plan using the insights from the worksheet.

Vision and Goals

1. Write the three to five key messages from your embedment vision. Make sure the messages are relevant for all employees.

2. Describe the goals that your company is using for results, embedment, and individual capability. Add some explanation about why these goals were chosen. Use your work from question 3 to help establish individual goals.

3. For individuals, describe the formal, psychology, and social dimension of the change. Use the questions for each dimension shown earlier in the chapter that are most relevant for the audience you are targeting.

Leader Accountability and Development

1. Identify the key leaders in your change process for embedment. Clearly write out their accountabilities. Think in terms of groups of leaders that need to drive innovation embedment: top leadership teams, executive committee or steering committees, strategic business unit heads, functional and business unit heads, middle managers, and first-line supervisors.

2. How do these accountabilities change as these leaders move up the commitment curve? Put a plan in place to share these with the leaders, and seek their input.

3. How will you communicate these accountabilities to the leaders? To the rest of the organization?

4. Be sure to tie these communications into the vision and goals for innovation embedment.

Culture and Values

1. What aspects of your culture and values will enable the change required for innovation embedment? What aspects of your culture will be the barriers to embedment?

2. Create a statement about how you will use the enablers of your culture and values to drive the change. How will you use the change management process to address the barriers?

3. How will you use communications to reinforce these elements of culture that are enablers? When you see positive changes in overturning the barriers, how

will you communicate these? Think about nondirect ways to communicate these changes, such as putting them into other key communications or using them to hold discussion on innovation.

Resources: Funds and People

1. What funds and people decisions require a change management plan?
2. How will you communicate the changes in these systems? How will you tie these new approaches to the overall vision and goals?
3. From the change management process, identify where most people in your organization are on the commitment curve. Using this insight, describe how you will communicate to people that new opportunities exist in innovation.
4. What vehicles will you use to communicate the successes of individuals and to underscore that innovation from everyone is possible?
5. How can you use these messages to help individuals move up the change curve?

Knowledge Management and Learning Systems

1. How will you use change management to get people to use the KM system?
2. How will you communicate the role of learning in innovation embedment?
3. What key messages need to be created about learning and KM?

Rewards and Recognition

1. How will you use change management to address changes to the reward system?
2. Are these changes seen as formal, psychological, or social?
3. Where are the individuals on the commitment curve in terms of how they view rewards for innovation? Create a plan to engage them in a discussion on this topic. Use the learnings to add to your change plan.
4. How will you communicate the rewards system's changes to all affected employees?
5. Use change management to understand how your employees would like to be recognized for their achievements.
6. How can you communicate employee recognition to a wider group of employees?

Systems Alignment

1. What changes will need to be made in these systems? How will you use change management to effect these changes?
2. How will you communicate these changes?

3. How will you engage people to internalize the changes? Think in formal, psychological, and social terms.

Measurement and Reporting Systems

1. How will you make the measurement system for embedment visible and meaningful?

2. What key messages need to be created?

3. How often will you communicate progress?

4. What channels will you use to get this information to everyone? Think in terms of the KM side, postings in high-traffic areas, and articles in newsletters.

5. How will you tie the measurements into the vision and goals?

CHAPTER NINE

Rewards and Recognition

The Informal Embedment Category

We all know that we get the behaviors that we measure, recognize, and reward. Going all the way back to the 1940s and 1950s, behavioral scientists have shown that people repeat behaviors that are rewarded—and avoid those that are not. In the quality movement of the 1980s and 1990s, they studied and leveraged the link joining attention, measurement, and focus.

The bottom line is that there is little chance a behavior will be a priority if you do not attend to it, measure it, and reward it. The dominant wisdom in most organizations today is that behavior is, at least in part, driven by the rewards and recognition it generates. If you want people to collaborate, you need to define collaboration, set behavioral expectations, and then reward collaborative behavior through formal and informal means such as management recognition, money, perks, and intangible benefits. Similarly, if you want innovation, you need to recognize and reward personal and team initiatives.

But as we all also know, even when the theory is clear, you can get stuck in the implementation. In our case, we found that innovation embedment needed to involve a complex variety of systematic and integrated techniques to recognize and reward innovation. For example, it needed to include monetary as well as nonmonetary rewards, formal and informal approaches, and recognition from internal as well as external sources.

Most important, we needed to align rewards at all levels of Whirlpool in an integrated and united fashion. Rewards and recognition could not be for just some people or levels in Whirlpool. We realized that our rewards and recognition embedment strategy needed to target rewards and recognition at three levels:

- The *individual* level, including the individual innovator or leader who participated in or promoted innovation
- The *team* level, for the effort of innovation teams or work units that worked on an innovation
- The *organizational* level, for rewarding people who addressed the systems and processes that focused the organization on risk taking, culture change, the customer, new business opportunities, and embedment itself

The following sections of this chapter will walk you through how we executed new strategies for rewards at Whirlpool, the successes we had, and the lessons we learned. We share stories relating the techniques we used for rewards, as well as which ones worked and which lost their steam or encountered resistance.

MONEY DOESN'T ALWAYS TALK: THE POWER OF INTRINSIC REWARDS

Before we lay out the details on how we aligned our rewards and recognition programs with embedment, it is useful to share some background on what we quickly learned concerning people's motivation to become involved with innovation. In the early stages of our efforts, we adopted a simple program using cash as incentives for innovation. Our use of monetary rewards occurred only during this early part of our efforts and diminished over time. For example, in our North America region, we offered $500 to individuals who joined an innovation team. To our surprise, this lure of cash did not work as well as we expected; few people raced toward winning this bonus. From our experience, it seemed to be far truer that our people were motivated by intangible and intrinsic rewards than by money or formal recognition.

Indeed, the rewards and recognition literature has always debated the effectiveness of extrinsic incentives (money and formal recognition) versus intrinsic incentives (feelings of contribution and personal satisfaction) on task interest. According to research by Alesander Stanjkovic and Fred Luthans (1999, 2001), intrinsic interest is actually reduced when task participants are offered extrinsic rewards such as money. When people enjoy their work for intrinsic reasons, it seems that they lose interest and motivation when offered extrinsic rewards such as money or formal recognition.

DUCT TAPE VERSION
Don't Cross That Line

One of the first distinct areas we identified for action on the embedment wheel was the category of rewards and recognition. We knew that we needed to select high-potential people to lead innovation efforts and change our human resource systems to align with new desired behaviors and career paths. However, we had not yet developed a strategic and integrated framework for rewarding and recognizing innovation across the organization. This area actually proved to be one of the more difficult categories on the embedment wheel to get our arms around. We struggled with what approach we should take to reward innovation. We spent time benchmarking other companies and found a wide array of approaches to evaluate.

Designing an integrated rewards and recognition system sparked intense debate among our senior leaders. They wanted complete clarity and specificity as to what types of behaviors we needed to change, reinforce, or extinguish. Revising our rewards system also pushed up against a prevailing belief, at least in the innovation folklore, that companies could make innovators millionaires by allowing them to share in the profits generated by their innovation.

Some of our debates about these topics were quite intense, but they moved our organization forward by virtue of inspiring us to have useful dialogue and hearty debate that ultimately helped us align our rewards and recognition with a new strategy.

One explanation for this phenomenon has been posited in what is called cognitive evaluation theory, which is based on cognitive dissonance and suggests that individuals must always have some type of internal justification for their work. In other words, we must always justify our behavior because it is illogical to do something for nothing. For example, if a volunteer donates eight hours of time working on a difficult project and receives no pay, the theory explains that the person will justify the hard labor by concluding that the work was enjoyable and personally satisfying. Alternatively, if the volunteer is paid for the time, he or she would report that the job was a lot of work and did it only for the money. In the second situation, the volunteer would have less task satisfaction just because he or she was paid.

In our case, it is possible that our early use of money as incentives for people to get involved in innovation detracted from the intrinsic motivations they may have had to participate on innovation teams. But whether it was the result of this phenomenon or some other factor we can't identify, our rewards and recognition, especially at the individual level, soon became far more focused on infor-

We now understand the primary reason behind the difficulties we had in this arena. Reward systems in organizations where innovation is not embedded, but arises out of a project or skunkworks, are designed to reinforce "separate" behaviors. But when innovation becomes embedded, it does not take the form of add-on duties for individuals or the form of isolated think tanks for groups; rather, it becomes part of the day-to-day work for everyone. Rewarding it in any other way would be counterproductive to what we were trying to do.

Second, when innovations come from embedded practices, it is very difficult to isolate the handful of people who are responsible for the innovation. The more we understood how innovations at Whirlpool needed to come to fruition, the more we acutely saw that would be hard to identify and reward every person who played a role in the innovation. Moreover, it could even be counterproductive because many people's perception of their own level of involvement may be different from the innovation leaders' perceptions. If we overlooked someone, it would have a detrimental effect on innovation embedment. The bottom line is that when innovation is embedded, there are many people in a large organization like Whirlpool who contribute.

From these two realizations, we began fashioning a rewards systems in line with our vision and culture. We focused our efforts on finding ways to reward the behaviors needed for embedment. We did not cross the rewards line and directly reward individuals for innovations, even major ones. Not crossing this rewards line is a key to truly understanding how Whirlpool found success in the rewards and recognition arena.

mal and intrinsic types of rewards than on rewards we designed up front. It truly seemed that people derived and defined rewards for themselves and that we did not need to adopt a formal system of extrinsic rewards.

In addition, we talked with other organizations about formal rewards and recognition systems. Their advice corresponded to our assumption that intangible programs might work best, at least at first.

It is also important to recognize another reason that we slowly focused on intangible rewards programs. Quite frankly, we were not yet ready in the beginning of our efforts to decide how to change our global compensation systems and structures in a major way. We were not prepared to tackle how to figure out if people on innovation teams would share in future profits or in the percentage of revenue generated from innovation. In fact, we were concerned that profit sharing might motivate people to join the teams for the wrong reasons. We did not want to reinforce innovation as a separate activity. Rather, we needed to guide everyone's focus toward the long-term embedment of innovation into the core of their jobs. A focus mainly on money would have skewed that critical goal.

Finally, one of the best parts of our organizational culture was the tendency for people within Whirlpool to be idealistic and value substance over money. We did not want to lose that. We wanted people who were more on the idealist side to be those who took a stand for innovation at Whirlpool. We figured that participation in innovation activities, at least in the beginning, would become highly rewarding to our people, because it provided them with opportunities to fulfill their creative potential, while applying ideas to make "their" company successful.

INFORMAL REWARD AND RECOGNITION PROGRAMS AT THE INDIVIDUAL LEVEL

As a result of all the above reasons, we ultimately developed a wide variety of informal and intangible rewards programs, with varying success, at the individual level. Many or most of these programs were not planned in advance; they evolved out of a small amount of formal research or, far more important, out of a discovery process we had to go through to implement and tweak reward programs that appealed to our people. Many of these programs emerged over time as the effort progressed.

Following are some of the strategies that did emerge and were built on over time. They are in no particular time order or sequence. We hope that you can adapt and build on these for your own organizations.

Getting Asked to the Party

Especially in the beginning of the innovation effort, being asked to join an innovation team was perceived as a respectable reward or recognition. It became clear that people who joined our first innovation teams felt a special pride. It was perceived that being on a team meant that you were unique and you could take time out from your normal role to learn about and participate in an area that was part of the company's core strategy. This was one of the most exciting times in Whirlpool, so to be asked to participate was considered an honor.

In a sense, our innovation teams may have touched on a core human need. Many behavior scientists recognize the need for inclusion as one of our most basic human needs. The noted group dynamics author and psychologist Will Schutz (1984) talked about three basic sets of needs: need for inclusion, for control, and for openness. We therefore accepted that inclusion was rewarding in and of itself, and we decided to accept and not diminish that feeling to reward people who were involved and to motivate others to become more involved.

There was a side to this type of recognition that we did not expect, did not want, and had to control. The fact that participants felt a need to attribute a "special" status to team members reflects something about human nature that was clearly antithetical to innovation from everyone, everywhere. In fact, we had one moment where one of the leaders of an innovation team casually mentioned to one of us that his team was being selective about whom "they let in." This type of protectionism let us know that inadvertently, we had created a clique mentality with special status and meaning. We therefore had to adjust this person's perception of role in embedment to ensure innovation could come from everyone. The incident reminded that we needed to balance the special feeling within team members with a broader base of inclusion and belonging among everyone.

Becoming a Strategic Thinker

Related to the above reward, we discovered that many people derived pleasure and recognition because they were participating in an activity that was considered strategic to Whirlpool. This allowed people who normally work at a more operational level to have an opportunity to get involved and contribute in an exciting new way to the company that was not available to them in their usual positions. The issue here is not status but quality of contribution that people believed they could make to their company. This reflects an important intrinsic reward that many people find motivating.

Until recently, one of Whirlpool's characteristics was that it had been a fairly top-down hierarchy. This was a definite strength when most change and direction were driven from the top and aligned down the organization. People knew what they had to do. However, it was also a liability because it contributed to creating two groups of people: those who were the strategic thinkers and those who were not.

Participation in innovation invited everyone to learn more about Whirlpool's business, particularly regarding how to contribute on a strategic level by developing new-to-the- world solutions for our customers. It fostered a greater sense of connection to the business for those who were interested and opted to participate.

Increased Marketability and Job Potential

Another important intrinsic reward was that through participation in the innovation process, participants could increase their marketability by collecting knowledge and learning new skills in areas many would not have had access to otherwise. Many participants learned about competitive awareness, trend analysis, customer analysis and segmentation, business opportunity analysis, business planning, venture capital processes, finance, new product development, and marketing.

Without a doubt, team members learned a broad range of portable knowledge and skills that could serve them well in any role in their future, whether it was within Whirlpool or in new jobs at other companies. Somewhat to our dismay, this turned out to be particularly true in regions other than North America, where people with new innovation skills were highly recruited by external firms. One reason was that in the early stages of embedment, we did not have innovation job tracks that were upwardly mobile within Whirlpool, so when headhunters called, external options looked appealing. We therefore had to work hard to ensure that our own people could apply these new skills to their own jobs.

Expanding Their Networks

Many team members gained open access to networking both within Whirlpool and outside the company with people whom many employees would not have had immediate access to before. Some team members were able to meet with senior Whirlpool leaders, venture capitalists, potential trade partners, and customers, as well as Whirlpool people from other innovation teams in different regions and functions. Their role as team members in innovation embedment allowed them to call up any colleague from around the world and talk about a common interest, thus creating forms of communications not possible in our previous culture.

Clearly, networking was a motivator in terms of increasing feelings of inclusion, which are important. Being part of a global group working on an exciting and interesting task was without doubt inherently motivating. It also had numerous practical benefits for the company that people noticed and reported as rewarding and motivating for them. For example, instead of reinventing everything in every region, people now had more of a network to share and leverage learning across regions, reducing work and leaving more time and resources for innovation. In addition, access to different ways of thinking about the customer and about the business enhanced our ability to be creative.

Being Free to Think Outside the Box

Another intangible but strong reward for joining innovation activities was the freedom to act and think differently. This reward yielded a significant benefit for the organization, in that many individuals found that they gained unanticipated skills from the techniques associated with innovation. They learned to broaden their thinking and their perspectives. They gained a perceived freedom that they could act and behave in ways that had previously been antithetical to Whirlpool's established culture and practice.

Whirlpool's former culture allowed anyone to say no, while hardly anyone could say yes. This created a culture that was risk averse and where the few really creative ideas we had were often slowed to a crawl or watered down. The innovation effort created a climate where people could try out ideas, through using the seed funds and experiments, to prove their concept.

Running Their Own Business

The individual-level reward that we might claim as the most meaningful was that people seemed to want the opportunity to run their own show. Innovation clearly tapped into an entrepreneurial sentiment or inclination among many people, imparting among innovators a sense that they were starting their own business within the company. And this became a reality for those whose ideas moved onto a business opportunity. More than a few people literally found themselves running a new business within the company—something that they may never had had the opportunity to do without this effort. Even if the idea, product, or concept ultimately failed, the chance for gaining entrepreneurial skills like scaling up a business was unprecedented in Whirlpool's eighty-year history.

There are a number of examples of this that we can cite. One individual proposed a small business that focused on in-home cooking demonstrations and retail businesses to create events where friends and family could learn new recipes, then buy from a catalogue the accessories or small appliances used to create the meal. This concept was ultimately shelved, but it offered great potential for innovative learnings that we intend to apply to other business opportunities and to customer loyalty efforts. Another example is the Gladiator product line, consisting of appliances for the garage, which is likely to become a major business for Whirlpool. This effort is being led by an individual from a marketing team who most likely under previous business models would be working on only the marketing aspect of Gladiator as opposed to leading the entire new business.

External Recognition

Probably the most unanticipated type of individual recognition came from outside the organization. Individuals on innovation teams found themselves being interviewed by such national publications as *Fortune Online,* the *Wall Street Journal,* and *Fast Company.* As soon as these publications came out on newsstands with someone's interview in it, the person became an instant celebrity inside Whirlpool. It literally opened people's eyes to what was possible for them, and some began to pursue these types of media opportunities. This type of behavior would have been antithetical to the culture before the innovation effort.

In hindsight, we should have made these interviews more inclusive, as well as leveraged their dissemination inside and outside Whirlpool more thoroughly for our own organizational purposes. This would have served as both an excellent recognition technique and a wonderful (and free) public relations communication technique for Whirlpool. As a result, our communications department has begun to work systematically to ensure that we get the type of coverage that provides broad exposure not only to our efforts but for the Whirlpool people who are leading and working on them.

Recognition and Rewards for Leaders at the Middle Manager Level

We also knew that we needed to create a strong incentive to reward and recognize leaders at the middle manager level and above for supporting innovation as a priority activity for everyone in their work unit. For example, leaders could encourage participation by making time and resources available for innovation activities, as well as promoting participation in innovation teams and encouraging people to learn and use the innovation tools and techniques. Leaders could also encourage their people to participate in innovation workshops (sessions where innovation techniques are used to generate new ideas or expand on existing business ideas) and for accessing I-Mentors or I-Consultants to work on innovation projects. Promoting this type of behavior among our leaders was difficult because they needed to juggle the demands of their everyday work with the longer-term potential of innovation, which was not a well-established business practice.

But given that we were interested in encouraging leaders to engage in these behaviors, we set aside a place on the company's performance evaluation form for goals associated with encouraging participation in innovation. We discuss the evaluation and appraisal process and its role in innovation embedment in other chapters relating to systems. In theory, leaders who encouraged participation in innovation were to be rewarded and recognized formally. The jury is still out on whether each leader who devoted time and effort and made time and space for his or her people to engage in innovation activities will be rewarded and recognized in a manner that is meaningful. But where innovation embedment was on an individual's performance appraisal, we saw tremendous impact.

It might be true that for individual leaders, as with individual contributors, more informal and intangible feedback is the most rewarding aspect of innovation. For example, one source of such feedback is clearly the use of 360-degree feedback for leaders about other people's perceptions of their commitment, knowledge, and skill in innovation. Leaders did receive feedback from their peers, managers, direct reports, and others about their perceptions of how the leader was emphasizing innovation in their area and how well the leader was using and encouraging the use of innovation tools and other items. There were not immediate rewards or formal public recognition for this feedback, but for leaders who obtained high scores, we believe that the kudos were a form of recognition and provided great intrinsic satisfaction.

Finally, leaders who made the choice to participate in innovation reaped all of the same possible rewards and recognition as any individual participant, such as learning new skills, increased marketability, and external recognition.

TEAM REWARDS AND RECOGNITION

Although we wanted to encourage innovation from everywhere and everyone in the form of individual initiative, we did not necessarily want to begin to create a culture of individual heroes. We recognized that it was important for us to avoid the tendency to make rewards and recognition focused only on the individual level.

Instead, we sought equally to foster a team approach to innovation. We knew a lot about the methodologies for rewarding and recognizing team behavior as opposed to individual heroics from our prior work on project management and product development teams. As with all other team issues, we did not want to create anything formal that gave the appearance of rewarding individuals who upstaged others, worked noncollaboratively, or exhibited competitive behavior within the team or between teams. Some organizations pit teams against one another to see who can create the best product or idea, but we did not adopt this approach and did not want our rewards strategy in any way to encourage these types of behavior. We wanted to be in line with one of our own values statements: "Focus competitive behavior on the competition, not on each other." On balance, however, we did not want to squash individual initiative and entrepreneurial behavior.

As with the individual-level rewards and recognition, it turned out that the most powerful methods were not formal but were focused on more intangible benefits, such as the following.

Becoming Part of an Innovation Team and Strategy

One of the biggest rewards for team members came when they were part of a team that came up with a winning idea that was sanctioned to migrate into a full-blown business opportunity with potential for revenue and real customers. Celebrating these successes as a team was cited as one of the biggest rewards to participating in an innovation. The camaraderie created within the teams was itself motivating. For example, the level of excitement from the team that ran the North American Innovation Days event would have been impossible to predict or design in advance. In fact, the psychological payoff for this team, along with the fact that the event was both worthy and successful in communicating what innovation was about motivated several other teams in other regions to consider this same strategy.

We also noticed that people took great pride in working on innovation teams even when their ideas did not develop into full-blown businesses. There was a certain pride about being able to say that one was involved in an innovation project on a specific team. This was not usually said as a competitive statement between teams in Whirlpool, but just a chance to say that you were involved.

Visibility with Senior Leadership

Team members also received attention and visibility from senior leadership. This was a big deal. Teams with new ideas were asked to present their business opportunity to the I-Boards, which were made up of senior leaders. For many members on these teams, it was a unique opportunity for recognition. It provided visibility for many people who might have never had the chance or platform to "strut their stuff" to senior management or to be exposed to different ways of thinking and to the process of high-level business decision making. It was also good for the company to have a natural way to meet its talented people.

We highly recommend that companies leverage this strategy and make visibility one of the keys to motivating team members. It is one area that is easily controlled and managed.

New Friends and Diverse Views

Given that most innovation teams were intentionally made up of a diverse set of people, many participants were motivated by having access to new ways of thinking and acting about the products, brand, service, and the business in general. Many team members mentioned that exposure to people who were different was enormously rewarding, even if no new business opportunities were uncovered. This exposure to diverse thinking in the long run benefited all team members in terms of broadening their perspectives. It also benefited Whirlpool itself in terms of new ideas and product.

For many people, being a member of such a diverse team composition was new in their work experience. Again, we found this was an area we could orchestrate and leverage. Diversity on teams was good not only for idea generation and out-of-the-box thinking but was motivating for participants.

News Ways of Working as a Team

For many participants of innovation teams, the type of teamwork required was a rewarding new learning experience. Teams learned to work together in an entrepreneurial setting where tasks were often loose (or even ill defined) and the outcomes were uncertain. Working in this type of team environment fostered an increased recognition of the value of teamwork, especially in such ambiguous situations. This was vital learning for us, as Whirlpool teams in the past had usually had a set of practices that reduced, rather than promoted, ambiguity such as extensive chartering and project planning. It was great that teams could pull out these methods and techniques when they needed them, so that working in a complex and vague business setting was an insightful development experience for all team members. Their knowledge also transferred back to the work settings, where many team members were able to apply a new-found patience and appreciation for complicated situations.

ORGANIZATIONAL-LEVEL REWARDS AND RECOGNITION

We knew that individual and team-level rewards and recognition needed to be supported by organizational-level processes and systems that played a role in our reward system, such as those owned by human resources and finance. We actually found it easier to adapt some of these processes to support rewards and recognition than to create new and different individual monetary rewards programs, probably because at the systems level, we were not dealing with people's motivations, feelings, and psychology. We were also not sure of the impact that these changes would have on people's motivation when compared to intangible rewards.

We conducted a readiness assessment to ensure that we could change the elements of the processes we needed to change without a lot of resistance. We focused on changing elements that were "ready" or "readying" rather than those that were not quite there. The importance of such a readiness assessment will be evident to you when you use the worksheets at the end of this chapter.

Following are the most significant systems and processes we put into place to support individual and team rewards systems. Note that some of these organizational systems dovetail with—and are further expanded by—what you will read about the many system and process changes that we made to allow us to measure our success, as covered in Chapter Ten.

Human Resource Systems

As with most other large corporations, Whirlpool's human resource systems such as performance management, merit and bonus pay, 360-degree feedback, and talent pool selection and development are linked to our organization's rewards and recognition systems. To support our innovation activities, we therefore had to adapt and revise many of these systems. For example, our leadership performance management process and our 360-degree feedback now have mandatory items focused on participation in and encouragement of innovation in their work units. Leaders are assessed by the performance appraisal process, and their merit and bonus pay are linked to participation.

We also adapted our talent pool system to make participation in innovation strongly encouraged for greater mobility and opportunities for promotion. This system was created to ensure that we have the right amount and type of talent in the pipeline and to ensure that people with potential are being developed to meet the demands of the future. We knew that if innovation was a core competence critical to our business, then we needed to provide people with assignments that would build their capability to lead and participate in innovation. As a result, leading an innovation team on a key new business area or spending time as vice president in a region for innovation became one of the assignments critical to upward movement.

Balanced Scorecard Measures

The balanced scorecard, developed by Kaplan and Norton (1996), is a way for organizations to ensure that they pay attention to a balanced set of measures, such as customer satisfaction, operational effectiveness, innovation, and financial results. The idea, consistent with core competency development, is that there are outcomes such as effectiveness, employee morale, innovation, and customer loyalty that drive financial success. Only by measuring, reporting on, and paying attention to all these can an organization achieve a true picture of its success. Measuring only financial success as an indication of the health of the enterprise is ignoring what drives financial results and motivating the wrong behavior for long-term success.

We modified our own balanced scorecard system to include measures associated with innovation embedment and results. We revised our scorecard to reflect our focus on how innovation and customer loyalty will affect financial results in the long term. This change was critical in focusing leader attention on innovation as a critical organizational measure and was also required from a rewards point of view, because scorecard measures determine a percentage of bonus pay for leaders. The balanced scorecard contains the global measures that the executive committee tracks throughout the year. At the end of the year, the board of directors reviews the results against the goals, assigning a numerical multiplier that is used to determine the amount of bonus that leaders receive.

Financial Systems

As mentioned in Chapter Six, we found that we needed to adapt our financial systems to measure not only the resources (funds and people) placed into our innovation effort, but also the outcomes in terms of revenue and profit associated with innovation projects. These changes were necessary to track the progress of innovation projects and their business potential, and they also rolled up into the global balanced scorecard that was used by the board of directors to set total bonus payout percentages for leaders.

Communications

Our formal communications systems did much to foster recognition. The *Innovation Field Journal* and other publications recognized through articles those involved in innovation. In our "all-hands" and "town hall" meetings, the meeting moderator was asked to mention people working on innovation teams and their accomplishments. These efforts served as a great advertisement and also a recognition mechanism for people involved in innovation. We would highlight accomplishments, new product, and service ideas from people around the world.

WHAT WE LEARNED

- Think about rewards from an embedment approach. This includes not reinforcing innovation as a separate activity through monetary rewards aimed solely at innovators.

- Make your rewards and recognition strategy align with your culture, such as focusing competitive behavior on competitors. At the same time, use it to create new cultural areas you want to focus on, such as fostering out-of-the-box thinking.

- Formal reward programs such as sign-on bonuses and cash do not seem to work as well as more intangible, informal, and peer-based recognition programs for participation in innovation. Motivation for innovation appears to be implicit. Organizations should leverage this phenomenon actively and not try to force monetary strategies, at least at first.

- Build the rewards on inclusion, but balance between being included and rewarding individuals.

- The development of new skills, knowledge, and networks is a primary motivator for many people to engage in innovation activities at the individual level. Making these benefits visible and leveraging them should be a major part of a rewards and recognition strategy. Development of new skills and ways of thinking benefit not only people but the organization's capacity in the long run.

- Recognition from new and unanticipated sources, such as outside publications, can be as strong a motivator as internal recognition. Be open to rewards from unusual places. These can have unexpected benefits for individuals and the company.

- Address organizational and systems rewards and recognition along with individual and team-level rewards. System- and process-level rewards are critical for alignment but, as the literature states, might not have as much force as more informal mechanisms.

SELF-ASSESSMENT: REWARDS AND RECOGNITION

You can use Worksheets 9.1, 9.2, and 9.3 to evaluate your efforts to create rewards and recognition programs at the individual, team, and organizational levels.

Worksheet 9.1. Readiness Checklist for Rewards and Recognition at the Organizational Level

This short assessment can tell you whether your organization is rewards and recognition "ready." It reflects some of our thinking about what areas we tackled first at the organizational level.

Item	Yes	No
1. In general, is it considered an honor to receive recognition or a reward formally sponsored by your organization?	___	___
2. Is there transparency and fairness around the criteria for monetary and nonmonetary rewards?	___	___
3. Is there transparency around actual rewards and recognition—that is, do others have access to who gets what?	___	___
4. Is there consistency across the organization in the manner that rewards and recognition are administered?	___	___
5. Recognition from leaders in this organization is an honor.	___	___
6. You describe your human resource systems as flexible and adaptable to new business practices.	___	___
7. You describe your performance review system as discriminating performance among low, medium, and high performers.	___	___
8. Can you describe your merit review system as discriminating performance among low, medium, and high performers?	___	___
9. Have rewards and recognition systems been adapted to link to other strategic initiatives in the past?	___	___
10. It is possible in your organization for lower-level people to receive significant monetary rewards?	___	___
11. Rewards here balance monetary with informal.	___	___
12. Top-level balanced scorecard (or "top sheet") balances financial with nonfinancial measures.	___	___
13. One person is assigned to be accountable for rewards and recognition for innovation.	___	___

Scoring: How many yes answers do you have?

10–13   You are in great shape to succeed in modifying your systems.

6–9   You probably have a few risk areas you need to address.

Below 6   Your new rewards and recognition strategy might be blocked before it starts by any existing history, culture, leadership, and systems issues within your organization.

Worksheet 9.2. Organizational Rewards and Recognition Alignment

Listed below are the primary organizational-level systems that we recommend be adapted to reward and recognize innovation at the team and individual levels. Check to see how many you have considered adapting to foster motivation for innovation.

Process or System	Elements of the System	Which Ones We Have Considered
Human resources	Compensation	
	Talent pool	
	Merit	
	Performance management	
	360-degree feedback	
Balanced scorecard	Measurement of results	
	Top sheet (regional or functional top seven to ten measures)	
	Bonus payout	
Finance	Revenue projection	
	Profit sharing	
Communications	Publications	
	All-hands meetings	
	Town meetings	

Worksheet 9.3. Individual Rewards Checklist

Use this suggested checklist for setting up individual rewards and recognition for participating in innovation. The questions answered "no" will give you a place to start. Use it to open the dialogue with leaders about how to create an environment that rewards individuals for innovating.

Question	Yes	No
1. Does your organization balance formal and informal rewards and recognition for participation in innovation?	____	____
2. Are sources of recognition balanced among senior leader, peer, internal, and external sources?	____	____
3. Are rewards balanced between traditional rewards and recognition and the opportunity for learning, networking, and skill development?	____	____
4. Are participants in innovation provided with the opportunity to contribute at a strategic level?	____	____
5. Is recognition from unusual sources, such as external publications and organizations, promoted and communicated?	____	____
6. Do individuals have the chance to become part of a new business from their participation in innovation?	____	____
7. Is there a chance for participants to enhance their visibility with senior leadership?	____	____

CHAPTER TEN

Measurement and Reporting Systems and Systems Alignment

Anyone who works at Whirlpool understands one thing: people want alignment. Of course, this is not unusual. Most people would like their world to make sense. We took this need seriously. We focused our attention on two areas: (1) alignment of our measurement systems with our goals and (2) alignment of our systems and processes with our goals and rewards and recognition programs. Our desire was to hear hallway conversations that went something like this: "Gee, they have really thought about this," or "This must be serious, it's on my performance review," or "The new systems support the goals of innovation."

This chapter covers what we did to align our measures and systems and processes with the goals of embedment. Note that it covers two elements of the embedment wheel: measurement and systems alignment.

MEASURING EMBEDMENT ALL AROUND

Whirlpool designed a comprehensive measurement system to assess our progress in embedment and to make midcourse adjustments. In order to ensure alignment between measures and our goals, we intentionally mapped our goals to existing and new measures. If you recall from Chapter Three, we had developed three types of goals: business results, embedment results, and individual results. We found that we not only needed to adapt some of our existing measurement systems, but we needed to create new measures. This work is ongoing.

BUSINESS RESULTS MEASURES

Results goals focus on the business results from the innovation effort. We considered a number of different options to measure progress and landed on three complementary approaches. First, we wanted to continuously assess the health of our pipeline for new business ideas. Second, we were interested in the revenue potential for ideas moving through the pipeline. Third, we wanted a solid set of measures regarding the amount of revenue we were generating as a direct result of our innovation effort.

To measure progress toward these goals, we found that we had to establish new data collection and reporting requirements that did not exist in the old system. It took us a year of hard work to do this. First, we put together a set of guidelines at the corporate level outlining the three requirements. The actual accountability for change, however, resided in a number of different places. At the regional level, the vice president of innovation and the chief financial officer were asked to modify their systems so that they would be able to track the progress of all ideas on I-Pipe in order to report on the revenue potential of ideas.

We used this reporting system for over a year to make decisions and track the health of the innovation effort from a business results standpoint. The data were reviewed regularly in I-Board meetings and during Executive Committee sessions. The method fulfilled our need to report on our progress against business results goals.

However, we had a sneaking sense that something was not quite right. One sign was that we kept getting into long debates about what we were measuring: specifically which innovations were directly linked to the innovation effort itself and which were not. We thought that it would be easy to identify specific projects that were a direct result of the innovation effort, but this proved untrue.

For example, there were business ideas with great potential that were shaped by the innovation tools and methods, but in fact, they did not arise as a result of the innovation effort. The business idea existed before the formal innovation process, but an innovation tool either moved it along, was used to modify the idea, or was used to shelve it. One example was the washer and dryer called Duet. Duet was not conceived or designed through the innovation process. It did, however, benefit from the process through rethinking the launch process and placing it into a larger context of the fabric care business.

As this dilemma began to make its way to the top of our "things to be concerned about" pile, the Executive Committee decided it was time to judge the overall progress of innovation embedment from an independent perspective. As they rightly decided, we would not be able to measure our progress until we had a good definition of what we were really measuring. The issue of how to measure business results was therefore not fully resolved at that point.

EMBEDMENT MEASURES

As discussed in Chapter Three, embedment goals are journey goals. They represent how we are progressing toward embedding innovation from everyone and everywhere. They are different from results goals in that they strive to describe how we know that innovation is embedded in our culture, values, knowledge sets, leadership systems, and the actual way of being. It turned out to be more difficult than we thought to come to terms with a discrete set of quantitative measures that made sense when talking about progress in changing culture, knowledge management, or learning. As a result, our measures in this area were often qualitative in nature.

This was a valuable learning experience within Whirlpool, since we have largely been a fact-driven company. One of our learnings from both this effort and from the high-performance culture change effort that we discussed in Chapter Five, was that the data we prefer to pay attention to must sometimes be soft and qualitative.

In this case, we had to accept three distinct qualitative perspectives by which we could measure our progress toward embedment: action around the embedment wheel, executive committee actions, and I-Board actions.

Measuring Embedment by Going Around the Wheel

This first measure of progress in embedment was to continuously assess the health of embedment by going around the wheel at the enterprise, functional, and regional levels. In some way, the mere fact that we were taking action in each of the embedment categories would be a measure of our focus and success. We therefore asked leaders from each region, function, and strategic business unit (SBU) to report regularly on the actions they were taking for each embedment category. We also performed this same check on ourselves at the enterprise level. We looked to see if our efforts were out of balance between and among the different categories of embedment, and we assessed our progress against what we said we were going to do in each category.

What we paid attention to versus what we did not proved to be quite indicative of our culture and our company, because when we assessed our activities and balance around the wheel, we found that we had paid more attention to elements on the top and right side of the wheel than those on the left. Activities such as vision and goals, leadership accountabilities, knowledge management, and resources fared better than areas such as strategic communications

DUCT TAPE STORY
An Awesome Audit

After two solid years in innovation embedment and measures, the Executive Committee charted a global innovation audit as a way to obtain a wide-ranging and integrated look at how innovation was progressing in Whirlpool, using a variety of indicators. It also focused on how people in different business functions and regions were defining innovation. The audit had eight major areas of data collection:

1. Definitions used in innovation in each region. We wanted to know if there was consistency in what we were counting as innovation globally.

2. Amount of new revenue and expense for innovation from 2001–2002, with projections for 2003. These data focused on three areas: revenue from projects due directly to the innovation effort, revenue from projects shaped by the innovation, and revenue from innovation projects that were not touched by innovation tools or methods.

3. Capital layout for 2001–2002 with projections for 2003. This category had to do with how much capital we had projected for use in innovation versus how much we actually used.

4. People resources, including percentage of engineering time for each innovation project by region. We wanted to know if our engineering resources were being sapped by the innovation effort and if they were being used evenly across regions.

5. The status and health of the I-Pipe in terms of types and numbers of ideas moving through different stages. We wanted to know if we had a robust pipeline in terms of types of ideas and in regard to where ideas actually were in the development process.

6. Qualitative perceptions of the progress of innovation embedment by all levels in the organization. We wanted to know if people were learning about innovation, how many people had been involved in innovation activities, and if people had positive perceptions and experiences associated with the effort.

7. Analysis of the effectiveness of strategic communications, both internal and external. Did people inside and outside the company know about innovation?

8. Whether leaders were being assessed on their efforts in innovation by embedded systems such as the performance appraisal process. We wanted to know if leaders were being measured and rewarded based on their leadership accountabilities in innovation.

It was one of the most extensive audits we every conducted at Whirlpool. In the Epilogue, we discuss the overall findings of the audit in more detail. Without question, the first two areas of inquiry, definitions and amount of new revenue generated, were the most cantankerous areas of the innovation audit.

The Executive Committee put the first area, definitions, on the audit to test their hypothesis that the strategic business unit (SBUs) or regions were using unique definitions and ultimately measuring innovation differently. This was a problem because we wanted to roll up the regional and business unit measures into a global innovation balanced scorecard measure. Obviously, this would not be impossible if we were using different definitions of innovation. It was also an issue in terms of assessing how we were doing on innovation.

Unfortunately, as we suspected, we immediately walked into a maze of definitions and measures. The crux of the issue centered on the SBUs' or regions' measurement of innovation versus growth. Innovation was defined by some regions or SBUs as a product or service that meets at least one of the following: creates distinctive and innovative solutions valued by the customer, creates real and sustainable competitive advantage, or creates exceptional value for shareholders and represents significant opportunity for new revenue growth. Other SBUs defined innovation as a new category of product or service and minimal cannibalization of existing business and significant market share or average sales value improvement.

You can see a stark difference between the two definitions. The difference is so great that when we reported our results to the Executive Committee at the conclusion of the audit, we told them that we could not provide definitive findings on how much revenue had been generated without a host of qualifiers that would allow us to compare apples to oranges! This was due to the differences that existed in definitions and, ultimately, to disparate measures.

As a result, the Executive Committee asked each SBU head to line up the definitions and measures to a common set. Although the differences in definitions and measures are significant, it is easy to see how we got there. In the first year, we had more consistency of definitions and measures. As embedment progressed, regional and SBU leadership teams took the accountability and autonomy to guide their innovation efforts given their unique business needs. In addition, the Executive Committee's global measure was reported on the balanced scorecard once a quarter. This meant that the details of innovation measures were not being scrutinized as often as was probably needed to catch this disconnect.

What we learned was that although each SBU and region was well intentioned, the differences resulted in a cumbersome process to roll up innovation revenue and confusion about what we had really accomplished. We are in the process of correcting this issue. Common measures and iron-clad definitions go hand in hand and are critical to tracking innovation embedment and innovation. In addition, without a focus on measures, we would have never discovered and corrected this disconnect.

and rewards and recognition. This was a valuable insight for us. It told us that we needed to focus on balancing our efforts, and in the long run, it pointed out that we might have to change our focus for future efforts that involved embedment of other core competencies.

Measuring by Executive Committee Measures

In Chapter Four, we said that we had laid out an explicit set of accountabilities for each Executive Committee member. We were stringent about the measurement of their action on those accountabilities. We figured that if the people at this level did not take action and if inaction was ignored, the entire effort was doomed. Lack of attention at the top meant that embedment will not last. Every Executive Committee member was measured on his or her execution of those accountabilities.

In addition, there are a few other measures we used at the Executive Committee level:

- Completing the Executive Committee leadership agenda for innovation embedment related to taking action on all areas of the embedment wheel at the enterprise level. Each Executive Committee member was accountable not only for his or her region or SBU, but also had the dual accountability for the enterprise. We repeatedly reviewed our progress and graded ourselves on these actions.
- In the first year, one of the ways we measured our success was that each region or SBU needed to generate at least three new business opportunities in their I-Pipeline that were directly from innovation work. Each executive committee member had a goal for his or her region or SBU around generating actual business opportunities in the region, even if these ideas did not move all the way through the pipeline.
- One of the most important elements of the embedment wheel, given our goal of innovation from everyone and everywhere, was to ensure that we had an infrastructure to share and capture knowledge. As a result, all Executive Committee members were measured on whether they enabled a knowledge management (KM) infrastructure in their region and whether their region had successfully launched the innovation E-space Web site and the customer loyalty site.

Measuring by Innovation Board Measures

Each regional I-Board also set up its own measures to see how it was progressing in areas related to embedment. To some extent, these reinforced Executive Committee focus on the health of the embedment system and the number of ideas actually entering the pipeline. Other measures targeted how well the I-Board itself was performing in terms of supporting innovation teams. Some examples of measures we used, in addition to supporting the embedment wheel work described above, included these:

- How many ideas in the innovation pipeline could be tracked to customer insights? One of the reasons we selected the innovation tools and methods that we did was that they used customer insights as one of the starting points for the innovation process. Because Whirlpool historically had an insufficient line of sight to its customers, we wanted to measure our progress across all functions toward using customers as our main source of insights. I-Boards tracked the alignment of ideas to customer insights and made a determination of how well we were doing using customer data to generate ideas for innovation.
- Consistency and support of the I-Board was an essential element to embedment. As a result, I-Boards measured their support by how often they met and focused on innovation. The measure of success was to meet at least once a month as an I-Board and hear from members of the I-Teams about funding for ideas during that period. One measure of success was that the I-Board was meeting and listening to I-Team members.
- A third measure of I-Board success was whether members helped develop ideas rather than just kill them. Remember that behaviors designed to *not* just say no were an important part of the culture change associated with innovation from everyone and everywhere.
- Providing resources (funds and people) for innovation was crucial for I-Board success. The I-Board in part measured its success in embedment by tracking how many I-Mentors and I-Consultants were available to help in innovation efforts, how often these resources were used by line managers and teams, and how much seed fund money had been agreed to be paid to teams.
- The I-Boards also tracked how many innovation events were happening in their SBU or region. The number of innovation events ranged from innovation work sessions where ideas were conceptualized to week-long I-Mentor training sessions. Clearly if these activities slowed or stopped, that would indicate a slower embedment pace, at least in the first few years.

Exhibit 10.1 shows one way that we graphically displayed the results of some of our business and embedment measures. You'll notice that the exhibit depicts the four stages of the I-Pipe, from concept to experiment to prototype to scale-up, and how many projects are at each stage. It also charts some of the relevant aspects of embedment, including number of I-Mentors and I-Consultants, and tracks revenue projections. Although this specific exhibit may not meet your needs, you can modify it to create something that summarizes your embedment and results measures and puts them into one picture. In this way, you can detect patterns that might lead to tweaking one system or another.

Exhibit 10.1. Innovation Business Results

Innovation scorecard: 2/23/2002
                85% of year remaining

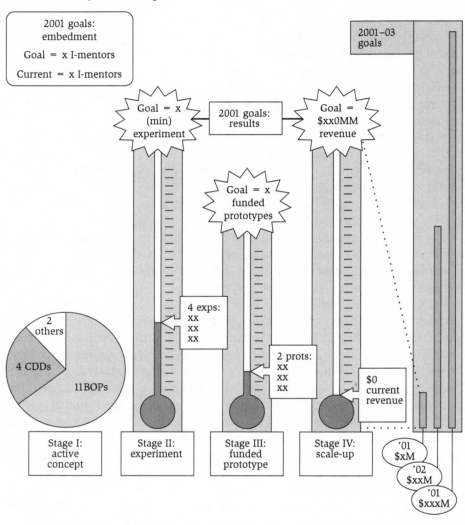

A NOTE ON INDIVIDUAL MEASURES

As we discussed in Chapter Three, we did not identify individual-level goals for embedment until almost three years into the embedment process. These goals targeted key job groups or key individuals in terms of what we expected from them in innovation—for example:

- Number or percentage of people in any work group who can describe how innovation has changed their job
- Number of job descriptions rewritten to include innovation
- Identification and removal of barriers to innovation in any work group
- Written statements about how an individual has used innovation tools
- Number of performance appraisals that have listed innovation goals for individuals

Because it was impossible to obtain a detailed picture of how we were doing on all individual goals (there are sixty thousand people in Whirlpool), we set up a pulse check system, using our intranet, designed to survey a random sample of people every quarter on the areas listed above. We asked people to describe their interaction with the innovation process, the extent of their involvement in it, and how much time they spent monthly on innovation. We also asked if people had written job descriptions for innovation and if their performance appraisal goals had changed.

Questions in the survey were in a quantitative format. We also left write-in space for people to share their thoughts, ideas, concerns, and any actual data they had from job descriptions or performance reviews. From this information, we were able to discern how we were doing on individual embedment goals.

To our surprise, the individual results were quite compelling. Our first survey showed that almost 50 percent of people who responded to the survey in any region had at least heard about innovation, and more than 20 percent had participated in an innovation activity such as training or an innovation team. If this 50 percent seems small, think about the amount of recall for any message in a communications or advertising sense, especially in a dynamic environment dense with many messages. If the message is not directly related to your job at the moment it is conveyed to you (and innovation embedment in the first two years was not directly related to everyone's job), it is unlikely you will recall it for long. Fifty percent of a random sample of people from anywhere in the world was much higher than the range of the 25 to 30 percent that we expected.

TO CHANGE OR CREATE MEASURES: THAT IS THE QUESTION

Whenever possible, we used existing measurement systems to track innovation embedment. For example, we already had a Web-based employee survey tool in place that we adjusted to meet our need for surveys on individual measures. Adding measures to existing systems is ideal in the first few years of embed- ment. It lessens the confusion about how many new terms and concepts peo- ple have to learn. But whether you adjust old systems or invent new ones, there is one important axiom of measurement systems to heed: the amount of energy expended to collect the data to report on the measure has to be reasonable. It does not make sense to set up systems where collecting the data requires extreme effort or the measurement system can overwhelm the effort itself.

SYSTEMS AND PROCESS ALIGNMENT

We have repeatedly made the point through this story that a critical success fac- tor in embedment is the alignment of systems and processes to support the intent of innovation embedment. Whirlpool has always had a strong process-oriented culture, probably due to our roots in manufacturing and quality excel- lence. Our people were quite accustomed to creating processes and systems that helped us reach our strategy as an organization. In this respect, adaptation and change of our existing processes and systems came naturally to us. In fact, many of our first conversations about embedment were focused on the need to align existing processes and systems.

It this section, we will share what existing processes we adapted and what changes we made to those processes. We will also remind you of some new processes and systems that we needed to create that we have already discussed in the book.

Leadership's Critical Role

First, everyone needs to understand that alignment is not a staff function. We did not go through a rigorous process to analyze each process and system from a corporate perspective. Rather each senior leader, usually an Executive Com- mittee member, was charged as part of his or her embedment accountabilities to examine the processes or systems under his or her bailiwick and ensure align- ment with the goals of innovation from everyone and everywhere. This align- ment targeted business results goals and embedment goals.

The close involvement of functional leaders and people in staff roles in this activity is an important point because one of the reasons that we believe we have been successful at embedment is the dedication and involvement of senior leaders: line and staff. Although each of them probably did not actually realign processes themselves, they were closely involved in providing direction and reviewing results. Functional leaders most involved in enterprise-wide alignment were human resources, finance, strategic planning, product development, and corporate technology organization and information systems. The accountabilities of leaders of regional or line organizations such as Europe, India, Latin America, and North America were to work with functional organizations to provide feedback on changes and to work to adopt those changes in their regions. Each region was given the prerogative to adapt the process to its specific situation and local environment if the intent of promoting innovation embedment and business results was maintained.

Criteria for Process Adaptation

At the time, we did not explicitly create a list of criteria for alignment or redesign of processes. But for purposes of this book, it is possible to retrofit a set of criteria that our leaders effectively used to look at processes and systems. They are listed below and can serve as guidelines to help you determine which processes you should adapt:

- *The system or process must be inclusive rather than exclusive in terms of input from certain types of people.* You should adapt systems that are not inclusive. For example, until recently, our product development process did not have a mechanism to accept ideas from anyone in the company. Most ideas considered came out of the technology organization. Now it has been modified to accept ideas from a broader range of people.
- *The system or process must reward and recognize people for participation in innovation.* Prior to embedment, there were no formal mechanisms to motivate people to participate in innovation or to reward or recognize them once they did. Now our talent pool process promotes participation in innovation activities and human resource processes such as performance management support innovation.
- *Include innovation embedment measures in analyzing the effectiveness of the system or process.* Before embedment, success measures for many processes had focused on efficiency or effectiveness in terms of cost and quality. These measures are still important to us. However, now we realize that when we measure the health of a system or process, we must also assess its worth against how well it is promoting or maintaining innovation results and embedment.
- *The system should be modified to take in inputs from innovation efforts and, if appropriate, feed its outputs back into innovation.* For example, our brand management process needed to be modified so that it accepted inputs from innovation efforts, such as new ideas about products, services, or relationship management strategies. Conversely, on the back end of the brand management process, we needed to make sure that data and information that were

being collected from research on how our brand drivers affect the customer were fed back into the innovation effort. In this way, the data could be used as raw material for further innovation. (Brand drivers, such as products, services, communications, relationship, and shopping experience, are the ways that we ensure the image of each of our brands is making the impact on the consumer that we intended it to have.)

SYSTEM AND PROCESS REDESIGN

Let's now take you through some of the systems and processes that we did redesign and point out some of the changes we made that in our view had the biggest effect on embedment. We will not cover all our systems and process— that would take an entire book—but we target the three main areas: human resources, product development, and finance.

DUCT TAPE VERSION
Another Case of Good Genes

Earlier in the book, we talked about the need to have someone in the leadership group who understands the three levels of goals and helps everyone else get to the right ones. We said our CEO had a "good goal gene." The same was true in the systems work. In fact, in many ways, the systems work should have been harder than the work on goals. It is more daunting to think about grabbing large cross-functional systems by the tail and wrestling them to the ground to ensure alignment with innovation embedment. Most leaders would prefer to look the other way.

However, our chief operating officer, Jeff Fettig, took systems alignment to innovation as a personal challenge. Jeff possessed the good systems gene, understanding the power of operating and management systems. He dove in with both feet to align them, no matter how hard the work.

Early in embedment, Jeff was leading the North American region in the transition between two heads of the region. During that brief time, his embedment focus was where no one else's was: on systems redesign. He was so serious that he had systems alignment put on the embedment measures for the North American I-Board. He asked them to start with a few key systems and redesign them with innovation embedment in mind. He continued this focus as he methodically guided the alignment and redesign of the major systems for alignment with the strategy and with innovation embedment.

Human Resources

One obvious place to look for system and process alignment and redesign was in the area of human resources. These are the systems and processes that support the acquisition, development, and maintenance of knowledge and skill development and utilization in innovation. It is also, at least in part, responsible for rewards and recognition from participation in innovation. We will cover three of the human resource systems that were adapted to reinforce innovation embedment: leader development, performance appraisal, and talent pool.

Leader Development. Whirlpool has had a strong history of leader development. We built our performance center, Brandywine Creek, in the mid-1990s as a testament to our commitment to leader development. Traditionally, our leader development targeted teaching our strategy and the leader's role in execution. With the change in our vision and mission and our innovation embedment strategy, the focus of our leadership development shifted the focus on strategy to ensure that leaders not only understood but embodied the behaviors, knowledge, and skills that would ensure that innovation came from everyone and everywhere.

Our leadership development curriculum targeted leaders from the Chairman's Council down to the manager level. At the Chairman's Council level, participants went through a two-week development program with a heavy emphasis on action learning (applying knowledge to real-world problems) around Whirlpool's competencies. The focus was on their role in creating a culture and environment that enabled innovation from everyone and everywhere.

At the director and manager levels, the focus was not necessarily on learning innovation tools or methods (they could join an innovation team for that) but on the work unit leader's role of making time and space for innovation. In addition, participants at these levels spent time talking about their role in promoting mobility and freedom for their employees to work on innovation projects. We discussed how to leverage learning when employees came back into the work unit and how to use the knowledge management system to influence learning from across the organization.

Performance Appraisal Process. Whitwam was convinced that the innovation effort would not be as far along as it is without using the performance appraisal system to set goals and assess against goals. In addition to the 360-degree feedback and development plan described in Chapter Nine, leaders used the annual performance appraisal process to set goals around innovation and receive assessments against these goals.

In year one of embedment, for our North American top leaders and our executive committee, 30 percent of their performance goals targeted innovation results and embedment. You can see in Exhibit 10.2 that we had a chart that listed each of the leader's names, the innovation domain each was accountable for, the revenue generation we expected, and the number of experiments we wanted them to promote. We also had collective embedment goals that each was assessed against.

In year two of our embedment efforts, all top leaders were asked to identify both results (for example, amount of revenue generated) and embedment goals (for example, processes to be put in place, number of I-Mentors to be certified). This helped to focus all our top leaders on their accountabilities and made them understand that the corporation was serious about their involvement in innovation.

Exhibit 10.3 shows the front part of our performance management form, which lists innovation as 30 percent of the assessment criteria. This is the form that is used with each leader to set individual goals at the beginning of the year and assess progress at the end of the year.

Lower-level managers also had goals for innovation in the performance appraisal process. Their goals were more likely to target embedment than revenue generation. We phased the goals at the director and manager level to coincide with expansion of the innovation effort and use of the 360-degree feedback process at these levels.

In retrospect, we learned that some leaders were concerned that we had required results goals in our appraisals too soon, causing some to attempt to move things through the pipeline too rapidly at the expense of a more authentic embedment timetable. In addition, no leader actually achieved his or her results goals in the first year. This was due less to a failure to act properly and much more to the impracticality of creating an innovation and booking new revenues in the same year. In hindsight, what we did certainly focused attention where it needed to be, but might have been slightly unrealistic in terms of getting real results. If we had it to do over again, we most likely would include goals in the performance management system but would have made them more realistic.

Talent Pool. Whirlpool has a robust talent pool process. We take development of our leadership seriously and spend considerable time assessing our talent and developing them. We adapted and used the talent pool process tool to drive innovation embedment. In years two or three, talent pool deliberations of leaders started to include assessments of how well they were doing in innovation embedment. These assessments were included in their overall potential evaluation. In addition, we used assignments in innovation, as the vice president of innovation in a region or as the leader of an innovation team, as development opportunities. The talent pool system reinforced the importance of innovation embedment by showing that it was going to be difficult to move up in the corporation without having been involved in innovation in a very real way.

Exhibit 10.2. Performance Management Goals

Individualizing North America Innovation Goals:
Executive Committee, North America Staff, Members of I-Board
Top 80 people, 30 percent of appraisal innovation

Innovation goals: 25 to 75 experiments, 15 funded prototypes, $xx new revenue

Leaders' Names	Domain Ownership Responsibilities	Revenue ($ millions)	Number of Experiments	Embedment Goals
	Home Wellness	x	10	All top 80 participate
	Fabric Care	x	10	
Smith	Personalized	xx	10	Collective measure
Jones	Appliances	x	5	
	Buy-Back Time	xx	10	Support experiments
	Purchase Experience	x	5	
		xx	10	Provide people resources
		x	5	
		x	2	
		x	2	
		x	2	
		x	2	
		X	2	
		$xxx Collective Measure	Individual Measure	

Product Development

One of our core processes that has been quite successful in the past decade has been the C2C (customer to customer) product development process. Clearly we would be negligent not to adapt this process to innovation. The front end of this product development process, where new product ideas formerly came from, was thus the first area that we modified.

In the past, ideas usually came from a specific function such as market research, engineering, or the corporate technology organization. Now we needed to add in the capacity to accept ideas from the innovation process—that

Exhibit 10.3. Performance Management Form

Performance Management Process (PMP)

Employee Name:	ID #:
Job Title:	Date of Mid Year Review:
Business Unit/Region:	Date of Year-End Review:
Department: Division:	Performance Period: To:

The *PMP Summary Form* is the end-of-year performance summary designed to:

- Align objectives and performance and convey priority by focusing on the following areas:
  - Innovation/Customer Focused Performance Model
  - Operations Goals and Projects
  - The final rating will be dictated by a 30/70 ratio of performance: 30% on Innovation and
  - 70% on Operations Goals and Projects
  - Increase communication between supervisors/team leaders and employees regarding expectations, measurements, and feedback about performance
  - Track improvements in performance by identifying specific results and valued behaviors that are critical for organizational and individual success

Results through Aligned Objectives. Consider results on individual and team objectives, key job and/or team responsibilities, and specific personal development objectives. To support your overall rating, give examples where performance was that of an outstanding contributor, or where it exceeded, met, or was below expectations. Consideration should be given to external reasons why objectives might not have been met (e.g., unexpected change in priorities, uncontrollable external factors, etc.).

1. Innovation:

Embedment	Pipeline	Results

2. Operations Goals and Projects

☐ Below Expectations   ☐ Meets Expectations   ☐ Exceeds Expectations   ☐ Outstanding Contributor means innovation from everyone and everywhere—not just formal functional areas. In addition, we needed to ensure that the documentation required in the C2C process to move a product idea from one phase to the next did not creep into the innovation process (we all knew and acknowledged that the C2C process was probably overly cumbersome in this regard).

How we addressed this is an inspiring story of cross-functional collaboration. The Corporate Technology Organization (CTO), the process owner for C2C, made it a priority to tackle these issues. There was no protection of the current process, only a willingness to integrate C2C with innovation. At a top level, the changes we made included:

- Using the I-Board approval of seed funds for product idea development as a feed into the C2C process itself. That way, if a product idea developed into a full-blown business opportunity, it would already be in the C2C pipeline.

- Differentiating the product ideas in the C2C process that did come from innovation from those that did not.

- Integrating the documentation from the innovation process with C2C documentation rather than imposing a new set of requirements on products entering the C2C process from innovation.

- Integrating the criteria for the C2C process go/no go gates with the gates for the innovation process. Again, our goal was not to make product ideas go through two sets of gates.

- Modifying training on C2C to integrate innovation processes. This broadened people's understanding of the intent and scope of the C2C process and made them more flexible in terms of how they engaged in product development. It helped clarify the real intentions of the C2C process: risk management and full exploration of the potential of an idea rather than process for process sake.

- Adapting our product development process to align with innovation sent a couple of strong messages: we are serious enough about innovation to integrate it with C2C, and there are no hidden agendas or power struggles about process ownership.

Financial Systems

Our financial systems clearly were affected by the innovation effort, most notably around the way we tracked new revenue and how we set up the resources for seed fund money. In Chapter Six, we made the point that we needed to change our mind-set in two ways, from a resource allocation framework to a resource creation framework. This change required moving the locus of control for seed fund money from the corporate level into the regions and that we set up financial systems that could track how money was being used.

The second major area of change for our financial systems was identified as a result of the Innovation Audit. While collecting information for the audit, it became clear to us that we had not done an effective job of capturing our costs or payback from innovation efforts. We could track large capital layout and upfront consultant expenses for innovation, but we could not really track the labor or indirect costs, such as travel associated with innovation.

In addition, we had a difficult time separating revenue generated from projects that were a direct result of innovation with revenue from projects that might not be directly related. We are in the process of making changes in our financial systems that will allow us to track these items, making it easier to understand the cost and benefits of our innovation activities.

Finally, at a more global level, we migrated to a major line item for innovation on our global balanced scorecard (this is our overall set of summary measures of how we are doing as a company). This measure centers on a high-level description of embedment plans being achieved in each business. The progress against the balanced scorecard measures was reviewed with the entire organization in quarterly business meetings. At the end of the year, this global balanced scorecard was reviewed by the Whirlpool Board of Directors to determine the organization's bonus payout percentage. The innovation measures on the global balanced scorecard were highly visible.

There are many other systems and processes that might be affected by innovation embedment, including procurement, legal, strategic planning, and brand management. For example, procurement processes might need to be changed to procure needed equipment and other materials more quickly to meet the pace of innovation. Similarly, partnership agreements might need to be more flexible as the organization takes on untraditional types of partners and strategic planning. Brand management processes might need to be adapted to take into account inputs from the innovation effort.

All of the systems and processes that might be affected by innovation are too numerous to mention here. We are, and recommend that your organization does the same, auditing all of them to make sure that they are aligned and supporting innovation embedment.

WHAT WE LEARNED

- Measures must follow the goals. We found we needed three sets of measures: results, embedment, and individual measures. Mixing results with embedment is confusing and minimizes the importance of both. This was a lot of work, but worthwhile in terms of accurate status and credibility of innovation embedment.

- Measures must be set, tracked, and then reported. Data collection and tracking cannot require inordinate amounts of time and energy. This will defeat the purpose.

- Where possible, add innovation embedment to existing measurement systems. This will cause less confusion and fewer new concepts to learn in the first years of innovation embedment.

- Trying to measure new phenomena might lead to discovering that people are not on the same page about what they thought they were measuring. This is natural and good, as it clarifies and integrates thinking about embedment.

- There are at least four criteria to use when realigning processes and systems to innovation embedment: the system must be inclusive, must recognize and reward people for participation in innovation, should use measures of innovation embedment as success criteria for the system, and should be modified to take in inputs from innovation efforts as well as feed the embedment of innovation.

- Human resource systems such as performance appraisal are perhaps the most powerful in terms of changing behavior in innovation embedment.

- Top leadership engagement and collaboration across organizational functions are critical for changing and adapting existing systems and processes.

SELF-ASSESSMENT: MEASURES, SYSTEMS, AND PROCESSES

The assessment in Worksheet 10.1 will help you to determine how well your measures, systems, and processes are aligned with embedment.

Worksheet 10.1. Determining Alignment of Measures, Systems, and Processes with Embedment

Check as many of the following statements as apply to your organization:

_____ We have intentionally aligned our measurement systems with our embedment goals.

_____ We have separated results measures from embedment measures.

_____ We continually check to make sure that we are all using the same definitions of innovation (or whatever else we are trying to measure).

_____ We have embedment measures for each embedment element or category.

_____ We have measures of how senior leadership is executing their accountabilities for embedment.

_____ We have used a set of criteria to assess alignment of our current systems and processes against our embedment goals and objectives.

_____ A senior leader is assigned accountability for system or process change.

_____ We have aligned our performance management system to our embedment goals.

_____ We have aligned our talent pool system to make sure it supports embedment.

_____ We have examined our product development system to make sure it is integrated with innovation embedment.

_____ We have looked at our financial systems to see if they support a resource creation mind-set.

_____ We have a way to monitor other systems and processes like procurement to see if they are in alignment with innovation embedment.

Scoring: How many checks do you have?

1–4 You need a lot of work on alignment.

5–8 You are getting there! You need some work on alignment.

9–12 Great job! You are aligned!

EPILOGUE

Writing this book was fun but not easy. As an original story, we did not start with someone else's work and then add ours to it. We started with a clean sheet of paper and tried to tell the Whirlpool story as candidly and robustly as it happened. We found that to be harder than either of us had imagined. We wanted desperately to do justice to the Whirlpool story and to the people of Whirlpool. We wanted to be balanced in our praise and critique.

In the three jam-packed years of innovation embedment, Whirlpool accomplished a great deal, almost too much to capture in one book. We had to make choices about what aspects of the story to tell and which to leave out. As a result, some wonderful stories and interesting learnings are not included here.

It may surprise you to know that we did not really start out to write a story on Whirlpool. We never saw ourselves as Whirlpool's innovation embedment biographers. We started out to write about innovation embedment in a generic sense and quickly realized that we were fortunate to be associated with a story that includes real heroes and heroines—and real successes and mishaps. Once we came to grips with this destiny, we changed course. Anyone could write a generic story. We were lucky enough to be part of a real one.

We were, and continue to be, part of an incredible initiative of unabashed courage to transform Whirlpool into a leading-edge customer-driven enterprise. Whirlpool is a great company and deserves to have the spotlight on it for trying to become an even greater company. Whirlpool is also a tremendous motivator of talent, whether you work for the company as Nancy does, or if you consult to the company as Deb does. There are always challenging and exciting projects to undertake, working with consummate and dedicated professionals to noodle things through with, along with unique and novel ways to try to create change. Add to this the very friendly and small-town Whirlpool flavor, and you get a sense of what makes Whirlpool, and this story, unique. From our point of view, what's not to like?

HAVING A "WHEEL" REVELATION

Much of this book revolves around our embedment wheel. When we started writing, we thought the wheel was useful for two important reasons: to serve as a useful construct for the entire book and to be useful to readers. Along the way, we confess to having some doubts.

But while we were working on this book, we also kept our day jobs, Nancy as the head of competency creation and leadership development at Whirlpool and Deb as strategic consultant to some of the world's greatest organizations. We found ourselves continuously learning from the wheel and using it in multiple applications of our jobs. We found that the wheel applied to more than just our situations at Whirlpool, and for more than just innovation. Deb has used it to help many senior leadership groups think through complex change strategies. She has also used it as a way to explain the dual strategy of change and embedment for competencies other than innovation. Within Whirlpool, the wheel has been used to refresh our product creation cycle, design a total leadership system for the company, and in many other uses.

The wheel works, but at the end of the day, it is, after all, only a wheel. Making the substantial changes that innovation embedment requires can be accomplished only by motivated and spirited leaders and people pulling together toward an extraordinary outcome. This formula of all the right people in the right places does not happen often in companies; in fact, it is rare. Whirlpool was fortunate; we had, and still have many, of the right people at all levels. It was only as a result of this that the wheel worked at all.

THE SECOND WAVE OF INNOVATION EMBEDMENT

The Whirlpool story of innovation and embedment is not over. In fact, we consider ourselves to be in the early stages. In human years, innovation embedment at Whirlpool is barely a toddler.

We are now in the process of identifying and tackling many more issues associated with embedment, enlarging the positive and moving innovation to a next phase of development. Innovation embedment is in its second wave. The first wave was the planning and our first steps toward execution. Now we have taken stock about how well we have done and are working to plan and execute this second wave. We've based many of these new plans on the innovation audit conducted in late 2002 and discussed in Chapter Ten. The overall findings for the audit point to the following:

- The innovation effort is making uneven progress in terms of embedment goals at the organizational and individual levels. In some ways, we have been more successful at changing systems and process than at making sure that everyone in Whirlpool has the knowledge and tools to innovate. We need to make progress at both levels. As a result, our second wave has a heavy individual component to it.

- Paradoxically, there have been extremely high levels of employee excitement and active participation in some pockets of the organization. People want to get involved, and many have had the opportunity. We want to get 100 percent participation in the second wave.

- The business outcomes in terms of new-to-the-world products and services, increases in customer loyalty, and revenue are slower than expected. We have made a lot of progress in many areas, but we plan to accelerate our progress in revenue and loyalty in the second wave with our customer touch points and new innovations just hitting the marketplace.

- The North America Region and the Corporate Technology Organization are ahead of all other regions (more people involved in innovation, more revenue, more systems and process change).

- People who are external to Whirlpool have very positive perceptions of our innovation achievements in the marketplace. The press we have received for our efforts is widespread and overwhelmingly complimentary. In the second wave, we want to leverage this phenomenon more fully.

- We need to attend to ensuring that we stick with common definitions of innovation around the world so we can track innovation on a global scale.

TWO OTHER NEW COMPETENCIES AT WHIRLPOOL

The revolution started by innovation that is underway at Whirlpool concerns our relationship with our customer, the end user. Innovation forced us to look at customer benefits along the path of innovations and developing economic engines that drive the innovations. Innovation embedment was the first major step at Whirlpool to put the customer in the center on an enterprise-wide basis. When we paired creating a relationship with customers with creative unique solutions, we started on a path of incredible learning and fun at Whirlpool. It is an unparalleled combination that will someday involve every person at Whirlpool.

In addition to innovation, we have also started to embed two new core competencies: customer-centered operational excellence (ccOPEX) and customer excellence. The latter is more than customer satisfaction. It is about having the most "impactful" customer insights in our industry. It is about chartering sixty thousand people to be customer champions: to know, be, and serve our customers. ccOPEX is equally grand in scale and novel in concepts as innovation. It aims to align all of our processes and practices toward the customer, using tools adapted from operational excellence strategies and customer excellence methods. We are using the embedment wheel with these two new competencies.

We are now learning to fully integrate these three competencies together into one approach that creates value for our customers, shareholders, and employees that cannot be duplicated by our competitors. It is a tall order, but the innovation embedment experience gave us the groundwork, experience, and confidence to take this on. Whirlpool is moving forward.

WHO "WE" HAVE BECOME

The penultimate section of the Preface to this book was headed "Who 'We' Are." Now that we think about it, the description we gave back there was a bit presumptuous. We wrote it, but moved into the next nine months of work and ten chapters that make up this book. Somewhere along the way (about a month into the work and Chapter Two), it began to haunt us. Who really are "WE"?

We don't go to parties much, but when we do, we dread the question: "So what do you do?" It is unanswerable. We've tried to answer the question, but after a minute of what will clearly be a long-winded response, the person looks for someone else to talk to, because it takes too much investment to get an answer to a question that might have been cursory to begin with. We wondered, Should we carry around the embedment wheel and pull it out, pointing to it while saying, "Here is what I do"?

For nine months, we struggled with how to define our role as we talked and debated the contents of the book. Then we realized it was the wrong question with the wrong emphasis. We shifted from "who we are" to "who were we becoming." The *chi* around that question even felt better.

We started to answer the question by counting our blessings. We feel fortunate for the experiences that we had in innovation embedment and with Whirlpool. It has changed the way we approach our work, and it has changed who we are. For example, we start our projects very differently. We start by thinking about the biggest outcome we can imagine and work our way back from that. We rarely start or end a change process with training. Now we understand that training alone is not the answer. We also now use innovation tools in our work. They forced us to learn out-of-the-box thinking.

We experienced the power of unleashing human potential through the most basic of human needs, to create and be recognized. We understand the power of grassroots, but for the magnitude of change we were looking at, leadership was pivotal. We know the value of knowledge sharing and the influence of open knowledge for everyone. And although we have both been very committed to diversity at every point in our lives, we have experienced far greater multifaceted diversity and inclusion around innovation. In all, we have helped Whirlpool move closer to innovation embedment, but, surprisingly, innovation embedment has changed us.

The story for Whirlpool is not over yet. It is just beginning. Its future is squarely in the hands of the dedicated and leading-edge people who make Whirlpool great. We think that Whirlpool's innovation embedment is on a path to help support the transformation of Whirlpool into a customer-driven company. Whirlpool is on the move and is changing. But it's not the embedment wheel that will transport it. It's the people who will do that through innovation from everyone and everywhere.

REFERENCES

California Management Review, 2002, 44(4).

Cameron, K. S., and Quinn, R. E. *Diagnosing and Changing Organizational Culture Based on the Competing Values Framework.* Reading, Mass.: Addison-Wesley, 1996.

Cameron, K. K., and Whetten, D. *Developing Management Skills.* Reading, Mass.: Addison-Wesley, 1998.

Collins, J. "Turning Goals into Results: The Power of Catalytic Mechanisms." *Harvard Business Review,* 1999, *77*(4), 70–82.

Collins, J. C., and Porras, J. I. "Building Your Company's Vision." *Harvard Business Review,* 1996, *74*(5), 65–78.

De Bono, E. *Serious Creativity: Using the Power of Lateral Thinking to Create New Ideas.* New York: HarperBusiness, 1992.

Drucker, P. F. *Innovation and Entrepreneurship: Practice and Principles.* New York: HarperCollins, 1985.

Hamel, G. "Strategy Innovation and the Quest for Value." *Sloan Management Review,* 1998, *39*(2), 78–85.

Hamel, G. "Bringing Silicon Valley Inside." *Harvard Business Review,* 1999, *77*(5), 70–84.

Kaplan, R. S., and Norton, D. P. *Balanced Scorecard.* Boston: Harvard Business School Press, 1996.

Kidder, T. *The Soul of a New Machine.* New York: Avon, 1982.

Kotter, J. P. "Leading Change: Why Transformation Efforts Fail." *Harvard Business Review,* 1995, *73*(2), 59–67.

Lewin, K., and Gold, M. (eds.). *The Complete Social Scientist: A Kurt Lewin Reader.* Washington, D.C.: American Psychological Association, 1999.

Markides, C. "Strategic Innovation." *Sloan Management Review,* 1997, *38*(3), 9–24.

Prahalad, C. K., and Hamel, G. "The Core Competence of the Corporation." *Harvard Business Review,* 1990, *68*(3), 79–92.

Schein, E. *Organizational Culture and Leadership.* San Francisco: Jossey-Bass, 1992.

Schutz, W. *The Truth Option: A Practical Technology for Human Affairs.* Berkeley, Calif.: Ten Speed Press, 1984.

Stanjkovic, A. D., and Luthans, F. "Differential Effects of Incentive Motivators on Work Performance." *Academy of Management Journal,* 1999, *44*(3), 580–590.

Stanjkovic, A. D., and Luthans, F. "Reinforce for Performance: The Need to Go Beyond Pay and Even Rewards." *Academy of Management Executive,* 2001, *13*(2), 49–57.

Strebel, P. "Why Do Employees Resist Change?" *Harvard Business Review,* May–June 1996.

INDEX

for, 185; working with trade partners, 114
Immersion workshops, 72-73
Incentives. *See* Rewards and recognition
Inclusion, 10, 85, *96*, 166, 168, 189
Incremental improvements, tracking, 126
Incremental revenue, estimated, *127*
India-focused products, 2
Individual change: accountability for, 62-63; change focus for, 151, *152, 157;* impact of, questions concerning, dimensions of, 153-156; need for, emphasizing, 82; new change model for, 153; strategic communications focus for, 156-157
Individual goals: assessing, *58;* difficulty addressing, 146-147; method of measuring, *152;* overlooking, 28, 50, 51; setting, *53,* 54, 192; uncovering need for, 52. *See also* Vision and goals
Individual measures, 36, *55, 152,* 187, *193*
Individual rewards and recognition, 163, 166-170, *177, 178*
Infighting, 81
Informal networking, 33
Informal talent pool system, 111
Information: access to, issue of, 124; forms of, 135-136; versus knowledge, *137. See also* Knowledge management (KM) and learning systems
Information systems, standard, 125, 132
Infrastructure: establishing, accountability for, 62; overview of, 26, 29-36. *See also specific elements*
Innate ability and capacity, belief in, 123
Innovation audit, 182-183, 196, 201
Innovation boards. *See* I-Boards
Innovation consultants. *See* I-Consultants
Innovation Days, *21,* 94-95, 114, 149, 171
Innovation Embedment Baseline Readiness Assessment, 39, *40-41*
Innovation embedment effort: concepts important for, 5-9; harnessing people resources for, 14-18; lessons learned for, 18, 22; organizational structure supporting, 18, *19-22;* purpose behind, 3-5; seeking models and partners for, 10-13; selecting a guide for, 13-14; successful, evidence of, 1-2; vision leading to, 9-10. *See also* Embedment wheel
Innovation E-Space, 126-131, 149, 184
Innovation events, tracking, 185
Innovation Field Journal, 128, 149, *150,* 174
Innovation mentors. *See* I-Mentors
Innovation projects: assigning talent to, issue with, 110-111; and employee mobility, 61; funding of, 53; mandating time for, 110; miti-

gating risk in, 91; participation in, 76; successful, number of, 51; volunteering for, 36, 111, *113,* 127, 128-129. *See also* Shelved innovation projects
Innovation teams. *See* I-Teams
Innovation, tenets of, 5-6, 10
Innovation Toolkit, evaluation tool from, *121-122*
Innovation tools and processes: encouraging use of, 170; goals for usage of, 54; learning and embracing, 63; teaching, workshops for, 72, 73; using and adapting, 66-67. *See also specific tools and processes*
Innovation vision. *See* Vision and goals; Vision creation
Innovation workshops, 17, 72, 73, 170
Innovator role: moving people into, 123; people seeing themselves in, 115
Inputting data, 140
Inside-out-view, *88*
Institutionalizing change, 25, 144; stage of, *145,* 146, 157
Integration, 146
Integrity, *96*
Intellectual property rights goals, 52
Internal consultants. *See* I-Consultants
Intervention, 81
Intranet sites, 111, 125, 149, 187
Intrinsic rewards versus extrinsic rewards, 163-166
Intro to Innovation page, 128, *129*
I-Pipe: audit of, 182; building new modules around, 127; development of, 125-126, *127;* funding flow through, stages of, *119-120;* versus idea portfolio, *88;* measures from, 180, 184, 185, *186;* and results goals, 52, 192
I-Teams: assignment to, opportunity in, 192; composition of, *20;* creation of, and roles of, 15-17; and I-Boards, 75; as key players, *22;* and leadership workshops, 73; listening to, 185; participation on, 76; promoting participation in, 170; recognition of, 95; and rewards and recognition, 166-167, 171; rotational assignments to, 68; and strategic communications, 95

J
Job description change: versus add-on work, 116; goals for, 53, 54; incentives for, 34; versus moving talent, 111; questions about, 154-155
Job potential, increased, reward of, 167-168
Job promotion opportunities, 173, 192
Johnson & Johnson, 13